CARIBBEAN WOMEN WRITERS
AND GLOBALIZATION

Caribbean Women Writers and Globalization
Fictions of Independence

HELEN SCOTT
University of Vermont, USA

ASHGATE

Published by
Ashgate Publishing Limited
Gower House
Croft Road
Aldershot
Hampshire GU11 3HR
England

Ashgate Publishing Company
Suite 420
101 Cherry Street
Burlington, VT 05401-4405
USA

Ashgate website: http://www.ashgate.com

British Library Cataloguing in Publication Data
Scott, Helen
Caribbean women writers and globalization : fictions of independence
    1.Caribbean literature (English) – 20th century – History and criticism 2.Caribbean
    literature (English) – Women authors – History and criticism 3.Globalization in
    literature
    I.Title
    810.9'9287'09729

Library of Congress Cataloging-in-Publication Data
Scott, Helen, 1966-
    Caribbean women writers and globalization : fictions of independence / by Helen Scott.
        p. cm.
    Includes bibliographical references and index.
    ISBN-13: 978-0-7546-5134-5 (alk. paper)
    ISBN-10: 0-7546-5134-7 (alk. paper)
    1. Caribbean literature (English)—Women authors—History and criticism. 2. Caribbean
literature (English)—Foreign countries—History and criticism. 3. Women and literature—
Caribbean Area—History—20th century. 4. Women and literature—Caribbean Area—
History—21st century. 5. Caribbean Area—In literature. 6. Postcolonialism—Caribbean
Area. 7. Globalization in literature. 8. Imperialism in literature. I. Title.

    PR9205.05S27 2006
    810.9'9287097290904—dc22

                                                                              2006016417
ISBN-13: 978-0-7546-5134-5

Printed and bound in Great Britain by MPG Books Ltd. Bodmin, Cornwall.

Reprinted 2008

Contents

List of Figures

Acknowledgements

So many people have helped me during the long years I have been working on this project, but I do owe a particular debt of gratitude to those who have read and responded to my work at various stages, especially Kathleen Balutansky, Anthony Bradley, William Keach, Neil Lazarus, Lokangaka Losambe, and Ashley Smith. Nagesh Rao and Pranav Jani in countless conversations have enriched my thinking about postcolonial literature. Thanks to Erin Burke for her custom-made maps, and to Peter McConville for his patient formatting. Ashgate's Ann Donahue has provided immense support and guidance throughout the process of converting manuscript to book. Thanks to my colleagues and students at the University of Vermont, and particularly to Robyn Warhol for her generous mentoring, and Nancy Welch for all her advice and support. My family on both sides of the Atlantic have sustained and inspired me. Helene Smith shared with me her love of Caribbean literature and culture, her zest for life, and her passion for global justice, and I dedicate this book to her memory.

List of Abbreviations

CDB   Caribbean Development Bank
CNG   National Government Council (Haiti)
IMF   International Monetary Fund
NJM   New Jewel Movement (Grenada)
OECS   Organization of Eastern Caribbean States
PAC   Political Affairs Committee (Guyana)
PNC   People's National Congress (Guyana)
PPP   People's Progressive Party (Guyana)
PRG   People's Revolutionary Government (Grenada)
SAP   Structural Adjustment Program
UWI   University of the West Indies
WTO   World Trade Organization

Literary Works

ABR   Kincaid, *At the Bottom of the River*
AD   Danticat, *After the Dance*
AJ   Kincaid, *Annie John*
AMM   Kincaid, *Autobiography of My Mother*
ASP   Kincaid, *A Small Place*
BEM   Danticat, *Breath, Eyes, Memory*
BS   Kempadoo, *Buxton Spice*
BW   Danticat, *The Butterfly's Way*
DB   Danticat, *Dew Breaker*
FH   Gilroy, *Frangipani House*
KK   Danticat, *Krik? Krak!*
L   Kincaid, *Lucy*
LP   Shinebourne, *Last English Plantation*
MGB   Kincaid, *My Garden Book*
MP   Kincaid, *Mr. Potter*
TP   Shinebourne, *Timepiece*
VT   Melville, *Ventriloquist's Tale*
WMS   Nichols, *Whole of a Morning Sky*

Introduction

Caribbean Women Writers and Postcolonial Imperialism

The brutal tectonics of neoliberal globalization since 1978 are analogous to the catastrophic processes that shaped a 'third world' in the first place, during the era of late Victorian imperialism (1870–1900). In the latter case, the forcible incorporation into the world market of the great subsistence peasantries of Asia and Africa entailed the famine deaths of millions and the uprooting of tens of millions more from traditional tenures. The end result, in Latin America as well, was rural 'semi-proletarianization:' the creation of a huge global class of immiserated semi-peasants and farm labourers lacking existential security of subsistence . . . Structural adjustment, it would appear, has recently worked an equally fundamental reshaping of human futures. As the authors of *Slums* conclude: 'instead of being a focus for growth and prosperity, the cities have become a dumping ground for a surplus population working in unskilled, unprotected and low-wage informal service industries and trade.' 'The rise of [this] informal sector,' they declare bluntly, 'is . . . a direct result of liberalization.'   Mike Davis, 'Planet of Slums'

With all her daydreams of a future in Brooklyn smashed, she had begun to wander around Georgetown and see, as if for the first time, the situation in which life had placed her.
    She saw streets of tumbling, ramshackle houses, hutches and sheds, slum dwellings tacked together with criss-cross pieces of fencing, and she felt as though she herself had become as dry and sucked of moisture as the sun-bleached grey timbers. Her own headscarf too was grey with wear and sweat. When she chanced to catch sight of it, her large face looked grey, the colour of old lava. The greyness was all around her and everything inside her too seemed to have crumbled into grey dust. Her shoes had more or less disintegrated, peeling open like old, blackened banana skins in their unequal battle against unpaved roads, stones, rains, mud, sun and dust. Every alley had its own stench of frying food, of fly-infested garbage, stagnant pools and rotting planks. She felt like a ghost in her own city. A jumbie. Nobody seemed to notice her. She could have been invisible.
                    Pauline Melville, 'Erzulie'

The Historical Framework of U.S.–Caribbean Relations

Caribbean Women Writers and Globalization: Fictions of Independence reads recent anglophone literature by Caribbean women in the context of that nexus of socioeconomic and political forces referred to variously as 'neoliberalism,' 'the Washington consensus,' 'corporate globalization,' or simply 'globalization.' The fiction, from and about Haiti, Antigua, Guyana, and Grenada, mostly written during and about the 1980s and 1990s, bespeaks a reality where new mechanisms of foreign control have replaced formal colonialism, making a mockery of the notion of 'independence' in any genuine sense.[1] Thus the subtitle 'fictions of independence' simultaneously designates creative literature from and about the postindependence era, suggests the growing autonomy of women writers, and acknowledges the reality that 'independence' is rendered fictitious by enduring imperialism.

A response to the crises in global capitalism that began in the early 1970s, and implemented by the main global powers and the multilateral financial institutions they govern, most importantly the World Bank and the International Monetary Fund (IMF), neoliberal globalization rests on economic deregulation, financialization, and privatization, in the name of the 'free market' and 'free trade.' From the 1970s 'Third World' nations were encouraged to take out loans from foreign governments, private banks, and international institutions.[2] With the debt crisis of 1982 many indebted countries were forced to carry out Structural Adjustment Programs (SAPs) in return for loan assistance from the World Bank or IMF. SAPs involve devaluation of currency; an orientation on exports and foreign capital investment; liberalization of financial markets; and cuts in government spending, subsidies, and wages. In his global study *Your Money or Your Life* Eric Toussaint explains the underlying dynamics: 'This is not a mere draining of the periphery's resources by the center. Rather, a class analysis reveals that this transfer of wealth is part of the . . . generalised offensive of capital against labour. This offensive aims specifically to re-establish the capitalists' rate of profit— known as "company performance"—in the long term' (8). Neoliberalism is typified by the Caribbean Basin Initiative, which replaced economic aid with a policy of trade benefits and investment incentives.[3] The rhetoric of free trade was belied by terms and regulations that benefited foreign corporations; as Petras and Morley point out, 'the CBI experiment was a windfall for U.S. manufacturers able to take advantage of low-cost labour, not a boon to Caribbean traders' (55). In much of the Caribbean such policies have been devastating to ordinary people (especially women, as we shall see), even when sometimes succeeding in shrinking budget deficits and maintaining debt payment.

Neoliberal globalization has economic and geopolitical motivations (strategic positioning vis-à-vis other powers; control over profits from oil refining, mineral extraction, offshore manufacturing, tourism, cheap labor); takes economic, political, and cultural forms; and is ultimately backed by the threat or reality of military force. It thus conforms to the definition of imperialism first developed at the start of the twentieth century and codified by Lenin in his *Imperialism: the Highest Stage of Capitalism*:

> In this view, colonialism, the conquest and direct control of other people's land, is a particular phase in the history of imperialism, which is now best understood as the globalisation of the capitalist mode of production, its penetration of previously non-capitalist regions of the world, and destruction of pre- or non-capitalist forms of social organisation. (Chrisman and Williams 2)

Such an analysis reveals the 'persistence of neo-colonialist or imperialist practices in the contemporary world' and forestalls what Anne McClintock has called the 'premature celebration of the pastness of colonialism, (which) runs the risk of obscuring the continuities and discontinuities of colonial and imperial power' (McClintock 294).[4]

This perspective is at the forefront of my study, which explores the impact of these processes on specific nations, as they are expressed in works of fiction. I begin with Haiti because it represents, as Paul Farmer has argued, a 'template of colony:' it illustrates in graphic, often early and extreme, form, circumstances familiar to the broader region (*Uses of Haiti* 53–90). While following a distinct course from other nations it is also prototypical of the post-colonial Caribbean. Michel-Rolph Trouillot argues that 'certain aspects of Haitian authoritarianism' in the nineteenth century anticipate more recent Caribbean regimes including Eric Gairy's Grenada, which is discussed here in Chapter Four (*Haiti: State Against Nation* 30). The ruling elites that developed after the Haitian revolution were 'products of a situation that anticipated neocolonialism in the rest of the world by a century and a half' (38–9). By the beginning of the twentieth century Haiti 'was a country poorly fitted into the world system, torn by its dual and fragmented dependence on France and the United States, both of which were . . . unable and unwilling to integrate it fully within their spheres of influence' (56–7); it was, in short, 'the first testing ground of neocolonialism' (57).

Jean-Claude Duvalier encouraged foreign corporations to exploit Haitian workers in low-wage agriculture and industry, and worked with neoliberal agencies as they imposed unequal terms of trade and structural adjustment programs. The other countries considered here have seen similar patterns of U.S. collusion with domestic regimes: Antigua under the Bird dynasty welcomed American military bases and tourist companies; Guyana's major industries have been owned by American corporations, and the U.S., with the aid of Britain, toppled the government of Cheddi Jagan and replaced it with the brutally repressive militarized regime of Forbes Burnham; in an operation informally referred to as 'the sledgehammer and the nutmeg' the U.S. invaded Grenada in 1983 and installed a friendly though repressive government.

Caribbean Literary Traditions

Just as the countries of the anglophone Caribbean have shared histories, albeit in distinct and varied forms, so do their literatures follow analogous trajectories.[5] While some nations, such as Guyana, have much more developed and distinctive national literary traditions than others, marked regional patterns nonetheless allow for some generalized periodization.[6] It is generally acknowledged that the era of national liberation struggles was one of immense cultural productivity in the Caribbean when many writers saw revolutionary potential in artistic endeavors, explicitly aligned themselves with projects of liberation, and produced what Frantz Fanon termed 'anti-colonial national literature' or a 'literature of combat, in the sense that it calls on the whole people to fight for their existence as a nation . . . because it molds the national consciousness . . . because it assumes responsibility, and because it is the will to liberty expressed in terms of time and space' (Fanon 240).

The greater prominence of, and more sustained critical interest in, women writers in the closing decades of the twentieth century are also broadly acknowledged.[7] The years after 1970 saw both increased attention to women writers of earlier periods, some of whom previously had received little regional or international attention, and the emergence in greater numbers of new women writers of the Caribbean and its diaspora.[8] Marina Maxwell in 1981 addressed the conditions that had both prevented women from becoming writers and made women authors invisible: "'It is a marvel that there have been so many creative women artists in the Caribbean. Too many have fallen silent or been driven underground, smothered by husbands, children or jobs'" (qtd. in Davies and Fido 14). Simultaneously with this impulse to excavate earlier works,

> [a] substantial number of women writers, living both at home and abroad, have emerged, giving different shape and voice to this literature and challenging the preeminence of the largely male writers whom we used to think of as 'Caribbean literature.' The reality of gender presents, perhaps, the crucial difference between this group of writers and the preceding generation. (Davies and Fido 59)

The process that began in the 1970s accelerated in subsequent decades. According to Alison Donnell and Sarah Lawson Welsh, '[o]ne of the most significant developments of the 1970s was the increased publication of Caribbean women's writing, and in the 1980s some highly significant new voices came into print' (368) and '[a]t the close of the 1980s and into the 1990s, there has been a flurry of articles and books addressing the issue of reading and evaluating women's writing from the region' (443). Caribbean women writers thus came into their own during the neoliberal period of imperialism.

Many scholars of this new wave literature eschew generalization in the face of its immense range. This is particularly the case for comparative studies: while, for example, the region's Spanish literature shares some patterns with the English literature—the Boom writers of mid-century were disproportionately male, women writers become much more visible after 1970—in other respects the two diverge. Many critics associate the Boom writers with postmodern experimentation, and the post-Boom generation with a 'return to a simpler concept of fiction' and a 'need to return to more popular and socially oriented novels' (Shaw 7); this is the reverse of the anglophone pattern.[9]

Perhaps inevitably, however, critics *have* attempted to generalize about the Anglophone literature, variously characterizing women's texts, in contradistinction to the extant canon, as more concerned with issues of personal relationships, gender and sexuality; less engaged with imperialism, class, economics and collective struggle; and radical more for its formal innovation that its political content.[10] Writing in 1996 E.A. Markham holds that while earlier writers challenged class divisions, 'the taboos which are being broken now are sexual and gender ones' (xxxi). Kathleen Renk's book-length study of 1999 looks at 'how post-independence women's narratives differ from their British and Caribbean nationalist precursors' (2). She argues that 'anticolonial narratives produced during the nationalist era undermined the colonial regime and fostered political and cultural independence' but 'the form and realism of this literature is based on the nineteenth century classic realist text' (4) and ultimately therefore such works 'do not overturn the basic assumptions of English nationalist literature, which encode monolithic national and gender identities and hierarchical gender systems' (5).

This supposition—that the new literature's break with 'European' and 'masculine' formal conventions represents a more fundamental challenge to colonial discourse than explicitly anti-imperialist literature—is repeated by many critics. Antonia MacDonald-Smythe observes that 'the eclectic, fragmented form favored by [Michelle] Cliff and [Jamaica] Kincaid for encoding the female experience is a rejection of the linear polemic of some earlier male-authored West Indian texts' (2), and suggests that despite thematic parallels between Caribbean women writers and 'their male antecedents,' attention should be paid to 'the ways in which the gendered locations from which they speak affect the shape of these thematics' (4). Emilia Ippolito develops a similar argument in her *Caribbean Women Writers: Identity and Gender*, contending that 'one paradigmatic writing strategy is that of formal innovation' and 'there has been a trend toward a rejection of the linear, realistic narrative' (7). Gina Wisker's broad introductory survey of Caribbean and African-American women's writing reiterates these observations:

> while, earlier in the twentieth century, modernism was enabling for Black men, who transferred the power of utterance from the coloniser to the male colonised, its formal experimentation did not, however, liberate doubly burdened women writers. They have, latterly, turned to the narrative structure of post-modernism—to fragmentation, intertextuality, parody, and doubling, locating gender differences as a site for representing and reconstructing new identities. (99)

Many critics, then, discern in contemporary women's texts a shift away from the anti-imperialist, nationalist, and/or class-based political agenda of the earlier (predominantly) male texts and a concomitant rejection of realist (sometimes 'modernist') literary forms in favor of experimental (sometimes 'postmodernist') narrative strategies. The latter formal developments are often equated with a more radical stance, and assumed to be more appropriate to a female sensibility.

While there is certainly much to support these observations, gendered generic generalizations are hard to sustain. Writers such as Dionne Brand, Michelle Cliff, Pauline Melville, Shani Mootoo, and others, including some of the writers discussed in this book, use experimental formal techniques as they interrogate gender inequality and interrupt conventional notions of (hetero-) sexual roles and identities. Yet similar thematic and formal developments can be seen in many male writers both old and new: The work of Wilson Harris, for example, certainly displays the 'fragmentation, intertextuality, parody, and doubling,' (Wisker 99) attributed to female authors; Barbara Lalla, in her reading of Anthony Winkler and John Hearne, convincingly demonstrates that male as well as female '[c]urrent Jamaican writers interfere with those features of discourse that anchor it in a single, stable perspective' (173). At the same time, while some new wave Caribbean women writers use what could be described as experimental narrative techniques—the distinction between modern and postmodern is less definitive than often asserted—others use realism or other 'linear' forms, and many write texts that could quite comfortably sit under the heading of 'protest literature.'[11] In this study I hold that ideological positions (anti-imperialist/pro-imperialist, sexist/antisexist, racist/antiracist) do not inhere in the identity of authors or in particular discursive or artistic forms, and that attempts to neatly categorize narrative techniques as 'male' or 'female' or as 'western or 'nonwestern' often rest on idealist, essentialist, and unsustainable foundations.

Identity, Class, Oppression

Contemporary scholarship on postcolonial women's literature is often concerned with questions of 'identity,' according to which class, gender, race, sexuality, nationality, ethnicity are primarily understood discursively. Drawing on Foucauldian paradigms, Irene Gedalof identifies a key question facing theorists of identity: 'can feminists keep open a space in which to consider the intersections of sex, gender, race, nation and the "embarrassed *et cetera*" in constituting identities . . . while holding on to a category 'women' that is sufficiently coherent to form the basis of effective theory and politics?' (1). What is noticeable about this and many other critical commentaries is the absence or marginalization of the category 'class.' Gedalof acknowledges and explains this omission in her investigation of postcolonial feminisms:

> Because of this particular focus on the relationship between community identities, origins and women . . . my 'embarrassed *et cetera*' only occasionally includes class. I would agree with some aspects of recent feminist criticisms that the turn to questions of identity in feminist theory has led to losing sight of questions of class and economic inequalities. . . . But I also suspect that questions of class-belonging and class-positions,

while certainly engaging women in very important ways, might not relate to the question of origins in the same way as do narratives of racial and ethnic identities. (15)

For Gedalof the material coordinates of oppression are secondary to the 'conceptual space where the social and the self meet . . . within particular discourses of gender, race, national and class identities' (2). Her focus is on 'narratives' and 'discourses,' and she subscribes to a Foucauldian understanding of power as 'not just a privilege possessed by a dominant group; it is rather exercised by and through us all, situated as we are in multiple networks of "nonegalitarian and mobile relations"' (19). This formulation effectively jettisons the primacy of social structures and class antagonism and instead generalizes power as something omnipresent, equating the expression of a system of ideas with the exercise of social domination.[12] It thus has much in common with the post-Althusserian 'rejection of economism and . . . reprioritization of ideology,' and disposal of 'Althusser's rather nebulous but necessary affirmation of the primacy of the material "in the last instance" in favor of a conception of ideology as absolutely autonomous' (Brenner 12–13). For materialists the problem with discourse theory is that 'once ideology is severed from material reality it no longer has any analytical usefulness, for it becomes impossible to posit a theory of determination—of historical change based on contradiction' (Brenner, paraphrasing Michèle Barrett, 13). The theoretical framework of *Caribbean Women Writers and Globalization* understands class not as an 'identity' but rather as a process and a material relationship to the governing mode of production, one that is the definitive divide globally in 'rich countries' and 'poor countries' alike.[13] In extension, all forms of oppression—racial, national, gender, and sexual—have specific material causes and effects, and are inseparable from each other and from capitalism.[14] Any critical investigation of capitalism would be incomplete without recognition of the centrality of racism to its inauguration and continuation. And as many, especially Third World, feminists have shown, the consequences of any attempt to prioritize either race or gender have been dire, especially for black women. Many Caribbean feminists have exposed and rejected the politics of either 'race first' national liberation/black nationalism or race-blind feminism.[15]

Similarly, as Deborah Levenson-Estrada maintains in her study of women union activists in 1970s Guatemala: 'There is no "more important" or "prior" issue—class or gender—these are inside one another, and the struggle against gender conventions and sexist ideologies is integral to any project of liberation. A critical consciousness about class needs a critical consciousness about gender, and vice versa' (227). Considered as material coordinates rather than systems of thought, gender and class are inseparable and interdependent: '"Gender is created not simply outside production but within it. . . . It is not a set of ideas developed separately from the economic structure but a part of it, built into the organization and social relations of work"' (French and James, quoting Ava Baron, 7). Women's oppression is not a transhistorical constant but rather arises with class society and serves particular economic interests under capitalism.[16] Women both provide the unpaid labor of privatized reproduction—the childcare and other domestic responsibilities that are necessary to service future generations of workers and, under capitalism, performed within individual households—and form a low paid work force: In the United States women still earn less than 80 percent of the average male wage, according to Census Bureau figures; UNIFEM finds that women in Export Processing Zones earn 20–50 percent less than men.[17]

These dynamics are particularly pertinent for discussion of Caribbean countries in the neoliberal period:

> The vanguard of industrial investment in the world capitalist system is in the lowest paid segment of those countries paying the lowest wages. Young women in developing countries are the labor force on this frontier . . . Escaping the patriarchal restrictions of domestic production, young women workers are segregated in the new industrial compounds where they are subject to the patriarchal control of managers. (Nash and Fernandez-Kelly, x)

While gender-based oppression, like racism and like heterosexism, cuts across class to the extent that sexism impacts all women, as racism impacts all people of color, and homophobia all whose sexual orientation or identity falls outside the sanctioned 'norm,' the *experience* of oppression varies qualitatively and quantitatively with class. In both colonial and postcolonial societies, while a minority of women are in positions of economic and social privilege the vast majority are of the working class; this is the case also for men, for the plurality of whom the idea of 'male privilege' is but a chimera; the absence of specific oppression does not translate into active advantage. At the same time, in the Caribbean as elsewhere, gender inequality keeps working-class women in 'the most marginalized, lowest paid occupations' (Senior 119), and overwhelmingly responsible for unpaid domestic labor. Working-class women are therefore particularly vulnerable at times of economic crisis (of the sort that swept much of the Caribbean in the 1970s and 1980s), absorbing the devastating impact of layoffs and structural adjustment programs, while not experiencing tangible benefits at times of economic expansion. Writing in 1997 Mary Johnson Osirim summarized the situation: 'At the close of the twentieth century . . . the majority of women in the English-speaking Caribbean persist in unrewarding, gender-segregated activities that severely restrict their upward mobility' (55).

These realities, albeit sometimes in sublimated shape, are omnipresent in much contemporaneous anglophone literature by Caribbean women. This book is interested in how literary works are shaped by, *speak to,* transform, mystify or crystallize these material conditions; it strives to remain, as Edward Said says of Gramsci's critical oeuvre, 'sensitive to the fact the world is made up of "ruler and ruled," that there are leaders and led; that nothing in the world is natural . . . politics and power and collectivity are always involved when culture, ideas, and texts are to be studied and/or analyzed' ('History, Literature and Geography' 465–6).

Independence, Postcolonialism, and Postmodernism

In critical discussions of Caribbean women's literature, the failures of independence are often seen primarily through the lens of gender in isolation from class: national liberation is not infrequently positioned in opposition to women's liberation and understood as empowering men while leaving women in subjugation: 'if a masculinist nationalism informed cultural and political life in the 1940s and 1950s, the late 1960s and especially the 1970s opened up to Caribbean feminism' (Hoving 5). It is true that independence did not lead to women's liberation; as Natasha Barnes argues, 'no Caribbean nationalist movement ever made "gender" a central conceptual category in its discourse of anticolonial revolution' (35), and certainly the movement for women's rights and its academic and cultural corollaries took on new momentum 'within an international feminist climate and the growing body of feminist literary criticism' in the 1970s (Davies and Fido 12). Nonetheless, women were crucially involved with national liberation struggles, and independence at least initially raised greater possibilities for sexual equality in spheres such as education, employment, and social services. In her study of Caribbean women Olive Senior points out that after 1962 newly independent nations addressed educational development in a systematic way, and '[w]hile the five-year plans which became the new blueprints for state policies might have contained no explicit references to female education, they implicitly conveyed the idea of equality between the sexes' (47). Senior also emphasizes the involvement of women in the political movements and institutions that accompanied independence: 'A great deal of the women's activism of the 1970s took place within the framework of political parties, in Jamaica and Guyana especially, where there were socialist governments, and through other small but active left-wing parties and organizations in these and other countries such as Trinidad' (183). In her 1986 overview Pat Ellis confirms that despite their restricted role in formal politics women were active in independence era revolutionary parties and governments in Grenada and Guyana, at the same time that they developed their own grassroots organizations such as the Sistren theatre collective in Jamaica and Concerned Women for Progress in Jamaica and Trinidad. Ellis also finds that '[m]any women in the region participate in trade unions; like political parties many trade unions have a women's auxiliary' and again despite a limited official role 'they actively participate in union activity and support strike action when necessary' (13–14).

However, national liberation did not fulfill its promise for the majority of women *or* men. Independence failed to bring equality and justice to all formerly colonized subjects; political independence did not fundamentally transform social relations and structures, but rather installed national bourgeoisies whose task was to manage capitalism, while the world's superpowers developed new systems to maintain their influence over strategically significant regions. In 'The Pitfalls of National Consciousness' Frantz Fanon famously describes the treacherous role of the national bourgeoisie: 'To them, nationalization quite simply means the transfer into native hands of those unfair advantages which are a legacy of the colonial period' (Fanon 152). The new ruling class reaches agreements with 'foreign capitalists' but 'does not share its profits with the people, and in no way allows them to enjoy any of the dues that are paid to it by the big foreign companies' (165). While women remain a small but growing minority of this ruling class, their structural role when in this position is indistinguishable from their male equivalents.[18]

The climate of postindependence disillusion understandably for some underscored the need to reject 'western' discursive and epistemological frameworks and create 'nonwestern' ways of thinking and communicating:

> Anglophone Caribbean women writers reject a narrow nationalism as they seek to redefine the term nation by reimagining what constitutes national community. . . . Given the diversity of the Caribbean and the cross-cultural process in the Caribbean as a whole, it is easy to see why the national ideal, based on one truth, is rejected by these writers. (Renk 143)

For Renk and some other critics of Caribbean literature, the failures of nationalism, including its patriarchy, lie in its eurocentrism, which is equated with particular formal and epistemological qualities: Nationalism, like imperialism, is held to be oppressive because it is 'singular,' 'hierarchical,' and 'linear.'

While in part an outgrowth of postindependence skepticism, this reflexive suspicion is also associated with the postmodernist orthodoxy that accompanies many spheres of postcolonial criticism.[19] While there is an explicit tension between the central tenets of poststructuralist theory and postcolonial critical investigations, the figures associated with the former—Derrida, Lyotard, Lacan, Foucault, Kristeva, Deleuze, and Guatarri, and interpreters thereof—pervade the latter. Caribbean writers and scholars not infrequently express suspicion of such 'high theory,' but much critical scholarship, while noting 'its universalism and eurocentrism,' nonetheless accepts the 'perfect relevance of poststructuralism in any anticolonial, anti-Enlightenment project' (Hoving, following Stuart Hall, 8). And yet postmodern paradigms can, ironically, given their habitual celebration of multiplicity and specificity, lead to formulaic—one dimensional, mono-focused, reductive—readings of texts as linguistic, discursive allegories, and exclude multiple possibilities for more specific, grounded readings. And, as many of postmodernism's critics have argued, the 'linguistic turn' and 'descent into discourse' in postcolonial studies risk obscuring the material coordinates of imperialism, and depoliticizing a field of study that is from its inception engaged with inherently political questions of empire, race, colonialism, and their relationship to cultural production.[20] In her study of Caribbean women writers Isabel Hoving equates 'high theory' with 'political criticism' and attributes the crisis in postcolonial studies to 'weariness with the issues of gender, class and race,' which is met with a 'return to the literary' (7). Yet it could be argued that it is 'high theory' that insistently pulls us *away* from concrete histories, lived experiences of oppression and resistance, and specific artistic movements and works, and leads us towards monotonous questions of discourse, representation, language, and identity.[21]

In his account of the critical challenges posed by 'the new and complex varieties of historical experiences now available to us all in the post-Eurocentric world' (470), Edward Said finds 'the various post-modern theories put forward by J.F. Lyotard and his disciples, with this disdain for the grand historical narratives, their interest in mimicry and weightless pastiche, their unrelenting Eurocentrism' unequal to the task ('History' 471). This eurocentrism is endemic to criticism that artificially homogenizes competing ideologies and cultures while accepting that the world can be broken down into 'West' and 'East,' although the so-called 'western tradition' is itself a historically recent construct, one that is only sustainable by ruthlessly masking the nonwestern roots of classical thought and obscuring the cultural cross-pollination that is central to human history. The anticolonialists of the national liberation period opposed eurocentrism, but in the words of Said, 'they did not at all mean that all whites and Europeans, or all white and European culture, were to be thrown out and rejected' (*Reflections* xvii). Rather the anti-imperialist giants of this era saw that within 'western societies' dominant ideologies have always been in tension and conflict with oppositional currents, in correspondence with capitalism's antagonistic class forces and relationships. In his book-length study of postcolonial theory, African scholar Ato Quayson reiterates this position:

> [U]nlike most postcolonial commentators I do not think it is possible or desirable completely to debunk Western-inspired theories. . . . It is undeniably the case, of course, that discourses manufactured in the West have regularly been used as tools for marginalizing others. And yet at the same time these same tools, in the hands of both Westerners and others have also been used in serious struggles for liberation, not just from the West but from constrictive patterns of thought. There is no question, for instance, of the efficacy of Marxism in providing progressive ways by which non-Western nations have grasped the processes of globalization and helping them to position themselves strategically with regard to these processes. In fact, there is no question that without Marxism, some of the best ideas that postcolonialism has produced, from Fanon through to C.L.R. James and Gayatri Spivak, would have been much less interesting than they have turned out to be. (12–13)

This figuration of discursive and cultural forms as 'tools' is very helpful for discussions of Caribbean literature, which even more obviously than other regional literatures is multifaceted and plural, drawing on and synthesizing multiple influences—from Amerindian, African, European, Asian traditions—to produce something unique. Concepts such as transnationalism, hybridity, nomadism, syncretism, creolization continue to be central to critical exploration of Caribbean culture. But as Quayson argues, we cannot afford to overlook 'the efficacy of Marxism in providing progressive ways by which non-Western nations have grasped the processes of globalization' (12). While a straw-man version is assumed to be unable to negotiate multiplicity or to challenge oppression around nation, race, gender, and sexuality, Marxism can provide a framework from which to probe the interdependence of class exploitation and other forms of oppression, and to apprehend imperialism as an integral, though flexible, feature of capitalism. The materialist dialectic, moreover, provides an apt starting point for analysis of postcolonial literature, capable as it is of engaging with the material coordinates of imperialism without reductively placing 'the literary' in a mimetic relationship to an unproblematic empirical reality. In advocating such a critical theory I follow the many materialist scholars in the field of postcolonial studies.[22]

Historical Materialism and Literature

Georg Lukács' *History and Class Consciousness* illustrates how the materialist dialectic can enable a grounded, nuanced, and specific analysis of the ideological and aesthetic ramifications of literary texts and movements. This work, encompassing, in the words of Edward Said, 'almost all the area now settled on by critical discourse: representation, reflection, reification, reception, epistemic unity, dynamism in the artwork, sign-systems, the relations of theory with practice, the problems of the "subject"' ('Between Chance and Determinism' 63), is particularly useful at the current conjuncture, as Timothy Bewes argues in his book-length exploration of the theory of reification:

> For all that the concept of reification is criticized as embodying a dualistic topography of truth and appearance, use-value and exchange-value, transcendence and worldliness, pre-revolution and post-revolution, the consciousness of the bourgeoisie and the consciousness of the proletariat, etc., the concept elucidated by Lukács is at every moment set against such a dualistic topography. Reification, potentially, is as nuanced as any term within the post-structuralist arsenal of elaborate metaphors and 'non-originary' concepts. (14)

Lukács' *tour de force* was germinated during an era of revolutionary upheaval that fostered attendant convulsions in the world of ideas; it provides a remarkably pliant framework for tracing the relationship between social and ideological forces while avoiding the twin perils of Cartesian reductionism and idealism.[23]

Lukács develops an incisive critique of 'the antinomies of bourgeois thought,' and the assumed opposition between subject and object, which he describes thus:

> The belief that the transformation of the immediately given into a truly understood (and not merely an immediately perceived) and for that reason really objective reality, i.e. the belief that the impact of the category of mediation upon the picture of the world is merely 'subjective', i.e. is no more than an 'evaluation' of a reality that 'remains unchanged' . . . (150)

Bourgeois empiricism further specializes and compartmentalizes knowledge into discrete self-contained units, or 'monads,' making 'of every historical object a variable monad which is denied any interaction with other—similarly viewed—monads and which possesses characteristics that appear to be absolutely immutable essences' (153). The predominance of the idea that literature should be separate from 'politics' illustrates the continuing force of such habitual artificial specialization, as though political science, geography, economics, literature, are not linked and interdependent faces of what Edward Said has called 'one worldly space.'[24] Lukács explains that this 'specialisation of skills leads to the destruction of every image of the whole' (*History* 103), but this fragmentation is not the *product* of the disciplines, rather the disciplines themselves are *constituted* by historical material forces:

> [T]he more intricate a modern science becomes and the better it understands itself methodologically, the more resolutely it will turn its back on the ontological problems of its own sphere of influence and eliminate them from the realm where it has achieved some insight. The more highly developed it becomes and the more scientific, the more it will become a formally closed system of partial laws. It will then find that the world lying beyond its confines, and in particular the material base which it is its task to understand, *its own concrete underlying reality* lies, methodologically and in principle *beyond its grasp*. (104)

While empiricism is thus mired in disconnected specializations, the flip side of bourgeois thought consists of holistic accounts couched in mystical or idealist terms—in other words explicitly disconnected from material reality, and still altogether dependent on the original antinomy between object and subject.

In many ways the postmodernist rejection of enlightenment thought enacts precisely such a retreat from the seemingly intractable problems faced by bourgeois empiricism. The Foucauldian notion that history is not intelligible by the human subject; Lyotard's radical dislocation of subjective knowledge and the objective world; Baudrillard's exorbitant claim that the Gulf War did not occur. All of these ultimately accept the antinomies of bourgeois thought while jettisoning the possibility of reaching anything other than purely idealist, mystified accounts, at the expense of history. In his *Bodies of Meaning* David McNally extends this argument, showing that ironically, given the seemingly ubiquitous critical focus on 'the body,' such theories 'eliminate the messier precincts' (as Said would put it) of corporeality:

> postmodernist theory, whether it calls itself post-structuralism, deconstruction or post-Marxism, is constituted by a radical attempt to banish the real human body—the sensate, biocultural, laboring body—from the sphere of language and social life. As a result, I argue, these outlooks reproduce a central feature of commodified society: the abstraction of social products and practices from the laboring bodies that generate them. (1)

This elision can be seen in readings of Caribbean literature that constantly move away from material relationships and the experiences of actual bodies towards allegorical interpretations emphasizing language and representation.[25]

In contrast, historical materialism takes the key components of Hegel's dialectic—'the unity of opposites,' the 'transformation of quantity into quality,' and the 'negation of the negation'—and transforms them into a historically grounded and dynamic system of thought with working-class self-activity at its center (Rees 8–9). As British Marxist John Rees explains, this dialectic 'is not a suprahistorical master key whose only advantage is to turn up when no real historical knowledge is available' (9). Its starting point is that all truth is relative, and 'there is no final, faultless, criterion for truth which hovers, like god, outside the historical process' but nonetheless 'some theories . . . are less internally contradictory and have greater explanatory power than others' (Rees 235). While bourgeois ideology is systemically compromised by the necessity of maintaining the status quo, thus 'the unexplained and inexplicable facticity of bourgeois existence as it is here and now acquires the patina of an eternal law of nature or a cultural value enduring for all time' (Lukács 157), the perspective of the oppressed has the potential to achieve a less compromised position by generalizing from the lessons of collective struggle—the end goal of which is the 'fundamental transformation of the whole of society' (Lukács 163)—and in turn testing those generalizations in praxis. This does not imply a pristine, unified, and unproblematic proletarian consciousness. On the contrary, consciousness is always uneven, riven with contradictions and divisions, and kinetic rather than static. What is implied is rather a method and perspective that is more likely to achieve 'superior explanatory power . . . in comparison with its competitors' (Rees 237).

Lukács' *History and Class Consciousness* is not the academic product of a 'great individual' but rather the distillation of the lessons of a period of revolutionary upheaval.[26] Its key terms are 'totality,' 'contradiction,' 'mediation,' and 'change:' Capitalist society is a totality, yet is immediately experienced as disconnected parts; the parts are in a relationship of mutual conditioning, or mediation, and this relationship is not static but contradictory and fluid. First and foremost, 'the dialectical method aims at understanding society as a whole . . . (it) simultaneously raises and reduces all specializations to the level of aspects in a dialectical process' (*History* 28). While acknowledging the illusory nature of empirical reality, Lukács replaces the subject/object antinomy with a model of change that does not 'abandon immanent (social) reality:'

> to leave empirical reality behind can only mean that the objects of the empirical world are to be understood as aspects of a totality, i.e. as the aspects of a total social situation caught up in the process of historical change. Thus the category of mediation is a lever with which to overcome the mere immediacy of the empirical world . . . Mediation would not be possible were it not for the fact that the empirical existence of objects is itself mediated and only appears to be unmediated in so far as the awareness of mediation is lacking so that the objects are torn from the complex of their true determinants and placed in artificial isolation. (162–3)

Lukács' formulations in *History and Class Consciousness* bear no relation to the version of Marxism that is linear, rigid, reductive, simplistically unified: 'it is the nature of the dialectical method constantly to produce and reproduce its own essential aspects, as its very being constitutes the denial of any smooth, linear development of ideas' (164); 'the dialectical antithesis of quantity and quality . . .

with all its implications is only the beginning of the complex process of mediation whose goal is the knowledge of society as a historical totality' (169);

> the single aspect is not a segment of a mechanical totality that could be put together out of such segments, for this would lead us to see knowledge as an infinite progression. It must be seen instead as containing the possibility of unraveling the whole abundance of the totality from within itself . . . if every movement beyond the immediacy that had made the aspect an aspect of the dialectical process . . . is not to freeze once more in a new rigidity and a new immediacy. (170)

As these quotations indicate, although *History* does not discuss 'what it is like to read or experience an author, or . . . what impresses and disorients one in a given novel' (Said, 'Between Chance' 63), it locates culture as an arena where 'fissures and dissonances are crucial' (Lukács 53), and provides a framework which can 'systematize the processes by which reality gets into and is reflected by art' (Said, 'Between Chance' 69). In this way it resembles another Marxist work born in a period of revolution, Leon Trotsky's *Literature and Revolution*, which insists that while form cannot be prioritized over sociohistorical content, '[A] work of art should, in the first place, be judged by its own law, that is, by the law of art' (150).[27]

Reading Caribbean Women's Literature

Taking this approach, the materialist *starting point* from which to situate the recent developments in Caribbean literature discussed above—the greater prominence of women writers, the shift away from the self-consciously anti-imperialist themes of the national liberation writers—must be the broader historical processes of the second half of the twentieth century. The mid-twentieth century development of national literatures was bound up with the consolidation under colonial rule of a domestic petty bourgeoisie, an outgrowth of the expanded educational and therefore professional opportunities for a minority of Caribbean men under colonialism; similar developments for women occurred later. Olive Senior draws out the connection between political independence and reforms beneficial to women, noting that 'in the post-war years, educational reforms went hand in hand with the expansion of the economic and political systems of the West Indian territories, which began to move to greater autonomy from Britain' (47). In 1991 she was able to observe that

> the progress of Caribbean women . . . is quite remarkable, though it is far more so in the larger territories where women have greater access to education and job opportunities. In these countries, females are now prominent in government and administration and in some of the professions, and are proving themselves as entrepreneurs and business-women. There are in some of our larger cities and towns numbers of highly visible, well-dressed, apparently self-confident women, who in their life styles and manner appear to have gained equality with their male counterparts. (Senior 187)

Senior is quick to point out that this new middle class represents only a minority, adding 'while some women are moving upwards, and very rapidly too, most women remain at the bottom' (187). However, expansion in educational opportunities and the opening of some sectors of employment previously closed to women importantly contributed to the greater visibility of women writers after the 1970s (Senior 45–51). The broader women's liberation movement, facilitated by the same socioeconomic forces, in turn fostered institutions—women's studies programs and departments in universities, research centers, writers' collectives, and publishing houses—which further enabled the emergence of women writers.[28]

While much new wave Caribbean women's fiction is not as explicitly 'political' as the literature of national liberation, there are certainly many exceptions to this rule.[29] However, there seems to be a kernel of truth in the notion that the literature of recent decades is, overall, less engaged with movements against imperialism than was the consciously nationalist literature of the period of independence struggles. The broader socioeconomic and political contexts, and particularly the class character of the national liberation movements, are vital explanatory factors. During the middle decades of the twentieth century temporary alliances were forged between the Caribbean working and middle classes, as Edward Brathwaite explains:

> In the British West Indies, it was a time when the educated middle classes began to press for a greater say in the government of their territories, when the labourers of plantation and city began to organize themselves in large tough unions, a coalition of the two (middle and labouring classes) pressing for better social conditions, universal adult suffrage, and self-government. This, in other words, was the age of West Indian nationalism. For young men of energy and talent, there was a great deal to do. (Introduction vi)

This alliance was never without tensions, as Clive Thomas argues in his 1988 socioeconomic study of the Caribbean: 'While the main supporters of this resistance were the poor and powerless masses, its leadership (when organized) was invariably recruited from the educated professional middle classes or other intermediate strata that had developed under colonial tutelage' (60). After independence, this anticolonial cross-class alliance disintegrated as the different poles of the national liberation movements pursued their antagonistic class interests. Opposition to postcolonial imperialism continued in multiple arenas, and the language of nationalism—sometimes explicitly 'anti-American' and for sovereign sustainable development—was and is sometimes used by political leaders, social movements, and elected officials during U.S. imperialism's cold war and neoliberal phases. However, the capital-intensive industrialization programs of the postwar period sharpened class divisions within Caribbean nations, as the ruling class benefited from the economic boom while the working class bore the brunt of the crises that followed. These incompatible class allegiances are no less acute among women, as has been noted by feminists seeking common ground:

> Despite the obvious and growing dependency of working and professional women on the services provided by domestic workers, and obversely on the need for many women to find employment as domestic workers, there exists a strong element of distrust between employer and employee, rooted in the class differences between the women. (Ellis 43)

Class antagonisms between women emerge thematically and figuratively in a broad range of Caribbean women's literature.

The same period that saw the increased visibility of women writers, then, witnessed a decline in middle-class participation in emancipatory, anti-imperialist politics, in conjunction with heightened class divisions between women and within society as a whole. Published writers, who overwhelmingly are of the middle class, were less likely to be part of anti-imperialist cross-class coalitions or other collective oppositional movements. For the middle class, political anomie, rather than the engaged optimism of mid century, characterizes the period. While there are exceptions, much later-century literature confirms the absence of a close relationship between the middle-class writer (and protagonist) and political struggle. In many cases class divisions haunt the literary work, and the gap between the world of the writer, and her fictional characters, and that of the majority of Caribbean women, is cavernous. Yet despite the class character of the novel—strongly associated with the rise of the bourgeoisie—we are often also able to see beyond this limited perspective and to grasp broader truths about postindependence Caribbean societies. The writer is neither simply a representative of their class position and social environment nor the autonomous subject of bourgeois ideology: the two coexist dialectically.[30]

Raymond Williams' discussion of authors remains helpful in clarifying the relationship between individual artists and social formations. He starts with the Marxist principle that 'the separated concepts of "individual" and "society" are radically unified, but reciprocally and indeed dialectically,' and quotes the following passage from Marx's *Economic and Philosophical Manuscripts of 1844*:

> The individual is a *social* being. The manifestation of his life—even when it does not appear directly in the form of a social manifestation, accomplished in association with other men—is therefore a manifestation of *social life*. . . . Though man is a unique individual—and it is just his particularity which makes him an individual, a really *individual* social being—he is equally the whole, the ideal whole, the subjective existence of society as thought and experienced. (194)

Williams then elaborates 'more precise theoretical positions' to assist in drawing out the implications for considering authors, and specifies different 'levels of sociality—from the external forms of the political economy of literature, through the inherited forms of genres, notations, and conventions, to the constitutive forms of the social production of consciousness' (195). Turning to the latter, Williams identifies 'effective social relations in which, even while individual projects are being pursued, what is being drawn on is trans-individual, not only in the sense of shared (initial) forms and experiences, but in the specifically creative sense of new

responses and formation' (195). Such forces are apparent in the periodic
emergence of 'specific new forms and structures of feeling' that are shared by
many different authors (195). At the same time any such pattern will show
variations, with some authors conforming to and others departing from the
archetype, and 'this very process of development can be grasped as a complex of
active relations, within which the emergence of an individual project, and the real
history of other contemporary projects and of the developing forms and structures,
are continuously and substantially interactive' (196). We are left with the
'reciprocal discovery of the truly social in the individual, and the truly individual
in the social' (197) as a model for contemplating authorship. Williams draws on
Goldmann for much of this, but departs from his distinction (which deploys
Lukács' 'actual' and 'possible' consciousnesses) between 'great writers . . . who
integrate a vision at the level of the possible ("complete") consciousness of a social
formation' and 'most writers (who) reproduce the contents of ("incomplete")
actual consciousness' (197). Williams acknowledges that this may at times be the
case, but warns against broad categorical abstractions: 'The real relations of the
individual, the trans-individual, and the social may include radical tension and
disturbance, even actual and irresolvable contradictions of a conscious kind, as
often as they include integration' (197).

Such a model is able to apprehend the commonalities and specificities of the
writers—from four nations of diverse geographic, demographic and economic
scale—explored in *Caribbean Women Writers and Globalization*, and has
informed my choices at every level.[31] My decision to organize the literature by
nation stems from the principle that while regional characteristics are strong, and
countries cannot be extricated from a global system, nonetheless each nation
experiences regional and international influences in distinct ways, and also
possesses particular social and cultural characteristics. In taking the nation state as
the primary organizing principle I am departing from a trend towards comparative
explorations of black women's writing that emphasize diasporic, global
connections between authors, many of whom are based in metropolitan centers in
North America and Europe and whose work defies easy national categorization.[32]
Such studies are valuable and pertinent, particularly in light of high levels of out-
migration from the Caribbean and the intensified globalization of culture in the last
50 years. Benedict Anderson's influential study rightly points out that nations are
'imagined communities' rather than historical or current realities.

And yet the nation remains as a stubborn material fact, and borders and states
continue to circumscribe peoples' mobility and lived experience. As Michel-Rolph
Trouillot explains, generalizing from the example of Haiti, a nation is 'a cultural
construct that operates *against the background of political power*' (*Haiti: State
Against Nation* 25). It is not a transhistorical essence, rather 'the nation is the
culture and history of a class-divided civil society, as they relate to issues of state
power. It is that part of the historically derived cultural repertoire that is translated
in political terms' (25). In its turn, nationalism is 'a political claim made on the
basis of culture and history' (26). Both are in some senses invented, but in others
grounded in lived realities inhabited by 'sensate, biocultural laboring bodies,' to

paraphrase McNally. While the global economy facilitates the free movement of capital (at least that of the most powerful nations), and trade agreements demolish barriers to ideally untrammeled corporate development, corporations continue to rely on close ties to their respective states, while the mobility of labor is carefully monitored, controlled, and contained.[33] Even while many of the writers explored here themselves have resided in, and written from, multiple countries, their literature remains acutely conscious of formative national experiences, and of the limits placed on most peoples' mobility. Jamaica Kincaid, herself a native of Antigua who migrated to the U.S.A., provides an epigrammatic reminder of the relativity of transnational freedom:

> Every native of every place is a potential tourist, and every tourist is a native of somewhere. Every native everywhere lives a life of overwhelming and crushing banality and boredom and desperation and depression, and every deed, good and bad, is an attempt to forget this. Every native would like to find a way out, every native would like a rest, every native would like a tour. But some natives—most natives in the world—cannot go anywhere. They are too poor. They are too poor to go anywhere. They are too poor to escape the reality of their lives; and they are too poor to live properly in the place where they live . . . (*A Small Place* 18–19)

The nation thus has negative and positive resonance—as a confining space and as a self-anchoring point of reference. The literature explored here is acutely aware of national specificities—of flora, fauna, language, art, food, religion—and of the force of the national economy and institutions—political, military, juridical—even while affirming strong affinities with other nations in the region and the globe.[34]

While the nation is axiomatic, it is also ultimately inextricable from the global system. This truth, so often erased from the dominant discourses of the dominant powers, which mystify the causal relationships between wealth and poverty, mobility and immobility, is laid bare in the literature considered here. Each text is grounded in national specificity, but the same global structures are clearly visible, in the omnipresent themes of migration and the journey, the global workplace (fruit picking in Florida, domestic labor in Toronto, childcare in New York City, nursing in London, export processing in Haiti), IMF and World Bank imposed structural adjustment, the tourist industry, the American businessman, poverty amid plenty, the threat or reality of foreign political and military intervention. My study unearths these profound continuities, following Edward Said's notion of 'worldliness,' which he describes as 'the restoration to . . . works and interpretations of their place in the global setting, a restoration that can only be accomplished by an appreciation not of some tiny defensively constituted corner of the world, but of the large, many-windowed house of culture as a whole' ('Criticism' 43).

All the texts considered here have a distinctive national character and at the same time global forces generate structural continuities that in turn emerge as thematic and figurative patterns.[35] Edwidge Danticat is currently perhaps the best-known anglophone Haitian writer in the U.S.A. In chapter one I develop a reading of her fiction that traces its distinctive combination of social and magical realism, and explores the emotional impact of the texts' intensely visual figurative patterns that express Haiti's brutal history and political realities while, with references to Haitian history and myth, especially Vodou, constructing alternative realities. In chapter two I read the literature of Jamaica Kincaid, arguably the best-known Caribbean woman writer in the U.S.A. While many critics of Kincaid's work have identified the figurative 'maternal-colonial matrix' and the postmodern 'indeterminacy' of its prose poetry, my reading highlights instead the recurrent articulation of, and protest against, global inequalities especially in their particular Antiguan manifestations. Kincaid explicitly addresses the postcolonial 'language debate' when she talks of the irony of exposing the crime in the language of the criminal, yet her texts themselves exemplify the ideological flexibility of language. Simultaneously, her entire oeuvre to date makes visible the immense gap between the world of the writer and that of the majority of Caribbean women while also revealing 'the objects of the empirical world . . . as aspects of a total situation caught up in the process of historical change' (Lukács 162).

Chapter three develops consecutive readings of Pauline Melville's *Ventriloquist's Tale*, Jan Shinebourne's *Timepiece* and *Last English Plantation*, and Oonya Kempadoo's *Buxton Spice* (all three global writers with formative ties to Guyana) in conjunction with Grace Nichols' *Whole of a Morning Sky* and Beryl Gilroy's *Frangipani House* (both Guyanese-British writers firmly established in the canon of Caribbean women authors but whose novels are nonetheless out of print in the U.S.). Melville's distinctive writing remains grounded in the Guyanese tradition—the legend of El Dorado, the voyage in to the interior, Wapisiana mythology, the tension between multiculturalism and communalism—even while resonating with Latin American magical realism and the cultural globalism of a Salman Rushdie. Kempadoo's intensely personal coming-of-age narrative, like the earlier works by Nichols and Gilroy, reveals the interdependence of political and domestic violence, social and sexual relationships. *Buxton Spice* also evokes the emotional and sensual experience of 1970s Guyana through rich images of flora and fauna combined with those of graphic, visceral violence. Taken together these novels reveal the extent to which national sociocultural and literary forces cohere in to a distinctively Guyanese voice and aesthetic.

The Grenadian novel *Angel* by Merle Collins is the subject of the fourth chapter. This work explicitly takes up questions of imperialism and resistance, attempts to tell history from the perspective of poor women whose lives are indelibly marked by local and global structures of power, and pays tribute to the possibility of collective struggle. Using the Creole continuum as it recreates the cultural and physical character of Grenada, *Angel* communicates a deep commitment to Grenadian self-determination, despite the narrative's bleak depiction of the destruction of a people's revolutionary aspirations. This work raises questions about the troubled relationship between political propaganda and artistic affect, and suggests some of the inherent contradictions within any attempt to give voice to working-class aspirations within the confines of the novel form.

My reading has led me to the conclusion that this literature *expresses* the historical moment—and the new forms of imperialism that replace formal

European colonialism after independence—just as the earlier fiction gave voice to the sociopolitical realities of the period of national liberation. The very economic and social conditions that form the backdrop of the literature are themselves shaped and exacerbated by new global forces. Even where there is no explicit engagement with foreign domination, these dynamics emerge nonetheless in the 'fissures and dissonances' of fictional works ostensibly rooted in the 'personal' realm of relationships and individual growth; often even the most personal issues are shown to be embedded in broader societal structures. These texts are not *less* political, but rather expressive of a *changed* political context.

While this study forefronts historical materiality it also strives to appreciate the specific creative qualities of works of literature. While socioeconomic forces and power relationships define our world, art constantly chafes against the confines of this lived reality and provides visions of alternative possibilities. Any such perspective inevitably raises definitional and analytical questions about the categories 'art' and 'aesthetics,' questions that are often superseded in ideology critiques and metaphorical readings. Lukács worked towards a definition of 'art' as a distinct realm of human activity that 'represents a human generality: a real mediation between (isolated) subjectivity and (abstract) universality; a specific process of the "identical subject/object"' (qtd. in *Marxism and Literature* Williams 151). Raymond Williams addresses the difficulty behind this formulation:

> The problem is to sustain such a distinction through the inevitable extension to an indissoluble social material process: not only indissoluble in the social conditions of the making and reception of art, within a general social process from which these can not be excised; but also indissoluble in the actual making and reception, which are connecting material processes within a social system of the use and transformation of material (including language) by material means. (152)

Two different kinds of error are possible in trying to reach a materialist understanding of culture: one is to hold that 'all literature is "ideology," in the crude sense that its dominant intention (and then our only response) is the communication or imposition of "social" or "political" meanings and value;' the other is to accept 'that all literature is "aesthetic" in the crude sense that its dominant intention (and then our only response) is the beauty of language or form' (155). Williams suggests that we reject 'the aesthetic' as a separate and abstract phenomenon but 'recognize and indeed emphasize the specific variable intentions and the specific variable responses that have been grouped as aesthetic in distinction from other isolated intentions and responses' (156). The very idea of 'literature' as a special area of life separate from the realm of human production is itself specific to capitalism and rests on ruthless suppression of the material and ideological conditions that shape literary production. But literature for that reason has the potential to crystallize certain elements of human existence, to imagine a world other than this and to communicate at the level of emotion. The definitive organizing principle for this book is the dialectical supposition that art is inseparable from social forces and yet always strains against the limits imposed by them. The literature explored here reveals the international relations of domination that continue to delimit human experience; it also expresses the indefatigable human impulse towards something more.

Notes

1 I use the designation 'anglophone Caribbean' rather than 'West Indian' although most of my study pertains to the West Indies, because I do include a chapter on Haiti. My study is in no way claiming to be broadly representative of all anglophone literature in the region: I do not, for example, include detailed discussion of writers from Jamaica and Trinidad, although both nations have produced significant literary traditions. I do not attempt, either, to discuss the region's Dutch, French, or Spanish literatures. Some, though not all, of the broad tendencies I identify are shared by other language groups. In their rich and diverse 1995 collection of Hispanic short stories, Margarite Fernández Olmos and Lizabeth Paravisini-Gebert draw attention to what is distinctive about Spanish Caribbean literature and also some of the regional continuities: 'The ample representation of female writing in this anthology attests to the fact that women writers have been at the forefront of literary innovation, not only in Puerto Rico, but in the region as a whole, having produced some of the most daring and controversial works in recent years' (13–14).

2 'Third World' is an inaccurate and at this time considered by many to be an obsolete term, but in the postwar decades, sections of the newly emerging colonies of Asia, Africa and Latin America used this designation as they attempted to develop a 'new international economic order' and built new political groupings under such headings as 'Non-Aligned Movement'—in other words subservient to neither Washington nor Moscow. Some see in the term 'postcolonial' a move away from the politically oppositional implications of the old term: 'with all its problems, the term *Third World* still retains heuristic value as a convenient label for the imperialized formations . . . replacing the term *Third World* with *postcolonial* is a liability' (Shohat 137–8).

3 Kathy McAfee explains in her summary of developments in the 1980s: 'The Caribbean region became the object of heightened attention and involvement by the United States. Washington enacted a set of new aid and trade policies and revived old practices, including direct military intervention, to strengthen US influence in the region. The Caribbean provides a particularly well-defined example of the policy agenda which the US has thrust upon low-income countries throughout the world under the banners of privatization and market-led economic development' (33).

4 See also work by Aijaz Ahmad, Arjun Appadurai, Timothy Brennan, Arif Dirlik, Neil Lazarus, Masao Miyoshi, and Benita Parry, to name but a few.

5 Haiti is obviously not part of the anglophone Caribbean, though it has produced some writers in English. In terms of francophone literature Haiti is again often seen as prototypical of region-wide trends. For example, G.R. Coulthard has traced the négritude made famous by Aimé Césaire to the work of Haitian Stephen Alexis in the 1930s, when opposition to the U.S. occupation fostered *l'indigenisme, l'haitianisme,* and *l'africanisme,* all cultural movements that celebrated Haitians' black ancestry and African cultural heritage while breaking with French cultural influences, and were precursors to many other forms of cultural nationalism across the region.

6 Birbalsingh, while stressing overlaps and exceptions, identifies four stages of writing: 'the first of which lasted virtually throughout the first half of the twentieth century; the second from 1950–1965; the third from 1965 to 1980; and the fourth from 1980 to the

present' (*Frontiers* xi); He sees the first group as largely 'colonial in outlook,' 'while the 1950–1965 writers probe and question this outlook [and those] after 1965 espouse post-Independence interests' (xi). Others may categorize differently: writing about the short story in 1996, E.A. Markham finds it convenient to assume three broad phases: pre-1950s; a transition embodied by Samuel Selvon; and a 'New Phase' after the 1990s. Alison Donnell and Sarah Lawson Welsh, in their extensive 1996 *Routledge Reader in Caribbean Literature*, work with more specific divisions: 1900–30; 1930–49; 1950–65; 1966–79; 1980–89; the 1990s.

7   Significant early publications addressing this new development include Selwyn Cudjoe's *Caribbean Women Writers*; Carole Boyce Davies and Elaine Savory Fido's *Out of the Kumbla*; Pamela Mordecai and Betty Wilson's *Her True-True Name*; Evelyn O'Callaghan's *Woman Version*. See also the more recent *Caribbean Women Writers: Fiction in English* edited by Mary Condé and Thorunn Lonsdale.

8   Evelyn O'Callaghan's 2004 study of narratives of the nineteenth and early twentieth century by (mostly) elite and middle class white women in the West Indies is a recent example of the former that problematizes the notion of female 'silence' prior to the late twentieth century.

9   Many critics of Hispanic literature note the coincidence of women's greater visibility, a more explicitly resistant literary voice, and a commitment to historical investigation and social justice that challenges postmodern theoretical assumptions. See Jehenson, McClennen, Shaw.

10 Barbara Lalla's *Defining Jamaican Fiction* is relatively unusual in its move away from a decisive distinction between two waves of literary development, and between male and female writing: it instead traces thematic continuity in the context of Jamaican literature by both men and women. Not all critics identify the ideological shifts with gender: Donnell and Welsh, for example, talking about poetry after the 1970s see in general 'a shift in concern from anti-colonial, oppositional modes . . . to more introspective and "non-colonial" attempts to reclaim a Caribbean subjectivity' (286).

11 As I argue in '"Dem tief, dem a dam tief:" Jamaica Kincaid's Literature of Protest,' many of the literary features habitually associated with 'postmodernism' are in fact identifiable in the high British modernism of the early mid-twentieth century.

12 This move can be seen through the lens of the 'retreat from class' analyzed by Ellen Meiksins Wood in her book of that title. Ironically, in a period when neoliberalism exacerbates class divisions within rich and poor nations alike, and cultural and political discourses recognize the heavy hand of the market and transnational corporations globally, class is problematized if not dismissed as an explanatory framework for understanding postcolonial culture.

13 The UN Human Development Report of 2002, which can be read on line at http://hdr.undp.org/reports/global/2002/en/ confirms this: 'The level of inequality worldwide is grotesque . . . the world's richest 1% of people receive as much income as the poorest 57%' (Chapter One, 7); at the same time '[T]he limited available evidence indicates that worldwide within-country income inequality has been increasing for the past 30 years' (8).

14 For materialist accounts of the roots of racism in capitalist slavery, see Robin Blackburn, *The Making of New World Slavery* and Eric Williams, *Capitalism and Slavery*. For a brief overview of the marxist account of racism see my chapter 'Was There a Time Before Race?: Capitalist Modernity and the Origins of Racism' in Bartolovich and Lazarus.

15 Chandra Talpade Mohanty's *Third World Women and the Politics of Feminism* launched an important critique on both fronts. Gayatri Spivak's 1985 article, 'Three Women's Texts and a Critique of Imperialism' significantly developed a critique of feminism that fails to interrogate imperialist structures and ideologies, and her opus has significantly contributed to an anti-imperialist critique informed by Marxism and feminism. Natasha Barnes' 1999 article, 'Reluctant Matriarch,' develops a thoughtful analysis of the pitfalls of nationalism and the necessity for a Caribbean feminism informed by opposition to racism and imperialism.

16 In *The Origin of the Family, Private Property and the State*, Engels developed an account of the simultaneous rise of women's oppression and class society. While some of the anthropological data on which this argument drew has been subsequently found to be incorrect, much of the argument has been substantiated. See, for example, Eleanor Leacock's *Myths of Male Dominance*, Rayna Reiter, *Toward an Anthropology of Women*. For debates around the merits and weaknesses of Engels' argument see Sayers et al *Engels Revisited*.

17 According to a recent report by UNCTAD (United Nations Conference on Trade and Development), '[w]omen account for about 40% of all workers worldwide, and their participation rate has risen steadily. The largest increase over the past 20 years was in South America (up from 26% to 45%), while the lowest rates were in North Africa and West Asia, where only a third of all women are economically active. But women still earn about two thirds of what men earn. The manufacturing wage gap ranges from 52% in Botswana and 75% in Egypt to 81% in Costa Rica and 86% in Sri Lanka' <www.unctadxi.org/templates/Page____509.aspx>.

18 This is vividly demonstrated by women who become heads of state: Margaret Thatcher as Prime Minister of the United Kingdom promoted neoliberal policies at home and abroad that had devastating consequences for working-class women, as did Eugenia Charles as head of the right-wing Freedom Party and Prime Minister of Dominica.

19 Postmodernism is itself a product of the same historical moment. Terry Eagleton argues in *The Idea of Culture* that postmodernism 'has abandoned a belief in radical mass movements, having precious few of them to remember. As a theory, postmodernism comes after the great mid-century national liberation movements, and is either literally or metaphorically too young to recollect such seismic upheavals' (14). Others make a distinction between ludic and resistant postmodernism: the latter, which is more pervasive in Latin America, 'has not renounced the need to seek theories and engage in politics that can lead to social change' (McClennen 24).

20 Aijaz Ahmad's *In Theory* of 1992 developed a far-reaching critical analysis of the ideological moorings of postcolonial studies. As Neil Larsen observes: 'What makes a consideration of Ahmad's critique of postcolonialism even more compelling is the fact that he locates poststructuralism squarely within its ideological field. Here, he confronts directly what must be one of the crucial issues in any critical or theoretical discussion of postcolonialism, namely, its demonstrable affinities for a philosophy that has declared itself the enemy of all notions of identity and fixed meaning' (*Determinations* 141). The following are just some of the works that have in recent decades developed political critiques of postmodernism: Paul Bové, *In the Wake of Theory* and *Mastering Discourse*; Alex Callinicos, *Against Postmodernism*; Christopher Norris, *The Truth About Postmodernism, What's Wrong with Postmodernism, Uncritical Theory*; David McNally, *Bodies of Meaning*; Alan Sokal, *Fashionable Nonsense*. See McClennen's excellent Glossary entries for the terms 'poststructuralism' and 'postmodernism.'

21 The immense body of work produced by Edward Said, which has undeniably influenced the development of postcolonial literary studies, is indelibly marked by a persistent investment in political praxis beyond academic study, most noticeably his enduring commitment to Palestinian liberation. While not Marxist, Said's work is characterized by a materialist attention to history, combined with a sensitivity to the aesthetic and cultural, and has informed my attempts to read postcolonial literature; *Caribbean Women Writers* is thus indebted to this towering intellect. Ahmad's critique of Said's 'loosely poststructuralist celebration of postcolonial "difference" and hybridity' (*Determinations* Larsen 153) remains an important corrective to his culturalism and hostility to Marxism, yet does not negate the significance of Said's distinctive contribution.

22 See Crystal Bartolovich's introduction to *Marxism, Modernity and Postcolonial Studies* for a thoughtful discussion of these debates. Within Caribbean literary studies M. Keith Booker and Dubravka Juraga, Carole Boyce Davies, Selwyn Cudjoe, have variously contributed to a Marxist current. Interdisciplinarily there is a strong strain of materialist-feminist scholarship, exemplified by June Nash, Helen Safa, Maria Patricia Fernandez-Kelly, addressing the Caribbean within the broader context of Latin America and the global economy. Alison Donnell has similarly brought a materialist perspective to analysis of Caribbean women's literature. Marxist politics have of course been extremely influential in the anti-imperialist movements of the region, as figures such as C.L.R. James and Eric Williams illustrate. These forces are clearly visible within the region's fiction throughout the last half century.

23 In *The Dialectical Biologist* Marxist biologists Richard Levins and Richard Lewontin use the term 'Cartesian Reductionism' to describe positivist systems of thought that accept isolated empirical facts on face value and understand them not as the products of larger historical forces mediated by particular ideological frameworks but as discrete facts with inherent and unchanging attributes. 'Idealist' systems of thought uncouple ideas from their sociohistorical moorings and endow the former with determinant power.

24 Edward Said observes that the naturalization of specialized divisions is such as to impact even academic marxists otherwise alert to the workings of ideology. He points out that in *The Political Unconscious* Fredric Jameson betrays 'an unadmitted dichotomy between two kinds of "'Politics'": (1) the politics defined by political theory from Hegel to Louis Althusser and Ernst Bloch; (2) the politics of struggle and power in the everyday world . . .' The latter is 'only discussed once, in the course of a long footnote' and 'in a general way' ('Opponents' 133). Jameson thus reinscribes the supposition that literature, criticism, and culture broadly understood are separable from the social forces that give rise to them.

25 My argument here shares common ground with Julian Markels' discussion of Dickens criticism: 'those metaphorical readings which are the built-in reflex of contemporary scholarship and which inexorably mask the narratology of overdetermination by which these novels approach or avoid a possible point of entry' (33). 'This reifying criticism, by virtue of its point of entry, is obliged to treat the integrity of detail in a novel's actual progression as irrelevant. It selects for interpretation only those details that serve its chosen principle of symbolic coherence, ignores the rest, and in effect transforms the novel into a lyric poem monologically stripped of the narratological overdeterminations through which a writer might find a point of entry by telling her entire story' (39). See Chapter Four, n21.

26 Timothy Bewes argues that Lukács' later renunciation of his theory of reification should be seen as contiguous rather than manichean: 'Immanent in the "total reification" thesis is its own immediate repudiation. . . . Reification is a self-reflexive, or dialectical concept. . . . Lukács' repudiation of his theory was an enactment of its logic that was at worst "premature" . . . ' (89). Yet such an analysis erases the impact of the historical shift from an environment of revolutionary upheaval to one of Stalinist counter-revolution and thus '"divorces the concept from its foundations in the economic base,"' a move warned against by Lukács (qtd. in Bewes 93). In 'Traveling Theory' Said describes how the fluidity and subtlety of *History and Class Consciousness* is later turned in to static, confining dogma by the author and others.

27 See William Keach's introduction to the new publication of this classic by Haymarket Books.

28 The deep connections between grass roots movements for women's liberation, the institutionalization of women's studies, and the expansion of Caribbean women's literature were made graphically clear to me during a 2002 research trip to the University of West Indies' Cave Hill campus in Barbados. The library possesses numerous pamphlets, leaflets, and collections of poetry and essays produced by women's writing groups and community projects of the 1970s.

29 The literature of Dionne Brand, Michelle Cliff, Merle Collins, Edwidge Danticat, representing a wide variety of formal technique and content, could be described as explicitly political, in that the texts describe collective projects of liberation. A much broader body of literature could be described as 'political' due to its engagement with structures of oppression—around gender, sexuality, class, race—and the interconnectedness of social and personal forces.

30 Edward Said departs from Foucault even in his most Foucauldian works on the question of the role of the individual author in the process of textual production of meaning; in *Orientalism* and *The World, the Text, the Critic* Said's consistent attention to historical and social forces of power and inequality generates interest in *conflicting* ideological positions as they are expressed by particular voices with specific relationships to the dominant class.

31 One aspect of the debate around Caribbean literature has long been the question of residence. With exceptionally high levels of out-migration, in the past predominantly to Europe and more recently to North America, many Caribbean writers do not live in their countries of origin. As many writers and critics have asserted, diasporic writers are clearly part of the Caribbean literary tradition. In the case of the writers explored in this book, some reside in the Caribbean, many in the U.S.A., some in Canada or Europe. The condition of voluntary exile could well be described as transindividual.

32 See for example recent books published by Myriam Chancy, Isabel Hoving, Emilia Ippolito, Tommie Lee Jackson, Caroline Rody, Gina Wisker.

33 Saskia Sassen's *Mobility of Labor and Capital* provides an insightful and compelling analysis of these dynamics.

34 See Chapter Two, n18.

35 My simultaneous attention to both national specificity and 'worldliness' is augmented by a desire to include writers who are famous and those who are less well known internationally and to represent a plurality of styles, techniques and influences. My focus is primarily on narrative fiction.

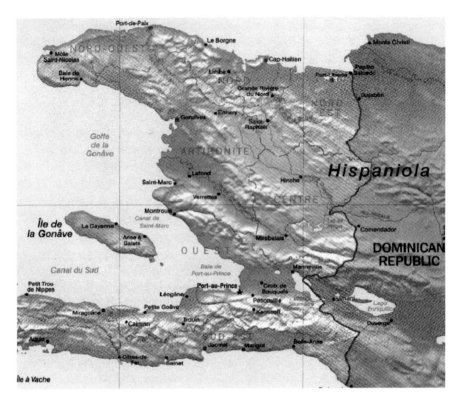

Figure 1   Map of Haiti

Chapter 1

Land of Mountains

The tradition of all the dead generations weighs like a nightmare on the brain of the living.   Karl Marx, *The 18ᵗʰ Brumaire of Louis Bonaparte*

History . . . is a nightmare from which I am trying to awake.

James Joyce, *Ulysses*

There is always a place where nightmares are passed on through generations like heirlooms.   Edwidge Danticat, *Breath Eyes Memory*

The Scars of History

When we are first introduced to the title character of Edwidge Danticat's *Dew Breaker* he has gone missing during a trip to Tampa, Florida from his current home in Brooklyn. His daughter Ka, the story's narrator, recounts the description of him she gives to the police:

> 'Sixty-five, five feet eight inches, one hundred and eighty pounds, with a widow's peak, thinning salt-and-pepper hair, and velvet-brown eyes—' . . . My father has had partial frontal dentures since he fell off his and my mother's bed and landed on his face ten years ago when he was having one of his prison nightmares. I mention that too. Just the dentures, not the nightmares. I also bring up the blunt, ropelike scar that runs from my father's right cheek down to the corner of his mouth, the only visible reminder of the year he spent in prison in Haiti. (*DB* 4–5)

We are thus introduced to two of the central tropes of the book, both suggesting the inescapable weight of the past as it bears down upon people in the present: nightmares and scarring. Like his daughter not yet knowing the truth, the reader initially assumes that in his past her father had been a victim of the Duvalier regime, and that memories of his imprisonment continue to torture him. Later in the collection we meet many other characters who carry the physical marks and manifestations of past trauma: the soles of a woman's feet are 'thin and sheer like an albino baby's skin' because they were whipped as punishment when she refused to dance with a *shoukèt laroze* (dew breaker) (131–2); another woman has been blind since agents of the dictatorship set fire to her home (95); and yet another stammers in fear decades after being tortured (198). We are soon dispossessed of the misapprehension that Ka's father is such a victim, however, when he returns to

his daughter and confesses that he 'was the hunter, he was not the prey' (20).[1] Far from bearing the marks of torture, he *inflicted* wounds like those felt by the other characters; his own scar is the result of the last desperate act of resistance from an activist priest, his final victim. As the collection continues we are given many more descriptions of this man that, despite superficial differences, match up with this first one, and he is remembered variously by survivors as a wanton sadist, by his wife as one who has undergone a miraculous transfiguration, by himself as both hunter and prey.

Many times we witness cases of mistaken identity, and despite the recurrent descriptive details proving that Ka's father was a *shoukèt laroze*, enough doubt is planted to make us sporadically question whether this is indeed the infamous dew breaker, and to look beyond surfaces to a possibly more complicated truth. One could conclude that the text wants us to reject such simple formulae as 'hunter and prey' in favor of complexity and indeterminacy: every story can be told from more than one perspective; every truth is relative; even torturers may be loving fathers and were once vulnerable children. In this way Danticat's fiction seems to conform to the critical generalizations about Caribbean women writers sketched in the introduction. In extension, like *Breath, Eyes, Memory, Krik? Krak!,* and *Farming of Bones*—texts that also deploy intertextuality, fragmentation, plural narrative voices—*The Dew Breaker* concentrates on the particular experiences of women, and is concerned with gender, sexuality, and familial relationships.

But these elements are interwoven with others shared by earlier Haitian writers (in French and *kreyòl*), including the *Indigénistes* of the 1920s and the revolutionary writers such as René Depestre and Jacques Stephen Alexis of the post-World War Two period:[2] Consciousness of history and the immense gulf between Haitian (and global) elites and the impoverished majority ('men and women whose tremendous agonies filled every blank space in their lives' [*DB* 137]); opposition to imperialism and domestic dictatorships; a commitment to justice and the struggle for liberation. Danticat helped translate one of Alexis' novels, *L'espace d'un Cillement* in to *In the Flicker of an Eye* (Shea 14*)*. Alexis also wrote a novel, *Compère Général Soleil*, about Trujillo's 1937 massacre of Haitians living in the Dominican Republic, which Danticat treats in her short story '1937' and novel, *Farming of Bones*. Danticat's fiction is always aware of the continuing dynamics of imperialism that combine with domestic forces to thwart Haitians' periodic mass revolts. Writing in the shadow of the end of *dechoukaj*,[3] the defeat of the Lavalas movement, and renewed repression and economic crisis, Danticat transforms these realities in to emotionally and visually powerful fiction laced with motifs of suicide, dead infants, breech and still births, scars and nightmares, all of which symbolize lost hope and political despair, but also those of fire, flight, transformation, and resurrection that suggest continued hope for social change and renewal.

Sugar, Slaves, and Occupation

In 'Monkey Tails' in late 1980s Haiti a student quotes the words of Voltaire to his younger friend: '"C'est a ce prix qu'ils mangent du sucre en Europe . . . in Europe they eat sugar with our blood in it"' (153). This moment typifies the way Haiti's history of slavery and sugar production, and that of revolutionary heroism, find their way into Danticat's narratives. In *Breath, Eyes, Memory* the narrator's Tante Atie 'would talk about the sugar cane fields, where she and my mother practically lived' (4) while retelling tales of Guineans—'the people of creation'—who were appointed the task of carrying the sky due to their immense strength (24–5); in 'Wall of Fire Rising' the child Guy learns by heart the lines of slave revolutionary Boukman while living in a shantytown 'under the shadow' of a sugar mill (66). Danticat's works thus illustrate how 'a living history' is 'powerfully embodied in Haitian culture' (Renda 45). The past continues to weigh on the present in very literal ways—sugar production continues to be central to the economy long after slavery ends, semi-feudal conditions persist in rural areas—as well as in folklore handed down across the generations. Most importantly, imperialism continues to circumscribe the lives of Haitians 200 years after their successful revolution gave birth to the world's first independent black nation.

Many historians of Haiti see in this nation's development what Paul Farmer has called a 'template of colony:' Relations and events that become central to the Caribbean (and often the entire colonized world) happen earlier and in starker form here. In *After the Dance*, her tribute to Jacmel's carnival, Danticat tells of the myths of Anacaona, the Arawak high priestess, that survived the post-Columbus decimation of her people and subsequent division, in 1697, of the island into the French Saint Domingue, now Haiti, and the Spanish Santo Domingo, now the Dominican Republic: 'Anacaona [has had] schools and shops named after her . . . [and] has inspired a well-known play by Jacmel-born novelist Jean Metellus, along with countless poems and songs on both sides of the island' (*AD* 41). While the ensuing plantation economy and slave trade mirrored those of much of the Caribbean, Saint Domingue was exceptional in that it 'became France's richest colony, the brightest jewel of the French crown, as was often said in the 1700s' (41). Maroon resistance against slavery was also common to other plantation societies, but Haiti's was again the only one to defeat the combined armies of Spain, Britain and France and overcome the divisions between slaves, mulattoes, and free blacks in order to become 'the first—and for some long decades the only—independent nation in the American hemisphere, where the notion of Liberty applied equally to all citizens' (*Haiti: State Against Nation* Trouillot 44).

But if this remarkable success anticipated the mass realization of independence region-wide in the second half of the twentieth century, so too did it usher in the structural contradictions of the postcolonial era. As Michel-Rolph Trouillot asserts, Haiti was 'the first testing ground of neocolonialism' (57), as noncolonial forms of imperialist domination quickly moved in to replace the colonial system: 'No longer a colony, yet a country standing outside the international political order conceived by the West, Haiti could not fully benefit from its hard-gained independence in a world that was not ready to accept the implications of its existence' (58). The powers of the world ostracized Haiti, refusing to respect its sovereignty and repeatedly invading its waters: France extended recognition in 1825 only in return for 150 million francs as compensation for the planters who lost their 'property' in the revolution, saddling Haiti with a crippling debt; the U.S.A. did not formalize relationships until 1862. This global pariah status ensured that terms of trade were against Haiti while 'the foreign trader has always operated in Haiti with the assurance that he can call in a foreign power if necessary' (67). The constraints of the post-colonial era—debt, unfair trade, foreign military invasion, and continuing economic dependence—thus hampered Haiti's development one 150 years earlier than the other nations considered here.

American imperialism also supplanted European colonialism earlier in Haiti: the 19-year-long occupation beginning in 1915 was the climax of decades of gunboat diplomacy designed to establish U.S. supremacy and displace Germany, the primary rival in the region. The narrator of Danticat's '1937' says that '[t]he Americans taught us how to build prisons. By the end of the 1915 occupation, the police in the city really knew how to hold human beings trapped in cages' (*KK* 35). Mary Renda's account of the occupation fleshes out this passing comment:

> While in Haiti, marines installed a puppet president, dissolved the legislature at gunpoint, denied freedom of speech, and forced a new constitution on the Caribbean nation—one more favorable to foreign investment. With the help of the marines, U.S. officials seized the customshouses, took control of Haitian finances . . . Meanwhile, marines waged war against insurgents (called Cacos) who for several years maintained an armed resistance in the countryside, and imposed a brutal system of forced labor that engendered even more fierce Haitian resistance. By official U.S. estimates, more than 3,000 Haitians were killed during this period; a more thorough accounting reveals that the death toll may have reached 11,500. The occupation also reorganized and strengthened the Haitian military. (10)

Haiti played an important role for the U.S. in its early imperialist plan for the region: Trouillot explains that the occupation paved the way for the Duvalier dictatorships of the second half of the twentieth century, both by heightening latent socioeconomic contradictions and by prefiguring methods of repression. In turn, the regimes of François, 'Papa Doc,' and then his son, Jean-Claude, 'Baby Doc,' Duvalier continued to serve the needs of U.S. imperialism: the former importantly became an unconditional ally of American capitalism and an 'anti-communist' counterweight to Cuba during the cold war;[4] the latter was a willing champion of the 'Puerto Rican' model of economic development, offering up Haiti's poor as a cheap, nonunionized workforce for foreign-owned offshore manufacture. Between 1970 and 1976 the U.S. installed 230 new industrial plants as investors eagerly exploited the cheap labor created through dispossession, immiseration, and political repression (Haiti Films).[5]

Hunter and Prey

Danticat's *Breath, Eyes, Memory* and *Krik? Krak!* illustrate the impact of Duvalierism's relentless regime of terror. In the novel the narrator is herself the product of her mother's rape by an anonymous Macoute, the memory of which forces her to leave her home country for New York City, where she is haunted by nightmares and eventually kills herself. In the Haitian scenes we see the casual brutality of the Macoutes, whose presence is overtly sexualized and intimidating. A gang gather close to the food stand of Tante Atie's friend Louise when Sophie is passing with her grandmother: 'One of them was staring at me . . . He stood on the tip of his boots and shoved an old man aside to get a better look. I walked faster. He grabbed his crotch with one hand, blew me a kiss, then turned back to the others' (*Breath, Eyes, Memory* 117). Moments later this Macoute accuses the coal vendor, ironically called Dessalines, of stepping on his foot, and pounds his gun butt into the man. As her grandmother fearfully pulls her away, Sophie looks back: 'The coal vendor was curled in a fetal position on the ground. He was spitting blood. The other Macoutes joined in, pounding their boots on the coal seller's head. Every one watched in shocked silence, but no one said anything' (118). After we learn of Dessalines' death at their hands, Sophie reflects on the myth and reality of the Tonton Macoutes and her mother's brutal rape as a sixteen year old (138–140). In the course of this passage Sophie reflects on a common saying: 'Who invented the Macoutes? The devil didn't do it and God didn't do it' (138). The novel does not answer this question directly, but it allows us to see that state terror has its roots in Haiti's history, which has always been embedded in global relations.

In *Krik? Krak!* Macoutes loom over the characters in stories set before and after the ouster of Duvalier: in the latter the coup regime reimposes the climate of terror under which everyone was a potential victim and 'women were sometimes treated the same as men, often worse' (*Haiti: State Against Nation* Trouillot 167). In 'The Missing Peace' we meet a young boy and girl prematurely aged by social forces: the narrator, 14-year- old Lamort, so named because her mother died in childbirth; and teenage Raymond, a khaki-uniformed guard who somehow survived the transition between 'old' and 'new' regimes with only a leg wound. The title refers to the password—incongruously 'peace' for a while—that could be the difference between life and death for one caught out after curfew by a trigger-happy teenage guard. Lamort's grandmother makes a little money by renting a room to foreign journalists who come to view the mass grave in a nearby churchyard and take home decontextualized images of chaos and violence. The current tenant, though, tells Lamort that she is not a journalist, but a Haitian American, Emilie, in search of her mother who she fears is dead: '"My mother was old regime"' she tells Lamort, '"She was a journalist. For a newspaper called Libèté in Port-au-Prince"' (111). When she persuades Lamort to break curfew and take her to the churchyard to look for her mother's corpse the two narrowly escape being shot by Raymond and his fellow guard. As they stand pleading with them, the narrator describes this scene:

> Two soldiers passed us on their way to the field. They were dragging the blood-soaked body of a bearded man with an old election slogan written on a T-shirt across his chest: ALONE WE ARE WEAK. TOGETHER WE ARE A FLOOD. The guards were carrying him, feet first, like a breech birth. (117)

The blood-soaked body and the vulnerability of the girl and woman who bear witness are in painful contrast to the image of strength and unity evoked by the slogan.

Dew Breaker pursues the question, posed in *Krik? Krak!,* of what produces and motivates the Macoutes. By the 1950s the conflicts exacerbated by the occupation came to a head, as the peasantry, already drained to such an extent that it was at or below subsistence level, was hard hit by another collapse in the international coffee market. A series of short-lived governments were unable to offer any solution other than increased taxation and repression. In 1957 a campaign of military terror was unleashed on the suffering population: '[T]he totalitarian response ... was the brainchild of the army trained by the Marines, and particularly of the cadets of the graduating class of 1930–31, which included Magloire, Cantave, and Kébreau' (148). That year a decree banned 'drawings, prints, paintings, writings, or any other mode of expression of thought aimed at undermining the authority of the state' (151), and another outlawed the wearing of khaki 'or any other cloth of that shade'—the army was instructed to open fire on anyone wearing light brown or olive green.

In this context, François Duvalier won an election, in September 1957, using the rhetoric of *noirisme*—black nationalism—and promising to redistribute the wealth out of the hands of the light-skinned elite to the black majority. Once in power he favored the very elite he claimed to despise, and made sure that the share of coffee profits would grow for the merchants and middlemen, and fall for the peasants; Duvalierism thus increased the already extreme social polarization between an amazingly wealthy minority on the one hand, and the impoverished bulk of the population on the other.[6] The only wealth he redistributed was from the pockets of the poor via state coffers in to the pockets of his henchmen and lackeys. As Trouillot puts it, Duvalier 'formalized the crisis' of Haiti: he attacked all national institutions that could support an opposition, shut down the press, purged the Catholic church, schools and colleges, cracked down on the unions; punished his critics with torture and execution and rewarded his followers from his slush funds; created a climate of terror through random violent attacks by the military; and, drawing on the ranks of dispossessed and desperate youths as fascists do, built a new plainclothed body of armed thugs, the dreadful Tonton Macoutes, named after the frightening bogey man of folklore who steals children and puts them in his sack; the Macoutes made it clear that noone was immune from state terror—women, children, the elderly, state officials, all were vulnerable to indiscriminate attack at any time.

In *The Dew Breaker* we are given a portrait of one of their number. Significantly from the landowning peasantry, and educated in a 'school run by Belgian priests, a school that was also attended by the children of the cane and vanilla plantation owners in the south' (191), he is effectively orphaned when Duvalier's army requisition his parents' land. Roped in to a rally in honor of the new president, the boy, inebriated from his first tobacco and liquor, succumbs to the spectacle of power:

> He was mesmerized by the procession of humanity, standing before the whitest and biggest building in the whole country. Decorating the palace terraces were men with rifles, men dressed in uniforms with golden ropes like those he'd studied in pictures of the fathers of the independence in his own boyhood history book. And finally the president, slipping out onto the balcony dressed like a guardian of the cemetery in a black suit and coattails, a black hat, a .38 visibly attached to his belt, and a rifle at his side. (192)

We see the mixture of ideology and force employed by Duvalier: rhetorically he linked himself with the revolutionary heroes of old, using *noirisme* to draw support from those angered by the racism of the American occupation and the light-skinned elite; symbolically he invoked the Vodou deities linked to death: Papa Guede, master of the dead, and Papa Legba, gatekeeper and guardian of cemeteries. At the same time he militarized the nation and made it clear that any opposition would be crushed. The man we first met as Ka's father remembers joining 'the Miliciens, the Volunteers for National Security' (191), and reflects on his motivation:

> He thought of how hungry he'd been after the president's speech, when the crowd was left to find its own way home and when one of the many men in denim who were circling the palace that day had approached him and asked him whether he wanted to join the Miliciens, the Volunteers, what later would be called the macoutes. (195)

But any sympathy that this account may elicit is cancelled out by the descriptions of what he becomes:

> He liked questioning the prisoners, teaching them to play zo and bezik, stapling clothespins to their ears as they lost and removing them as he let them win, convincing them that their false victories would save their lives. He liked to paddle them with braided cowhide, stand on their cracking backs and jump up and down like a drunk on a trampoline, pound a rock on the protruding bone behind their earlobes until they couldn't hear the orders he was shouting at them, tie blocks of concrete to the end of sisal ropes and balance them off their testicles if they were men or their breasts if they were women. (198)

The fact that we hear of these scenes from his point of view, in the everyday tones of one who has become bored of his job and dreams of a new life, only intensifies the horror of the tortures; at the same time we also are given other accounts from victims, and see the devastating impact his actions continue to have on their lives decades later. In addition, and this is something I will return to, the collection ambiguously explores the possibility of redemption and resurrection; while Ka's father, Anne's husband, the Brooklyn barber, is shown to have successfully created a new life and identity, many others are denied this chance at a new life.

Desperate Resistance[7]

The breech birth metaphor at the heart of 'The Missing Peace' resonates with the motifs of dead babies and stillbirths recurring throughout Danticat's work, figuratively underscoring the theme of persistent but thwarted attempts at political and social rebirth. The metaphor of an unsuccessful birth is frequently used to describe Haiti's history, as in these words from Amy Wilentz: 'The Haitian Republic is still a unique phenomenon, born out of a successful slave revolt. Its freedom was not gained after a long transition to independence; the republic's was a bloody birth with no midwife present' (207). At the center of *Breath, Eyes, Memory* are three acts of violence connected with women's sexual and reproductive organs: the narrator breaks her own hymen with a pestle in order to forestall dreaded virginity testing; her mother commits suicide by repeatedly stabbing herself in the stomach in order to end her pregnancy; and in a folk tale a young girl bleeds to death when her new husband cuts her in order to prove her virginity on their wedding night.

In '1937' women who escaped Trujillo's massacre by swimming across the river at the border between the Dominican Republic and Haiti are figured as having experienced a rebirth, miraculously rising from the bloody water like the phoenix from the ashes, with special powers and psychic connections to each other. The phoenix imagery recalls the story of Makandal, the Guinean slave who escaped to the mountains in 1752, became legendary for his knowledge of herbal medicine and his connection with the African *lwa*, and led a slave rebellion before being caught by the French planters: 'They tracked him down and tried to burn him at the stake. As the flames licked up around his chest, the slaves who watched marveled as they saw his soul leap out, transformed into a fly, and escape high into the air to seek followers again' (Wucker 77). The idea of rising from the ashes also resonates with Haiti's postrevolution history, as Laurent Dubois writes of the beginning of the nineteenth century: 'Haiti needed to be healed, for it was a nation founded on ashes . . . there were dead beyond counting—it is estimated that 100,000 or more residents of the colony died during the revolution—and many others were permanently crippled' (Dubois 302).

In Danticat's work, images of birth and rebirth are matched by those of death and child mortality. In *Krik? Krak!* and in *Dew Breaker* we find related imagery of cleansing water, baptism, and floods, symbolically connecting with the name, 'Lavalas,' or cleansing wave, given to the movement that swept the Duvalier regime from power in 1986. The first story of *Krik? Krak!*, 'Children of the Sea,' tells of a teenage boy and girl separated during the coup regime: he, a former activist in the Lavalas youth movement, has fled the terror in a raft bound for the U.S., while she flees to the countryside with her parents. The boy contemplates the water spirit Agwe watching over him as he anticipates joining his ancestors:

I go to them now as though it was always meant to be, as though the very day that my mother birthed me, she had chosen me to live life eternal, among the children of the deep blue sea, those who have escaped the chains of slavery to form a world beneath the heavens and the blood-drenched earth where you live. (27)

Again birth, death, and water are interconnected, and Haiti's *botpipple*[8] are linked with the slaves in the middle passage and the Vodou deities.

In *Dew Breaker* we see many references to the births and deaths of infants, often interwoven with water symbolism: In 'Water Child' a woman who has had an abortion mourns the child she didn't have and thinks of 'a shrine to unborn children in Japan, where water was poured over altars of stone to honor them, so she had filled her favorite drinking glass with water and a pebble and had added that to her own shrine' (57).[9] In 'Book of Miracles' Anne remembers the death of her young brother:

Anne had gone swimming with her three-year-old brother on a beach in Grand Goave, and he had disappeared beneath the waves. Ever since then, she'd convinced herself that her brother was walking the earth looking for his grave. Whenever she went by a cemetery, any cemetery, she imagined him there, his tiny wet body bent over the tombstones, his ash-colored eyes surveying the letters, trying to find his name. . . . She held her breath the way she imagined her brother did before the weight of the sea collapsed his small lungs and he was forced to surrender to the water, sinking into a world of starfishes, sea turtles, weeds, and sharks. (71)

The only counterweight is the old woman, Estina, in 'Night Talkers' who, though blind, has long been a midwife, successfully birthing and mothering many babies. Yet she dies in the course of the story.

Even when functioning metaphorically, Danticat's images of early death are grounded not only in history but also in the material reality of contemporary Haiti, where rates of child mortality are among the world's highest, life expectancy is below 50 years, and more than 80 percent of the population lives in poverty. Woefully inadequate clean water, sanitation, health care, and diet ensure that premature death is a norm for most Haitians. As the narrator of *Breath, Eyes, Memory* says, 'we come from a place . . . where in one instant, you can lose your father and all your other dreams' (165). Impermanence and fragility are conveyed in haunting imagery often combining the organic—plants and human bodies—with glass or crystals, such as the tales told by the prostitute in 'Night Women' to her son: 'I whisper my mountain stories in his ear, stories of the ghost women and the stars in their hair. I tell him that if I cross a stream of glass-clear hibiscus, I can make myself a goddess . . . I want him to forget that we live in a place where nothing lasts' (*KK* 86). Or in 'Book of Miracles' in Anne's story of a girl who 'cried crystal tears' (*DB* 69).

Survival is contingent upon the mutability emblematized by the Haitian daffodils loved by Martine, mother of the narrator in *Breath, Eyes, Memory*: 'they grew in a place they were not supposed to. . . . A strain of daffodils . . . that could withstand the heat, but they were the color of pumpkins and golden summer squash, as though they had acquired a bronze tinge from the skins of the natives who had adopted them' (*BEM* 21). People, like the hardy daffodils, must know how to adapt to hostile environments. Images of attempted, thwarted, terrible and beautiful transformations recur. In *Breath, Eyes, Memory* an albino named Chabin is said to be able to change into a snake at will (50); Haitians in the cold of Northern America are turned into 'ghosts' (160); cane workers sing of a mermaid who becomes human (229); folk tales describe a 'little girl who was born out of the petals of roses, water from the stream, and a chunk of the sky' (47), and women who remove their skin at night or become butterflies or tears (85; 150; 234). And again and again bodies, especially women's bodies, are assaulted, mutilated, abused, become diseased, and die.

But many of the untimely deaths have a different character: they are self-inflicted, deliberate, and often defiantly understood as a blow for freedom even if driven by desperation. In 'Wall of Fire Rising' past and present are intertwined, forming the backdrop to the unfolding story of a family: The father, Guy, faces daily demoralization as he seeks work in the sugar mill, competing for a job scrubbing latrines; his wife Lili begins each day with the forage for food, and Guy, their son, learns by heart for a school play the words of the revolutionary hero Boukman. He rehearses for his parents in this moving scene:

> The boy closed his eyes and took a deep breath. At first, his lips parted but nothing came out. Lili pushed her head forward as though she were holding her breath. Then like the last burst of lightning out of clearing sky, the boy began.
>
> 'A wall of fire is rising and in the ashes, I see the bones of my people. Not only those people whose dark hollow faces I see daily in the fields, but all those souls who have gone ahead to haunt my dreams. At night I relive once more the last caresses from the hand of a loving father, a valiant love, a beloved friend.'
>
> . . . the speech made Lili and Guy stand on the tips of their toes from great pride. As their applause thundered in the small space of their shack that night, they felt as though for a moment they had been given the rare pleasure of hearing the voice of one of the forefathers of Haitian independence in the forced baritone of their only child. The experience left them both with a strange feeling that they could not explain. It left the hair on the back of their necks standing on end. It left them feeling much more love than they ever knew that they could add to their feeling for their son.
>
> 'Bravo,' Lili cheered, pressing her son into the folds of her apron. 'Long live Boukman and long live my boy.' 'Long live our supper,' Guy said, quickly batting his eyelashes to keep tears from rolling down his face.' ('Wall of Fire Rising,' *Krik? Krak!* 56–7)

Legend has it that the inaugural moment of the Haitian revolution was the Vodou ceremony in Bois-Caïman, alligator forest, in 1791, where the *oungan* (priest), the Jamaica-born slave Boukman, led a ceremony in which all present swore to fight for liberty (Dayan 29; Dubois 101; Renda 43–4; Wucker 77). Such willingness to sacrifice one's own life in battle is enshrined also in the popular song addressing another legendary revolutionary, Dessalines, in the line 'pito m'mouri passe m'couri'—better to die than to run away—and in the slave myth of rebirth in Guinea.

This folk tale of dead slaves flying back to Africa is evoked in 'Wall of Fire Rising' by the figure of the hot air balloon, a toy of the sugar mill owner's son, who 'occasionally flew over the shantytown skies' (*KK* 60). Guy the older becomes obsessed by this symbol of escape. He says to Lili '"pretend that this is the time of miracles and we believed in them . . . I think I can fly that balloon"' (67). '"If god wanted people to fly, he would have given us wings on our backs"' Lili warns him, and he replies '"You're right, Lili . . . but look what he gave us instead. He gave us reasons to want to fly"' (68). For Guy the father the gulf between aspiration and actuality is too great to bear, and as we know he will, one day he flies off in the balloon. Momentarily his flight offers a glimpse of the miraculous escape he had dreamed of: 'From the field behind the sugar mill a group of workers were watching the balloon floating in the air. Many were clapping and cheering, calling out Guy's name. A few of the women were waving their head rags at the sky, shouting, "Go! Beautiful, go!"' (76). But as his son and wife approach, the crowd looks on in horror as Guy climbs over the side of the basket: 'Within seconds, Guy was in the air hurtling down towards the crowd. Lili held her breath as she watched him fall. He crashed not far from where Lili and the boy were standing, his blood immediately soaking the landing spot' (78). Even while the story focuses our attention on the tragedy of this suicide, it links Guy's death to the historic acts of his revolutionary ancestors:

> The boy continued reciting his lines, his voice rising to a man's grieving roar. He kept his eyes closed, his fists balled at his side as he continued with his newest lines. 'There is so much sadness in the faces of my people. I have called on their gods, now I call on our gods. I call on our young. I call on our old. I call on our mighty and the weak. I call on everyone and anyone so that we shall all let out one piercing cry that we may either live freely or we should die.' (79–80)

The legend of course has its origins in history. In his *Black Jacobins* C.L.R. James explains the significance of this slogan during the revolution:

> When Boukman was killed (fighting bravely) the Assembly stuck up his head in Le Cap with a placard: 'This is the head of Boukman, chief of the rebels.' The whites built three scaffolds in Le Cap and broke 20 or 30 blacks on the wheel every day. With their usual disregard of the slave even as property they massacred all they met, even those on plantations which had not yet revolted. Masters denounced those who had helped them to escape. Slaves presenting themselves to their masters seeking refuge from the devastation of the countryside or merely because they were afraid or tired of revolution, were killed at sight. The result was that all, timid as well as bold, soon understood that there was no hope except with the revolution, and they flocked to join its ranks. (96)

Death in battle was preferable to brutal reprisals and murder at the hands of the plantocracy. In turn it was the willingness of the slaves to risk their lives—in the struggle that gave them their only hope for a better future—that enabled them to defeat the combined armies of Europe. Such willing self-sacrifice was also a feature of the mass opposition to the American occupation, led by the Cacos who took to the hills to organize against the hated corvée, the system of forced labor overseen at gunpoint by the marines. Even though the occupiers responded with curfew, military law, mass arrests, and censorship, the Cacos repeatedly recovered, again, phoenix-like, to renew their resistance. When Charlemagne Péralte, who in 1919 led a resistance army of 15,000 peasants, was killed by the marines, they tied his dead body to a door and paraded it around the country in an attempt to intimidate the population; but Haitians saw a resemblance to Jesus on the crucifix, and Péralte became, and remains today, a popular martyr.

The climax of *Breath, Eyes, Memory* is the suicide of the narrator's mother, Martine. The man who finds her describes the scene: "'She had a mountain of sheets on the floor. She had prepared this. . . . She stabbed her stomach with an old rusty knife. I counted, and they counted again in the hospital. Seventeen times'" (224). Even this grotesque self-immolation is linked to the history of revolutionary defiance. Martine's surname is Caco, which recalls the rebels who fought the occupation, as Sophie's aunt explains:

> Our family name, Caco, it is the name of a scarlet bird. A bird so crimson, it makes the reddest hibiscus or the brightest flame trees seem white. The Caco bird, when it dies, there is always a rush of blood that rises to its neck and the wings, they looked so bright, you would think them on fire. (150)

Mary Renda tells a similar tale about the association between the rebels and bird: 'The taco, a small but fierce bird native to the island of Hispaniola, probably inspired the name of the tradition. "God feeds the little birds" became the motto of some Cacos, including Charlemagne Péralte' (Renda 140).[10] The passage invokes the fire, flight, and color imagery that figuratively express resistance here and in *Krik? Krak!,* and brings heightened symbolic significance to the pervasive references to blood and redness surrounding Martine. The Cacos wore 'red hatbands and pieces of cloth' (Renda 144), which even U.S. marines sometimes understood as emblems of resistance: one, Faustin Wirkus, coauthor of the 1931 book, *The White King of La Gonave*, wrote "'The red badge is in itself a declaration of a holy war against wrong and oppression'" (qtd. in Renda 145).[11] What's more, Martine is closely associated with Erzulie, a Vodou spirit who dismantles the usual ideological dichotomies: a childless mother who embodies both Madonna and Jezebel. For the funeral, Sophie dresses her mother's body in a bright red suit she was always too afraid to wear to church and then reflects: "'It was too loud a color for a burial . . . She would look like a jezebel, hot-blooded Erzulie who feared no men, but rather made them her slaves, raped *them*, and killed *them*. She was the only woman with that power'" (227).

In Danticat's fiction each suicide represents defeat, and also a desperate gesture against injustice, demonstrating what Kesta Occident calls 'stubborn hope:'

> I believe in the future even if we have to fight against a strong and powerful empire. I believe in all grassroots alternative efforts: social, economic, political . . . We are rooted in a culture of resistance and stubborn hope. We believe strongly in life. We choose to risk our own lives in search of a better collective life. (*BW* 229)

Suicide can better be understood as self-assertion when seen in relation to the figure of the zombi:

> zombis were beings without souls . . . 'whose death was not real but resulted from the machinations of sorcerers who made them appear as dead and then, when buried, removed them from their grave and sold them into servitude in some far-away land.' Born out of the experience of slavery, the sea passage from Africa to the New World, and revolution on the soil of Saint-Domingue, the zombi tells the story of colonization. (Dayan 36–7, quoting anthropologist Melville Herskovits)

As Jamaican novelist Erna Brodber puts it, the zombi is "'flesh that takes directions from someone else'" (qtd. in Dayan 37); this is a fate worse than death. Suicide—determining the moment and fashion of one's own death—can be seen as the antithesis of zombification. Yet what we are left with, nonetheless, recalls the words of Aristide describing Haiti's position in global capitalism: 'the classic dilemma of the poor; a choice between death and death' (Aristide 16).

'Together We are a Flood'

These powerful currents in Danticat's fiction express Haiti's thwarted attempts at social renewal, most importantly, given that Danticat came of age as an author during the coup era, the birth and death of the Lavalas movement. Her fiction illuminates the impact of neoliberalism, which by the middle of the 1980s had transformed the nation. As Trouillot explains:

> Haitian labor and U.S. capital together were to spark an 'economic revolution.' Alas, the rapid spread of light assembly industries, subcontracting work from U.S. firms, simply reinforced the urban-rural polarization. The already huge gap between the haves and the have-nots widened at frightening speed. (*Haiti: State Against Nation* 17)

These economic forces accelerated the decline of the peasant system of agriculture, causing hundreds of thousands to flee rural poverty for the cities, only to end up in slums like Cité Soleil outside Port-au-Prince, where more than two hundred thousand people live in tin-roofed, cinderblock, and cardboard shacks, without electricity, water, or sewers.[12] Economic domination manifested itself also through international financial institutions: From the 1970s the IMF and other lending agencies imposed stringent austerity measures on Haiti in return for loans which worsened rather than improved the economic climate.[13]

But after a decade in which a minority continued to enrich itself and flaunt its extravagancies while the majority was squeezed and battered, Haiti's poor again rose up to fight against their enemies at home and abroad. By the late 1980s a mass movement had materialized, using the church and radio stations to organize opposition to the Duvalier regime and to the conditions brought to them by global capitalism. Despite repression, tens of thousands took to the streets until in 1986 they ousted Jean-Claude Duvalier.[14] Gage Averill's eyewitness account conveys the jubilant mood:

> As the news of Duvalier's exile spread throughout the country, throngs took to the street, stripping trees of their branches, and hoisting them high in the air as symbols of renewal. Crowds sang the French version of Burns's "Auld Lang Syne," a song of parting that takes on sarcastic overtones when bidding farewell to a humiliated or despised ruler. (60)

The people of Haiti, free of Duvalier, aspired to pull up the old regime by the roots now the top layer had gone:

> Dechoukaj ruled the land as Haitians administered a people's justice, looting the villas of the rich, lynching Tontons Macoutes and staging strikes and sit-down protests to drive Duvalierists out of their jobs and into hiding. The Macoutes' new national headquarters was turned into a school; some cabinet ministers handed back their salaries; communist historian Roger Gaillard was named head of the university; the Cité Simone slum, named for Duvalier's mother, was renamed after the Church's Radyo Soley; and women marched to demand their rights for the first time in Haitian history. (Chamberlain 19)

By the end of the decade the movement consolidated into Lavalas, and the slogan 'youn sel nou feb, ansanm nou fo, ansanm nou se lavalas' ('alone we are weak, together, we are strong, together, we are a flood') rang loud in the streets, on t-shirts and posters. Jean-Bertrand Aristide, a radical priest and activist for the rights of the poor, emerged as a leader who embodied the spirit of anti-Duvalierism and opposition to neoliberalism (Wucker 137; Ives 42–3). In 1990, Aristide was elected on a reform platform by a 67.5 percent majority—in a contest that had 14 candidates (including the neoliberal Bazin, backed by Washington, who came in second with only 14 percent)—and Haiti's masses celebrated their seeming liberation on the streets in cities and villages across the nation. This is represented in 'Monkey Tails' where the narrator as an expectant father in 2004 remembers 7 February 1986 when he was a child:

> There was a different feel to our neighborhood for sure. People were walking around looking dazed, exchanging bits of information they were gathering from the radio and television and from one another . . . many were collecting shrubs from the ground and waving them in the air. Some of the men were wearing red bandannas around their heads and swinging sticks and tree branches while pouring rum and beer on one another. Others were dancing and performing somersaults but stopping occasionally to yell slogans or phrases they had held too long in their chests: 'We are free' or 'We will never be prisoners again.' (*DB* 148)

Just nine months later, however, a military coup was launched, funded by the nation's seven richest families and orchestrated by Duvalierist thugs with the support of sections of the U.S. state. The coup regime took its revenge on the population with mass arrests, assassinations, torture, beatings, rape, and other atrocities for the next three years. In September 1994 U.S. troops again invaded Haiti, this time, so the official story goes, in order to liberate the Haitian people, remove a military regime, and reinstate a democratically elected president. In reality the substance remained the same; only the details were different. The goal of this as well as the first invasion was to protect the interests of American imperialism. The main threat to those interests now was not the coup regime, but rather the masses, who now were challenging the entire system of neoliberalism.

The evidence for this is everywhere. First, in the fact that the U.S. government consistently sponsored the Duvalier regime while it was in power, and when the uprising threatened to bring it down, they came to his rescue. Greg Chamberlain describes February 1986 this way: 'It was clear . . . that the longer the revolt went on, the more radical influences and anti-U.S. sentiment would grow. Washington had to act, organizing a night escape of the Duvaliers into exile in France' (Chamberlain 18). Duvalier actually drove his BMW to the airport where he was met by an American cargo plane and taken, with his family and his ill-gotten riches, to a happy retirement in France. The narrator of 'Monkey Tails' describes the scene:

> The wife ornately made up, her long brown hair hidden under a white turban, her carefully manicured fingers holding a long cigarette, the husband at the wheel of the family's BMW, driving his wife and himself to the tarmac of an airport named after his dead father, from whom he'd inherited the country at nineteen, to an American airplane that would carry them to permanent exile in France. (*DB* 140)

With Duvalier safely removed, the U.S. installed the National Government Council (CNG), led by rightwing General Henri Namphy and containing key figures of the old regime; the CNG officially abolished the Tonton Macoutes, but as Gage Averill explains, 'many simply changed uniforms and slipped quietly into the ranks of the army or police' (Averill 162). Many former Front for the Advancement and Progress of Haiti (FRAPH) members joined the Interim Police Security Force, '"Macoutes no matter what you call them, window dressing for the American military"' (qtd. in Shacochis 238). Trouillot calls the orchestrated removal of Duvalier and establishment of the CNG 'a multinational exercise in crisis management; a calculated break in the democratic path that the Haitian people had embarked on' (*Haiti: State Against Nation* 226). The U.S. government granted $2.8 million in military aid for CNG's first year, even as human rights organizations protested and Haitians demonstrated against the government, and with good reason: The CNG in its brief tenure gunned down more Haitians than had Duvalier in the previous fifteen years (Trouillot 222).

As Paul Farmer documents in his *Uses of Haiti*, powerful American agencies campaigned against Aristide while supporting Marc Bazin, former World Bank official and darling of the multinational corporations.[15] Aristide was 'considered anti-American by the U.S. State Department, his sermons were taped and analyzed for years by the U.S. Embassy in Haiti' (Averill 168). Journalist Bob Shacochis, who was in Haiti during the period, witnessed systematic institutional double-dealing:

> The CIA, in collusion with elements in the Defense and State Departments, Congress, the INS and the national press, was openly working to subvert the White House's stated policy. It launched a smear campaign against Titid's [Aristide's nickname] mental health with fabricated evidence recycled by . . . a senior analyst at the agency . . . the agency functioned as a behind the scenes architect of FRAPH, a paramilitary terrorist organization run by a media-slick, cocaine-snorting, self infatuated madman named Emmanuel 'Toto' Constant. (29)

The U.S. Defense Intelligence Agency's Colonel Patrick Collins met with Constant and 'urged him to organize an effective counterforce to Aristide's base of popular support among the masses' (29); Agents met with Constant almost daily, he and many of the other junta members and supporters received substantial funding, through the National Endowment for Democracy, the U.S. Agency of International Development, and the CIA. Ordinary Haitians, according to Averill, recognized that despite the rhetoric and Duvalier's removal, the fundamental balance of power was intact: 'Duvalierists still held state power, class relations were largely unchanged, and the transition was being managed by the State Department' (Averill 165). During the coup's reign of terror, in 1991–92, 38,000 Haitians fled the regime and sought refuge in the United States. Of those, fewer than five percent received asylum and the rest were repatriated, hundreds held in prison camps at Guantanamo Bay (Wucker 154–5). U.S. agencies even gave names and addresses of some of those who had attempted to flee to coup leaders, guaranteeing arrest, torture and execution for unknown numbers.[16]

The U.S. government agreed to an embargo on the coup regime, but its impact overwhelmingly hurt the poor, not the ruling class, as Shacochis noted with characteristic self-derision: 'The embargo's impact on one's opportunity for fine dining in Petionville was zero . . . except for the better hotels, the military caserns, central police stations, and homes flush enough to afford a generator, the entire country had been living in darkness, without electricity, for months' (87). Prior to the invasion, the U.S. secured a deal with the coup leaders in the infamous Governor's Island Accord, with former president Jimmy Carter as the American spokesperson, chosen, as Shacochis puts it, because 'Carter knows how to ingratiate himself with tyrants and dictators' (52). The accord secured the coup leaders a role in the new regime in return for Aristide's return to the presidency; Aristide, on the other hand, would only be allowed to serve out the rest of his term (even though most of it had been stolen by the coup), and with severe curbs on what he could do. The subsequent military occupation did not disarm but rehabilitated the thugs of the Duvalier and coup regimes, giving the old police force a facelift and a new name. In the process of supposedly monitoring the coup regime's activities, U.S. officials seized approximately 150,000 pages of documentation from the headquarters of FRAPH and the Haitian army; they refused to hand them over to Aristide, even though they doubtless contained evidence of years of atrocities. Shacochis observed a typical scene in Port au Prince, where attachés (armed Duvalierists) fired in to a crowd while the American army looked the other way: 'the objective of the U.S. military now seemed rather conclusive—to protect the well-heeled elites up on the mountainside from the wrath of a million poor people in the slums below, whom the troops had supposedly come to liberate' (Shacochis 133).

On Aristide's return in 1994, the Western Powers imposed a Structural Adjustment Plan through the IMF and World Bank that drastically lowered tariffs, dismissed a quarter of the country's 45,000 civil servants, privatized state enterprises, and dramatically devalued the gourde while raising the cost of living. The result of this deal with the devil was a divided and increasingly dysfunctional Lavalas regime and a generalized social climate of insecurity, violence, and desperation. These conditions culminated in 2004, when, instead of the planned bicentennial celebrations of Haitian independence, U.S. troops once more invaded and occupied Haiti following a destabilization campaign that toppled Aristide's government, and installed a client regime.[17]

Negative Confessions, Repentance, and Resurrection

During the early days of Lavalas the climate of newly found political freedom was captured in a Haitian phrase: 'babouket la tonbe'—the bridle has fallen off (Farmer, *Infections* 164). The movement between silence and speech figures highly in *Krik? Krak!* and *Breath, Eyes, Memory*: the former ends with an epilogue describing writing as 'testament to the way that these women lived and died and lived again' (*KK* 224); the latter concludes with a ritualized spoken exchange between women of older and younger generations. But in *The Dew Breaker* silence triumphs. In 'Water Child' Nadine works with patients recovering from laryngectomy: the terrified newly voiceless Ms. Hinds, who compares herself to a *basenji*, '"a dog that doesn't bark"' (62), becomes emblematic of the larger condition of political silence: 'Ms. Hinds opened her mouth wide, trying to force air past her lips, but all that came out was the hiss of oxygen and mucus filtering through the tube in her neck' (60). In 'Night Talkers' the narrator, Dany, and his aunt are 'both palannits, night talkers, people who wet their beds, not with urine but with words' (98), but Dany doesn't get 'the chance to talk again' with his aunt (109), because she dies in her sleep, leaving him 'not able to speak' (111) and although awake, in an 'unusual dream where everyone was able to speak except the two of them' (112). The priest who is the dew breaker's last victim watches his wife dying from poison: 'She had already lost her power to speak, her ability to answer when he called her name, begging her to tell him what was wrong. Her lips moved, but no sounds came out of them' (206). And as he dies the priest himself realizes that he will not be able to recount his fate:

Maybe his death would have no relevance at all. He would simply join a long list of martyrs and his name would vanish from his countrymen's lips as soon as his body was placed in the ground.

Oh, what a great sermon he could have preached about this, but alas he would never be able to. There would be no resurrection. (*DB* 227)

While many characters crave the release and absolution promised by the ritualized speech of confession, only the guilty realize it. Claude, the American former drug addict who is deported to Haiti and taken in by an extended family he hadn't known existed, pours out his story to the reticent Dany: 'He had gotten his chance to speak English and tell his entire life story in the process' (103). Claude admits to killing his own father, and refers to his past deed as 'something really bad that makes me want to live my life like a fucking angel now' (119), but he has miraculously been given a second chance, taken in by a village community who accept him regardless: 'Claude was a palannit, a night talker, one of those who spoke their nightmares out loud to themselves. Except Claude was even luckier than he realized, for he was able to speak his nightmares to himself as well as to others, in the nighttime as well as in the hours past dawn' (120). The dew breaker in his reincarnation as husband/father is obsessed with *The Book of the Dead*, and in particular the chapter 'Driving Back Slaughters' with its line '"My mouth is the keeper of both speech and silence"' (*DB* 31–2). Like Claude, he himself confesses, rocking the world of his daughter who reports his words: '"This man who cut my face . . . I shot and killed him, like I killed many people." I'm amazed that he managed to say all of this in one breath, like a monologue. I wish I too had had some rehearsal time, a chance to have learned what to say in response' (22). Confession is thus closely associated with forgiveness and redemption.

One strain in the collection seems to endorse the idea of 'truth and reconciliation,' suggesting that even those who have done terrible things are capable of reforming, and should be given another chance. Yet another ultimately more decisive impulse rejects this notion, linking it to the ideological function of religion to counsel quiescence and postponement of justice until the afterlife. Interestingly this dialogue resonates with those surrounding the tradition of liberation theology that Aristide came from. As Robert Fatton argues in his *Haiti's Predatory Republic*, the rapid transformation of Aristide 'from an anti-capitalist prophet into a staunch U.S. ally committed to the virtues of the market' (108) had both external (hostility from domestic elites and the global capitalist powers) and internal (the limitations of his political framework) causes. The language of moral critique and Christian forgiveness transmogrified during the rule of Lavalas into what Michele Montas, wife of murdered anti-Duvalier journalist Jean Dominique, described as '"unholy alliances not only between victims and former torturers but also between those aspiring to positions of power and the fierce and proven enemies of democratic principles who inspired the coup d'état"' (qtd. in Fatton 177). Aristide advocated the 'power of non-violence . . . the power of love' (Aristide 64); the priest in *Dew Breaker*, like Aristide, enraged the presidential palace by 'not sticking to the "more you suffer on earth, the more glorious your heavenly reward script'" (*DB* 185), but ultimately offered no practical strategy to dispossess the ruling class, only self-sacrifice and divine intervention: 'he'd already decided to give his life, had made a pact with Heaven to be sacrificed for his country . . . he always saw himself being resurrected' (*DB* 200).[18]

While miraculous resurrections recur throughout Danticat's fiction, in *Dew Breaker* the two figures who believe in them most avidly are the former torturer and his wife, and ultimately we understand this as little more than a balm for their guilty consciences. In the first story we can believe that this man regrets his past, has repented, and deserves a new life. Anne insists that '[h]e hadn't been a famous "dew breaker," or torturer, anyway, just one of hundreds who had done their jobs so well that their victims were never able to speak of them again' (77), and celebrates 'the simple miracle of her husband's transformation' from lackey of Duvalier's regime to loving family man (72–3). But the dew breaker's own story undercuts Anne's version: 'The way he acted at the inquisitions in his own private cell at Casernes eventually earned him a lofty reputation among his peers. He was the one who came up with the most physically and psychologically taxing trials for the prisoners in his block' (197). And it is Anne who, at the end of the book, abrogates the philosophy of forgiveness and redemption:

> maybe she would reach for a now useless cliché, one that she had been reciting to herself all these years, that atonement, reparation, was possible and available for everyone. Or maybe she would think of some unrelated anecdote, a parable, another miracle story, or even some pleasantry, a joke . . . (242)

Far from justice through redemption and renewal, only the guilty are given a second chance: Duvalier and his family were relocated with their money to the south of France, while the surviving victims of Duvalierism received no compensation, no possibility of a new beginning.[19] In *Dew Breaker* the priest and his wife are killed, other torture survivors live with physical and emotional scars that will never heal, while the former torturer and collaborator live a prosperous life and worship miracles. The collection is not cynical though: we do find redemption in the persistent humanity of the oppressed. The priest's cellmates urinate on his battered, semi-conscious body not as a sign of contempt but in order to perform 'a kind of ritual cure. They believed that their urine could help seal the open wounds on his face and body and keep his bones from feeling as though they were breaking apart and melting under his skin' (219). Dany doesn't take revenge on his former torturer when he has the opportunity, not from fear of discovery but from 'the dread of being wrong, of harming the wrong man, of making the wrong woman a widow and the wrong child an orphan' (107). Dany does not succumb to the bloodlust of the powerful but continues to identify with the victims.

Nonetheless, the more pervasive trope throughout *Dew Breaker*, and one that matches Haiti's social climate at the start of the new millennium, is that of negation. Ka's father remembers her response to the exhibits of the Ancient Egyptians at the Brooklyn museum: 'all you noticed was how there were pieces missing from them, eyes, noses, legs, sometimes even heads. You always noticed more what was not there than what was' (*DB* 19). He is also drawn to the 'negative confession' (23). Anne describes herself and her husband attempting to become invisible by keeping a low profile in their new life but recalls that, ironically, 'it was their lack of participation that made them stand out' (74). A defaced flyer announcing the crimes of Emmanuel Constant becomes 'a fragmented collage with as many additions as erasures' (79); later the prisoners in the preacher's cell are described 'being destroyed piece by piece, day by day, disappearing like the flesh from their bones' (225). The mother of the narrator in 'The Funeral Singer' 'used to say that we'll all have three deaths: the one when our breath leaves our bodies to rejoin the air, the one when we are put back in the earth, and the one that will erase us completely and no one will remember us at all' (177). Negation is closely connected to the idea of erasure, of disappearing without a trace; it again recalls that this is 'a place where nothing lasts' (*KK* 86). The collection ends with Anne overcome with 'fright that the most important relationships of her life were always on the verge of being severed or lost, that the people closest to her were always disappearing,' that the spirits that used to possess her during her fits 'left her for good the morning that the news was broadcast on the radio that her brother had set his body on fire in the prison yard at dawn, leaving behind no corpse to bury, no trace of himself at all' (*DB* 242).

The collection in this way recalls the countless 'disappeared' casualties of the dictatorship. And yet, of course, the radio report is a lie: we know Anne's future husband shot her brother. And we also know that the priest *did* leave a 'trace of himself' in the form of the scar on the Dew Breaker's face. We remember this fact because we are told of it twice: once from the perspective of the Dew Breaker's daughter and once from that of the Priest:

> Maybe the last person my father harmed had dreamed moments like this into my father's future, strangers seeing that scar furrowed into his face and taking turns staring at it and avoiding it, forcing him to conceal it with his hands, pretend it's not there, or make up some lie about it, to explain. (32)

> The wound on the fat man's face wasn't what he had hoped; he hadn't blinded him or removed some of his teeth, but at least he'd left a mark on him, a brand that he would carry for the rest of the life. Every time he looked in the mirror, he would have to confront this mark and remember him. Whenever people asked what happened to his face, he would have to tell a lie, a lie that would further remind him of the truth. (227–8)

The priest's thoughts remind us of Dany's aunt, left blind after the Dew Breaker torched her home, and Mariselle's husband, taken by the Macoutes, returned 'without a tooth left in his mouth' and then, 'with a mouth full of blood, vanished forever' (172). But they also reiterate the notion of 'leaving a mark:' not only the oppressors, but also history's oppressed leave their scars on the present. At the end of the collection the author thanks her 'cousin Hans Adonis' for his 'Duvalier-era research' and cites 'Patrick Lemoine for his extremely powerful memoir, *Fort Dimanche, Dungeon of Death*' (243). These references place *The Dew Breaker*, with Danticat's other works, in the context of historical record, even though it is fiction: these texts collectively leave a mark for those erased by Haiti's dictatorships.

'The day you see me fall is not the day I die'

Marx's characterization of history as nightmare in the *Eighteenth Brumaire* draws attention to the weight of prevailing social and material conditions in demarcating what is possible at any given moment in time. While historical materialism identifies the class antagonism that leads to revolutionary change, and therefore allows for the objective possibility of capitalism's demise and replacement with socialism, it does not suggest that such developments are predetermined or inevitable. By the twentieth century the liberal bourgeois concept of history as progress, like the idealist version articulated in *Ulysses* by Mr. Deasy—'All human history moves towards one great goal, the manifestation of God' (Joyce 28)—was no longer plausible. Stephen Dedalus' response to Deasy gestures towards both a recognition of Ireland's (not inevitable) failure to break with colonialism and sectarianism, and also a looming modernist fear that any attempt to make sense of history was doomed.[20] Danticat's work too seems balanced between the two impulses, but the greater pull is towards the former: Haiti has not yet escaped the horrors of foreign and domestic oppression, and periodic social convulsions have not produced lasting improvements; yet the possibility of revolutionary transformation remains. Such a reading is supported by the commitment to testimony and liberation that runs throughout Danticat's entire oeuvre, and is made explicit in her involvement in nonfiction projects, such as *The Butterfly's Way* and *Walking on Fire*.[21] As I have argued elsewhere, artistically Danticat communicates a sense of continued struggle that is at odds with any (post)modern counsel of despair.[22]

The Dew Breaker offers similar symbols, and reminds us not only of enduring struggle, but also of the unexpected potency of culture. In 'The Bridal Seamstress' the main character, Aline, is a Haitian-American journalism intern whose encounter with Beatrice (the seamstress of the title) provokes in her a desire to forego banal 'personal interest' stories and instead to write about 'men and women whose tremendous agonies filled every blank space in their lives' (*DB* 137), even if doing so jeopardizes her current position. The lasting image of the story is of falling leaves, which we are given twice. The first comes after Aline has heard Beatrice's story about her torture by the dew breaker, whom she now believes is living on her street, having pursued her wherever she has lived:

> Aline could see . . . the green ash shedding more leaves on Beatrice's porch. . . . The green ash . . . was still shaking ever so slightly in the afternoon breeze, letting loose a few more leaves. Beatrice was sitting on the steps in front of her house, watching the street, but mostly watching the leaves drop. It was an odd yet beautiful sight, the leaves seemingly suspended in the air, then falling ever so slowly as if cushioned by air

bubbles. It was an image worth closing another type of article with, Aline thought, but in many ways it was so ordinary. It was fall, after all. (133)

The second time is at the end of the story, after Aline has made her decision to shift to politically oppositional journalism: 'For now, she would simply sit with Beatrice and wait for some time to pass, so that she might see how the green ash leaves looked slowly falling from the tall tree in the very ordinary golden light of dusk' (138). This simple, 'ordinary' image evokes earlier examples of 'indirect signification on the political situation' (Averill 199): the band RAM's song 'Fèy,' itself modeled on an older 'traditional Vodou song,' in turn adapted from the proverb '*Jou yon fey tonbe nan dlo, se pa jou a li pouri/koule* (The day a leaf falls in the water is not the day it rots/sinks)' (Averill 199). RAM's Fèy, 'a harmless arrangement of folklore, traditional *vodou* lyrics for *petro* rhythm' nonetheless became 'an anthem for the movement, for freedom' (Shacochis 47) in the struggle against Duvalierism:

I'm a leaf.
Look at me on my branch.
A terrible storm came and knocked me off.
The day you see me fall is not the day I die.
And when they need me, where are they going to find me?
The good Lord, and St. Nicola,
I only have one son
And they made him leave the country.

This bare statement, 'the day you see me fall is not the day I die,' was taken as a refusal to bow to the regime, both by the authorities and those fighting against them. This same sentiment resonates throughout Danticat's fiction: the fall of the movement for liberation is not its demise, and art will continue to remind us of the continuing necessity for, and possibility of, future resistance.

Notes

1   As the father explains, the reference is to a Haitian proverb: 'One day for the hunter, one day for the prey.' See Gage Averill's study of popular music in Haiti: *A Day for the Hunter, A Day for the Prey.*
2   See the Introduction, by Marie-Agnès Sourieau and Kathleen Balutansky, to their edited collection, *Writing Under Siege,* and Paul Laraque's Introduction to *Open Gate: An Anthology of Haitian Creole Poetry.* Danticat has talked of her debt to Alexis, whom she describes as 'one of our greatest writers' (Shea 14). Danticat's narrative incorporates Alexis' murder by the Duvalier regime when the fictional dew breaker remembers 'one of his most famous victims, the novelist Jacques Alexis' (*DB* 197).
3   *Dechoukaj* is the Haitian word, translatable as 'uprooting,' used to describe the widespread challenges to entrenched power that surrounded the ouster of Jean Claude Duvalier in 1986.

4   Trouillot describes Francois Duvalier's decimation of the Haitian Communist Party, the PUCH (Parti Unifié des Communistes Haïtiens; Unified Party of Haitian Communists): Duvalier 'physically eliminated, imprisoned, or forced into exile hundreds of progressive intellectuals, writers, professors, journalists, and union and peasant leaders. The vast majority of these people had no contact with the PUCH or with any other political organization. In ideological terms, most of the victims were barely what U.S. nomenclature would describe as left of center. But that was all it took . . . Duvalier used the proven existence of a few armed communists to push the legislature into voting a legal monstrosity, the Anti-Communist Law of April 1969. Every "profession of communist belief, verbal or written, public or private" was declared a crime against national security and made its perpetrator into an "outlaw eligible for the death penalty meted out by a permanent military court"' (*Haiti: State Against Nation* 203–4).

5   While the economic and the political are clearly intimately related, dominant ideology works hard to separate the two, as when Haitians were labeled 'economic refugees' in an attempt to justify their repatriation and absolve the Duvalier governments of political repression. In 1981 while the Pentagon offered $300 million in military sales and a further $199 million in training to Duvalier's regime, 3000 refugees fleeing repression were detained for a year before most were forcibly repatriated. Thus the U.S. 'had the audacity to turn away the migrants who were a direct consequence of America's political and economic hegemony in the Caribbean' (Fernandez 389).

6   Class and race are more aligned in Haiti than in much of the Caribbean: 'a small elite with light skin counts for no more than a tenth of the population; the vast majority of Haitians occupy the darkest end of the color spectrum' (Wucker 34).

7   My discussion of political suicide in Danticat's fiction was part of a panel, 'Death and Power in Postcolonial Literature,' at the University of Kent's Connecting Cultures conference in April 2004, with presentations by Anthony Bradley on W.B. Yeats' *The King's Threshold* and Lokangaka Losambe on Wole Soyinka's *Death and the King's Horseman*. My conversations with my colleagues as we worked on this panel were immensely helpful.

8   Wucker explains that this Haitian word was coined in 1980, after a period of increased attempts by Haiti's urban poor to escape to the U.S. by boat (154).

9   This resonates with a moment towards the end of *Breath, Eyes, Memory* when Sophie and her relatives attend the funeral of her mother: 'My grandmother was watching for the black priest, the one they call Lavalas, to come through the door. The priest was the last missing pebble in the stream. Then we could take my mother to the hills' (231).

10   Balutansky and Sourieau talk of 'the *kako*, a twentieth-century version of an old nineteenth-century band of peasants from the Central Plateau [who] waged a guerilla war against the U.S. marines' (31).

11   Red is also the color associated with Ogou, the *lwa* of war and flames (Wucker 152).

12   The dire consequences of American influence in this period can be seen most graphically in the pig incident of the early 1980s. On the grounds that an outbreak of African swine fever threatened the North American pork industry, the U.S. government made the controversial decision to pay Duvalier to exterminate the entire stock of creole pigs, which had long played a crucial role in the peasant economy, and replace them with pigs imported from the U.S. Many, especially poorer, peasants never received the promised replacement pigs; those who did found that these animals failed miserably to adapt to the Haitian environment. This struck a terrible blow to the rural economy, and further contributed to the problem of deforestation, as many of the rural poor turned to charcoal production to supplement their depleted income.

13 This was apparent by the end of the 1980s: 'Loans and structural adjustment have not alleviated the country's horrendous poverty, reported by the World Bank in 1990 as 70 percent in the cities and 80 percent in rural areas' (McAfee 17). The U.S.-imposed embargo of 1999, ostensibly in response to electoral irregularities, heightened the economic crisis.

14 Arguably Duvalier's allies used his removal to forestall more far reaching upheaval: 'Confronted with the rise of Lavalas, the U.S. and Haitian ruling class decided to sacrifice Duvalier in order to reform and preserve the existing order ' (Ashley Smith 30).

15 Paul Farmer has worked for over two decades as medical director of a hospital in the village of Cange in Haiti that serves the rural poor. He helped establish two organizations—Zanmi Lasante in Haiti, and Partners in Health in Massachusetts—that aim to redress inequalities in access to health, and used a 1993 MacArthur 'genius' award to establish the Institute for Health and Social Justice, which has supported important research on the link between sickness and social and economic inequalities. Farmer has published several books that expose the connections between poverty, inequality, and infectious diseases, especially AIDS.

16 Nikol Payen, in Danticat's edited anthology of diasporic Haitians, tells a heartbreaking story about her sojourn as a translator for the Haitian refugees forcibly held at the American naval base in Guantanamo Bay. She documents the brutal treatment meted out to the refugees and the calculated dismissal of their claims of persecution, and she describes herself watching helplessly while those fleeing life-threatening political persecution were returned to Haiti. Her last illusions were stripped away when she accompanied a boatload of repatriated refugees. As they arrived in Haiti she watched an American State Department staff member hand over the refugees' identity bracelets to a Haitian soldier, removing their hope of escape and survival (*BW* 79).

17 For explanation of the circumstances surrounding these events see Ashley Smith's 'Aristide's Rise and Fall' and the 2004 collection edited by Pat Chin et al, Haiti: *A Slave Revolution: 200 Years After 1804,* which includes an essay by Danticat.

18 Aristide also, of course, enraged the Catholic church: he was expelled on the grounds that his sermons '"exalted violence and class struggle"' (Wilentz 401).

19 In an essay about U.S. immigration policy against Haitians, Danticat writes of the ruling against David Joseph, an 18 year old Haitian who 'fled Haiti with his younger brother after he was burned and stoned. His father had been severely beaten' ('No Greater Shame' 172): 'In his decision, [U.S Attorney General John] Ashcroft suggests that David Joseph and the others are a threat to national security. How come someone like David is considered a threat to national security, when Emmanuel Constant, the former head of FRAPH, a militia group that's suspected of having killed more than 5000 Haitians in the early 1980s, is not?' (171–2).

20 My gratitude to Anthony Bradley for sharing with me his insights into Joyce's particular understanding of history as nightmare in the context of the *Eighteenth Brumaire.*

21 The former collection brings together testimony from Haitians in the diaspora, and contests many forms of political oppression; the latter is a collection edited by Beverley Bell that records the voices of 38 Haitian women discussing their resistance to political and economic oppression.

22 'Replacing the "Wall of Disinformation:" *The Butterfly's Way, Krik? Krak!,* and Representation of Haiti in the USA.' *Journal of Haitian Studies* 7.2 (Fall 2001): 78–94; '"*Ou libéré?*" History, Transformation and the Struggle for Freedom in Edwidge Danticat's *Breath, Eyes, Memory.*' Sourieau and Balutansky, eds. 459–78.

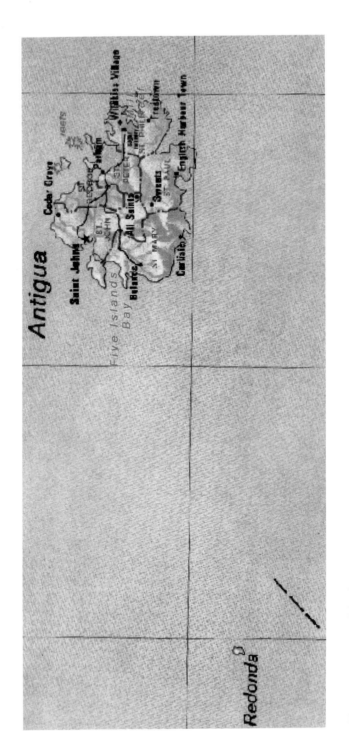

Figure 2   Map of Antigua

Chapter 2

Gateway to the Caribbean

> And when I blow things up and make life generally unlivable for the criminal (is my life not unlivable, too?) the criminal is shocked, surprised. But nothing can erase my rage—not an apology, not a large sum of money, not the death of the criminal—for this wrong can never be made right, and only the impossible can make me still: can a way be found to make what happened not have happened?
>
> Jamaica Kincaid, *A Small Place*

The literature of Jamaica Kincaid, arguably the most famous and prolific Caribbean woman writing in the U.S., has been read through the lenses of gender, particularly the mother-daughter relationship, patriarchy, psychoanalysis, and the postmodern-postcolonial refusal—via 'fluidity' and 'indeterminacy'—of the 'certainty' and 'determinacy' of Western discourse.[1] Paradigmatic moments include the problematization of English in *A Small Place*—'For isn't it odd that the only language I have in which to speak of this crime is the language of the criminal who committed the crime?' (31)—and the scene in *Lucy* where the eponymous Antiguan nanny associates her New York employer's beloved daffodils with the cultural imperialism of a British colonial education that forced her to learn Wordsworth's poetic tribute long before she ever saw the flower. While *At the Bottom of the River*, Kincaid's first major publication, perhaps lends itself most easily to the 'postmodern' characterization, with its ambiguous, dreamlike stream of consciousness and vivid images of metamorphoses and dissolved boundaries, postmodern strategies have been found in all her texts.[2] In the readings of Kincaid's texts that follow, I turn instead to the social inequalities and injustices that have shaped Antigua's history and continue through an 'independence' dominated by neoliberalism. In the process I highlight motifs that recur in the broader body of contemporary Caribbean women's writing: the distinctive subject position of the insider/outsider; consciousness of the material roots of women's oppression; a critique of imperialism past and present; vivid evocations of the physical world of the Caribbean juxtaposed with a critique of the 'tourist' image; a backdrop of local and global structures of inequality; complicated nodes of class affiliation and identification; and desire for an alternative to given conditions.

Kincaid's oeuvre repeats the dominant characteristics of Caribbean literature written from outside the country of origin. *Annie John* is the *bildungsroman* that remembers the paradisiacal island childhood, the fall from grace, and then the departure for metropolitan center; *Lucy* takes up the story from the other side of the journey, following the narrator through the early years of her life as an immigrant;

A Small Place describes the breaks and continuities in colonial and postcolonial national environments; *My Brother* tells of the return to the island home to attend to the illness (and then death) of a family member; *Autobiography of My Mother* and *Mr. Potter* imagine lives (in both cases fictionalized versions of the author's ancestors) in Antigua's colonial past; *My Garden Book* addresses the challenges of cultural relocation through the figure of the Caribbean gardener in Vermont remembering the flora of her original home.

'Corrupt men have given their country away to corrupt foreigners.'

As with the other literature considered here, Kincaid's work makes visible the effects of women's oppression and gender inequality. Most explicitly, the much-anthologized 'Girl' rehearses ideals of femininity while cataloguing the relentlessly repetitive chores of domestic labor. A two-page sentence consisting almost entirely of imperative clauses separated by semi-colons, 'Girl' presents a litany of appropriate feminine behavior as if spoken by a mother to a daughter, interrupted just twice by interjections from the latter. Mostly the list gives directions for domestic chores: laundry, gardening, cooking, serving, cleaning, shopping; looming over these is the condition of austerity that necessitates instruction in 'how to make ends meet' (*At the Bottom of the River* 5). Interspersed with the directions are injunctions on appropriate manners and demeanor and especially sexual conduct. Three times, with variation, the voice prescribes behavior that will produce something other than 'the slut you are so bent on becoming' and that the mother has 'warned you against becoming' (3–4). The perils of unwanted pregnancy are ever present, a fact that is underscored by the instruction, 'this is how to make a good medicine to throw away a child before it even becomes a child' (5). The voice is at times not unsympathetic, and, especially when cautioning against mistreatment at the hands of men, not only trains the girl to accept the terms of women's oppression but also provides her with a means to cope with it: 'This is how to bully a man; this is how a man bullies you; this is how to love a man, and if this doesn't work there are other ways, and if they don't work don't feel too bad about giving up; this is how to spit up in the air if you feel like it, and this is how to move quick so that it doesn't fall on you' (5). These last surprising pieces of advise hint at rebellion, but the overwhelming impression is of the oppressive weight of duties and impossibly demanding, often contradictory, expectations; the result produces *verfremdsungseffekt*, or the 'effect of making strange'—the term that Bertolt Brecht used to describe the impact of his revolutionary epic drama—as the process of socialization in to femininity is defamiliarized.

Seen in relation to the barrack yard tales of 'pioneer'[3] Caribbean writers such as C.L.R James and Eric Walrond, 'Girl' defamiliarizes the gender roles that are naturalized in the earlier work. Walrond's 'Wharf Rats' or James' 'Triumph' typify portraits of women whose lives are circumscribed by the challenges of domestic labor in conditions of scarcity and by their economic dependence on men, some of whom vent their own frustrations through violent abuse. At the same time the stories themselves are circumscribed to varying degrees by sexist stereotype. In 'Triumph' the women of the yard scheme and compete to secure themselves the financial attentions of men; while they are portrayed at times lovingly as plucky fighters usually coming out on top against the odds, their precarious condition is naturalized, as when we hear that the protagonist Mamitz does not regard beatings as more than 'minor incidents' ('Triumph' 110), or in 'Wharf Rats' when we see the vengeful character Maffi, seemingly driven by primal urges, using Obeah to kill the lovable Philip. In both of these stories women are routinely objectified, sometimes with a degree of misogyny. In 'Wharf Rats' Maffi is described as the 'black ominous Trinidad girl;' a man is said to have fathered 'a string of ulcered girls' before 'finally a pretty, opaque one' (Walrond 97); Maffi 'muttered diabolically' (102) while plotting the death of the boy she secretly loves. In 'Triumph' Mamitz is described as 'a black woman, too black to be pure negro, probably with some Madrasi East Indian blood in her . . . She was shortish and fat, voluptuously developed, tremendously developed' (James 110); 'fat, easy-going' (111); 'large, slow-moving, voluptuous, with her thick, smooth hair neatly plaited and her black skin shining' (116); while the despised Irene is 'a thin little whip of a brown-skinned woman' (111) whose public humiliation provides the gleeful culmination of the story. These depictions illustrate the color consciousness that is, for obvious historical reasons, a common feature of this period of Caribbean literature and can be seen also in the descriptions of the male characters, but they also reveal the extent to which the women are positioned as object rather than subject.[4]

Certainly the narratives 'write back' to the discourse of colonizer/tourist, embodied in the literature of British aristocrat and travel writer Alec Waugh and his ilk. Waugh's 'Antigua,' published in *Holiday Magazine* in 1951, turns the island in to a playground for wealthy Europeans and Americans and reduces Antiguans to the racist stereotype of colonialist fantasy: the lazy, superstitious child-native in need of colonial patronage:

> The Antiguans are a fascinating mixture of imported Africa and colonial England, and still retain the fetishes of the bush. 'Is good moon for planting tannias,' they will tell you. The moon rules their lives. If a girl cuts her hair when the moon is waxing, it will grow long and thin; at full moon it will grow short and thick. The best time is between the moons then it will be long and thick.
> Their belief in obeah—a kind of necromancy—persists. (259)

Waugh regards the 'natives' as part of the landscape or sees them as existing only to serve the wealthy visitors: 'wages and the cost of labor have kept their level. A maid is paid three-and-six a day, and feeds herself on that. She will steal a little, but within reason' (260); 'The cost of living is conditioned by the low rate of wages' (261). James' 'Triumph' animates Waugh's static caricatures and describes individual hardships, passions and emotions. While Waugh describes picturesque

local boys diving for pennies for his entertainment, Walrond reverses the gaze, and the tourists on the cruise liner become background to the drama of the 'wharf rats:'

> Philip drew in the oars. The *Kron Prinz Wilhelm* came near. Huddled in thick European coats, the passengers viewed from their lofty estate the spectacle of two naked Negro boys peeping up at them from a wiggly *bateau*. . . . For a Dutch guilder Philip gave an exhibition of 'cork'. Under something of a ledge on the side of the boat he had stuck a piece of cork. Now, after his and Ernest's mouths were full of coins, he could afford to be extravagant and treat the Europeans to a game of West Indian 'cork'. (Walrond 105)

But while James and Walrond write back to the appalling prejudices of the colonial writer, they also repeat ideological norms of feminine beauty and behavior that by the 1980s have been scrutinized and challenged by a new generation of writers who came of age in the era of mass movements for women's rights. 'Girl' is part of this shift in attention and identification, and it interrogates the mechanisms of gender interpellation that are unexamined in the earlier works.

All of Kincaid's texts in some form challenge sexist assumptions and the restricted roles available to women: *Annie John* fleshes out the unnamed almost silent character in 'Girl' and explores the processes by which mothers train their daughters to submit to the conditions of women's oppression; *Lucy* suggests that nanny and employer, though separated by race and class, nonetheless share many of the trials of womanhood; *Autobiography of My Mother* sketches the various ways in which black women have been brutalized; *My Brother*, while humanizing and identifying with Devon, also considers the women he has betrayed and abused.

But even while reflecting a gender critique that was less available in the early mid twentieth century, Kincaid's work represents an extension of the anticolonial address pioneered by James, Walrond, and others in the 1950s, the decade of Kincaid's childhood in Antigua. As I have discussed elsewhere, *A Small Place* asserts a direct response to Alec Waugh's travel narratives, and links the colonialist discourse of his era to the reductive and commodifying 'tourist image' of the present.[5] Kincaid's work places the history and continuity of imperialism at the heart of everything, even the most seemingly innocent of circumstances. This can be seen in *My Garden Book* perhaps most clearly because the subject matter, gardening, is within bourgeois ideology represented as being outside of politics, economics and power relationships. Kincaid rejects this separation: 'the fact is that the world cannot be left out of the garden' (*MGB* 82), asks 'what is the relationship between gardening and conquest?' (116), and reveals the myriad ways in which gardening and botany are inextricably linked to empire. One of the more striking truths revealed in the text is that most of the botanical species closely associated with Antigua (and more broadly the Caribbean)—including those that figure so highly in countless literary evocations of the specificity of the Caribbean home— are in fact, like the people of the region, imports of empire. Kincaid's earlier 'In the Night' echoes many other accounts that evoke the specific world of the Caribbean through depictions of the flora:

In the night, the flowers close up and thicken. The hibiscus flowers, the flamboyant flowers, the bachelor's buttons, the irises, the marigolds, the whiteheadbush flowers, the lilies, the flowers on the daggerbush, the flowers on the turtleberry bush, the flowers on the soursop tree, the flowers on the sugar-apple tree, the flowers on the mango tree, the flowers on the guava tree, the flowers on the cedar tree, the flowers on the stinking-toe tree, the flowers on the dumps tree, the flowers on the papaw tree, the flowers everywhere close up and thicken. (*ABR* 11)

In *My Garden Book* we learn that 'Caribbean' blooms are as often as not from other regions of the world also colonized by European powers:

The bougainvillea (named for another restless European, the sea adventurer Louis de Bougainville, the first Frenchman to cross the Pacific) is native to tropical South America; the plumbago is from southern Africa; the croton is from Malaysia; the hibiscus is from Asia (unfringed petal) and East Africa (fringed petal); the allamanda is from Brazil; the poinsettia (named for an American ambassador, Joseph Poinsett) is from Mexico; the bird of paradise is from southern Africa; the Bermuda lily is from Japan; the flamboyant tree is from Madagascar; the casuarina comes from Australia; the Norfolk pine comes from Norfolk Island in the South Pacific; the tamarind tree is from Africa and Asia. The mango is from Asia. The breadfruit is from the East Indies. (135)

Europe's imperialist powers roamed the globe, taking the best specimens of flora and fauna, distributing them across the far-flung colonies, and developing metropolitan botanical gardens such as 'Kew Gardens, which was then a clearinghouse for all the plants stolen from the various parts of the world these people had been' (135). As can be seen in the above list, the text meticulously dissects the act of cataloguing and naming that accompanied the process: the figure of Carolus Linnaeus is emblematic of the interdependence between colonial plunder and the development of modern disciplines. The text also returns repeatedly to the Dutch merchant George Clifford whose greenhouses were admired by Linnaeus. Clifford epitomizes the way that colonial exploitation is essential to capitalism's development but is simultaneously expunged from bourgeois history:

George Clifford is often described as a rich merchant banker—just like that, a rich merchant banker—and this description often seems to say that a rich merchant banker is merely a type of person one could be, an ordinary type of person, anyone could be that. And now how to go on, for on hearing that George Clifford was a rich merchant in the eighteenth century, I am sure I have become a part of the narrative of the binomial system of plant nomenclature. (163)

'I' here signifies 'descendant of slaves,' those who are written out of the disciplines that are themselves luxated from their material origins:

In almost every account of an event that has taken place sometime in the last five hundred years there is always a moment when I feel like placing an asterisk somewhere in its text and at the end of the official story making my own addition. This chapter in the history of botany is such a moment. But where shall I begin? George Clifford is interesting—shall I look at him? He long ago entered my narrative, I now feel I must enter his. What could it possibly mean to be a merchant banker in the eighteenth century? (164)

My Garden Book consistently demonstrates, through wry humor, unexpected juxtaposition, and sudden shifts of mood, that imperialism shapes even the most seemingly innocent and 'nonpolitical' aspect of life. History is understood in terms of class exploitation and the accumulation of profits through unpaid and underpaid labor. The history of gardening includes not only the record of imperial plunder but also those of plantations and subsistence farming. The text is interested in the difference between gardening as a leisure activity and gardening as labor. At one point Kincaid discusses *Nervous Conditions* by the Zimbabwean writer Tsitsi Dangarembga, and cites a passage about flowers: 'Bright and cheery, they had been planted for joy. What a strange idea that was.' She then describes the novel:

> The book is also a description of brutality, foreign and local. There are the ingredients for a garden—a plot of land, a hoe, some seeds—but they do not lead to little feasts; they lead to nothing or they lead to work, and not work as an act of self-definition, self-acclaim, but work as torture, work as hell. And so it is quite appropriate that the young narrator—her name is Tambu—finds in the sight of things growing just for the sheer joy of it, liberation.
> And what is the relationship between gardening and conquest?
> Is the conqueror a gardener and the conquered the person who works in the field? (116)

This typifies the constant impulse within Kincaid's work towards reconnecting seemingly disconnected situations and circumstances with the economic relationships—and class processes—that structure all human experience. This passage recalls a moment in *Lucy* when the nanny is traveling by train with her employer, Mariah, to the latter's family summer home:

> Early that morning, Mariah left her own compartment to come and tell me that we were passing through some of those freshly plowed fields she loved so much. She drew up my blind, and when I saw mile after mile of turned-up earth, I said, a cruel tone to my voice, 'Well, thank God I didn't have to do that.' I don't know if she understood what I meant, for in that one statement I meant many different things. (33)

Just as Alec Waugh looks at fields of sugar cane as an aesthetically pleasing backdrop for a vacation, Mariah delights in the beauty of farmlands. Lucy, on the other hand, like the narrator of *My Garden Book*, sees the backbreaking labor that went into plowing the land, identifies with the farm hands, and (implicitly) remembers the history of plantation slavery, when she sees the same fields. In another passage Lucy describes an environmental group that Mariah becomes involved with: 'Like her, all the members of this organization were well off but they made no connection between their comforts and the decline of the world that lay before them' (73). Lucy's thoughts, typically, lead her to recognize all sorts of connections that are invisible to Mariah and her husband Lewis:

> I couldn't bring myself to point out to her that if all the things she wanted to save in the world were saved, she might find herself in reduced circumstances; I couldn't bring myself to ask her to examine Lewis's daily conversations with his stock-broker, to see if they bore any relation to the things she saw passing away forever before her eyes. (73)

Here the destruction of the natural environment is tied to the capitalist development that generates the profits that ensure Mariah and Lewis's wealth. This reintegration of disparate social phenomena with capitalist economic structures and relationships is a striking feature of Kincaid's texts.

A Small Place displays very clearly the dialectical relationship between regional patterns and national specificity characteristic of the broader body of Caribbean women's literature. The fact that Kincaid was able to adapt the text to provide the commentary for Stephanie Black's documentary about neoliberalism in Jamaica, *Life and Debt,* indicates the extent to which the main concerns are regional rather than national. Both narrative frame and content exemplify the regionally archetypal relationships visible in Kincaid's other works: This is a text written about a remembered island childhood under British colonialism by someone who has left, settled abroad, and then returned after independence. The structural organization of the book highlights these familiar movements: the first section describes what the tourist, and the returning native, will see in the present (1988); the second remembers the Antigua of the colonial past (the 1950s and early 1960s); part three describes independent Antigua (after 1981); the final section shifts register in to an abstract mode and attempts to draw out generalizations about human nature from these distinct circumstances. At the same time, the particular vociferation of this and other Kincaid works can be traced to the specific personality of Antigua: its geography, particularly its size; the longevity of British colonialism; the peculiarly corrupt postindependence Bird political dynasty, whose neoliberal policies have ensured the omnipresence of American military bases and an economy heavily dependent on tourism. Periodically we are reminded of the broader population of Antiguans (West Indians) who now live and work abroad: at the airport white tourists are treated differently from an 'Antiguan black returning to Antigua from Europe or North America with cardboard boxes of much needed cheap clothes and food for relatives' (4). Sometimes the narrator is clearly located within this broader group of 'Antiguans returning to Antigua after a long absence—who are shocked and offended by the sight of the library sitting on top of a dry-goods store' (44). At the same time, and this is something I will return to, the subject position of the narrator is sufficiently ambiguous to require reminders that she is one of the Antiguans, not the tourists, as in statements like '[w]e Antiguans, for I am one' (8) and the oft repeated 'people like me.'

In keeping with the broader body of Caribbean literature, *A Small Place* is extremely conscious of the history of genocide, expropriation, violence, and exploitation, and lingers on the incongruity of this record and the region's breathtaking natural beauty. Like much contemporaneous Jamaican fiction, *A Small Place* is structured around the stark contrast between this beautiful paradise and the ugly social forces that have shaped it.[6] The text famously opens by describing what the tourist sees arriving in Antigua, again gesturing towards the region: 'what a beautiful island Antigua is—more beautiful than any of the other islands you have seen, and they were very beautiful' (3), and then quickly lays bare the antagonistic needs of tourist and inhabitant, in the process drawing attention to Antigua's particular geographic features: Antigua mainly consists of low-lying limestone and, due to the epidemic deforestation accompanying the sugar economy, tends towards dry soil and drought. While the tourist sees the lack of green lush vegetation as a positive indication of ideal vacation weather, the year-round resident must 'live day in, day out in a place that suffers constantly from drought, and so has to watch carefully every drop of fresh water used' (4).[7] Soon after, we get another graphic illustration of the unpleasant reality lying beneath the illusory beauty: the classic tourist brochure image of a blue sea is disrupted first by a reminder of the raw sewage that is inevitable because 'in Antigua, there is no proper sewage-disposal system,' then by a reference to the history of slavery, 'it would amaze even you to know the number of black slaves this ocean has swallowed up,' and then finally to the unfair trade relations that plague postcolonial Caribbean economies: 'most of what you are eating came off a plane from Miami. . . . A good guess is that it came from a place like Antigua first, where it was grown dirt-cheap, went to Miami, and came back. There is a world of something in this, but I can't go into it right now' (14). Here we see how Kincaid's 'constant flow' narrative technique provokes emotional response through successive graphic and often visceral images, and also persuasively reconnects the social forces and events that are habitually atomized in bourgeois consciousness: There are causal relationships between wealthy elites and impoverished majorities, profits and poverty, tourism and sweatshops. The unreliability of empirically observed reality is underscored again at the book's end, when an extensive portrait of exquisite landscape is simultaneously evoked, through sensuous, lovingly realized images, and undermined, by the repetition of 'unreal' and 'not real,' before we are again taken back to the history and continuity of conquest and expropriation that lies beneath. While such passages have been taken as indicative of a postmodern skepticism toward 'the real,' they could be seen instead as moments where the social *relations* underlying 'immediately given' phenomena are exposed.

Colonial ideology explains the 'underdevelopment' of the colonized world as the result of natural inferiority, and capitalist development as the result of European superiority; the causal relationship between colonial domination and economic underdevelopment is mystified. The imagined tourist in *A Small Place*, the latter day Alec Waugh, reduces the natives to a series of stereotypes—they are closer to nature, simpler, happier and so on—which stem from racist justifications for inequality. The logical conclusion of these seemingly benign stereotypes, the narrator shows us, is the idea that '[t]heir ancestors were not clever in the way yours were and not ruthless in the way yours were, for then would it not be you who would be in harmony with nature and backwards in that charming way?' (17). This extends the eurocentric myth contained in the book the tourist is reading:

> one of those new books about economic history, one of those books explaining how the West (meaning Europe and North America after its conquest and settlement by Europeans) got rich: the West got rich not from the free (free—in this case meaning got-for-nothing) and then undervalued labour, for generations, of the people like me you see walking around you in Antigua but from the ingenuity of small shopkeepers in Sheffield and Yorkshire and Lancashire, or wherever; and what a great part the invention of the wristwatch played in it . . . (10)

Kincaid's prose, characteristically consisting of long, often internally repetitive and rhythmic sentences broken up by many parenthetical asides, works to reconnect the pieces so ardently kept apart by bourgeois ideology while constantly reminding us to rethink, or un-think, the platitudes of colonial myth-making.

The text makes sense of the contradictions facing contemporary Antigua by returning us to the primitive accumulation of capital that was the driving force behind European plunder and conquest. Europe's nascent capitalism was fed by the region's gold, then sugar and slavery; *A Small Place* draws attention to the physical symbolic traces—and celebrations—of that early history in Kincaid's childhood: 'In the Antigua that I knew, we lived on a street named after an English maritime criminal, Horatio Nelson, and all the other streets around us were named after some other English maritime criminals. There was Rodney Street, there was Hood Street, there was Hawkins Street, and there was Drake Street' (24). This echoes a scene in *My Brother* where Devon (the brother of the title, who is dying of AIDS) idolizes these same heroified military figures even while he acknowledges their actual role in his own history:[8]

> He was obsessed with the great thieves who had inhabited his part of the world, the great hero-thieves of English maritime history: Horatio Nelson, John Hawkins, Francis Drake. He thought that the thing called history was an account of significant triumphs over significant defeats recorded by significant people who had benefited from the significant triumphs; he thought (as do I) that this history of ours was primarily an account of theft and murder ('Dem tief, dem a dam tief'), but presented in such a way as to make the account seem inevitable and even fun: he liked the costumes of it, he liked the endings, the outcomes; he liked the people who won, even though he was among the things that had been won. (94–5)

The very people who plundered and enslaved for profit are now remembered as saviors by the descendants of those whose commodification and exploitation were the source of the profits. In constantly reminding us of this history, the text refuses to participate in the process of euphemization that is central to the saccharin version of the past dealt up in textbooks, tourist brochures, and pageants.[9]

This also suggests a revaluation of the relative importance of a small island to the powerhouses of the world economy. For during the eighteenth century the sugar islands of which Antigua was one were arguably at the center of the world, as Eric Williams has argued: 'The eighteenth century was born in the glory that was sugar. "The profits of a sugar plantation in any of our West India Colonies," wrote Adam Smith, in 1776, "are generally much greater than those of any other cultivation that is known either in Europe or America"' (121). As early as 1697 Britain's triangular trade with Antigua accounted for 28,209 British pounds in imports and 8,029 in exports. While Antigua was a small player compared with Barbados or Jamaica, and these British islands were in turn dwarfed by the immense profitability first of France's Saint Domingue and later Spain's Cuba, it was nonetheless of considerable economic significance to Britain, and the competing European powers depended on, and constantly went to war over, their holdings in the region, no matter how small. In the Treaty of Paris of 1763, for example, Guadeloupe was settled on France in exchange for Canada, which went to Britain; the French were generally seen to have got the bargain.[10] Far from the 'ingenuity of shopkeepers' leading to Europe's supremacy, the Caribbean generated the wealth that fueled mercantile growth back home: 'What the West Indies had done for Seville in Spain in the sixteenth century, they did for Bristol in England and Bordeaux in France in the seventeenth. Each town became the metropolis of its country's trade with the Caribbean. . . . As a result of the triangular trade Bristol became a city of shopkeepers' (Eric Williams 143–4).

Of course, none of this would have been possible without the slaves, and *A Small Place* reminds us of this intimate connection between capitalist development (and underdevelopment) and slavery. Nowhere is this expressed more starkly than at the end of the second section, where the link is made between the commodification of Africans' bodies in the slave economy of the past and the gross national product of the present:

> Do you know why people like me are shy about being capitalists? Well, it's because we, for as long as we have known you, *were* capital, like bales of cotton and sacks of sugar, and you were the commanding, cruel capitalists, and the memory of this is so strong, the experience so recent, that we can't quite bring ourselves to embrace this idea that you think so much of. (36–7)

Slavery is present in all aspects of the present, including the living bodies that are descended from those enslaved. The text thus defies the habitual separation of English history and culture from slavery and disallows any 'innocent' anglophilia:

> I cannot tell you how angry it makes me to hear people from North America tell me how much they love England, how beautiful England is, with its traditions. All they see is some frumpy, wrinkled-up person passing by in a carriage waving at a crowd. But what I see is the millions of people, of whom I am just one, made orphans: no motherland, no fatherland, no gods, no mounds of earth for holy ground, no excess of love which might lead to the things that an excess of love sometimes brings, and worst and most painful of all, no tongue. (31)[11]

This passage precedes the sentence about the 'language of the criminal' referred to above, and it is significant that it is frequently skipped over: much notice has been given to the way language is emphasized here, but less to the consistent attentiveness to the economic forces structuring 'cultural' questions. It is generally acknowledged that the book condemns the legacy of British colonialism and draws connections between modern tourism and slavery. But *A Small Place* does much more than this: it lays bare the fundamental continuity of imperialism as an integral feature of capitalism, and it reveals the class interests served by it.

In a passage reminiscent of *Krik? Krak!*'s 'The Americans taught us how to build prisons,' the disposition of the independent nation is explained in terms of the colonial model:

> Have you ever wondered to yourself why it is that all people like me seem to have learned from you is how to imprison and murder each other, how to govern badly, and how to take the wealth of our country and place it in Swiss bank accounts? Have you ever wondered why it is that all we seem to have learned from you is how to corrupt our societies and how to be tyrants? You will have to accept that this is mostly your fault. (34–5)

A sardonic list of colonialism's record of murder and theft is then followed by an account of symbolic decolonization:

> The people like me, finally, after years and years of agitation, made deeply moving and eloquent speeches against the wrongness of your domination over us, and then finally, after the mutilated bodies of you, your wife, and your children were found in your beautiful and spacious bungalow at the edge of your rubber plantation—found by one of your many house servants (none of it was ever yours; it was never, ever yours)—you say to me, 'Well, I wash my hands of all of you, I am leaving now,' and you leave, and from afar you watch as we do to ourselves the very things you used to do to us. (35–6)

The third section of the book, which opens with the question, '[i]s the Antigua I see before me, self-ruled, a worse place than what it was when it was dominated by the bad-minded English and all the bad-minded things they brought with them?' (41) resonates with Fanon's 'Pitfalls of National Consciousness' in its portrait of the role of the national bourgeoisie during and after independence. The connection between the new government and the maritime criminals of old is established straight away when we are told the statement that is 'on every Antiguan's lips:' '"The government is corrupt. Them are thief, them are big thief"' (41), recalling Devon's '"dem tief, dem a dam tief"' (*MB* 95). What follows is a catalogue of their crimes.

Kincaid's portrait is of the Bird dynasty of Antigua, the embodiment of the postindependence regime based on patronage and a friendly relationship with American imperialism: 'All the ministers have "green cards"—a document that makes them legal residents of the United States of America. The ministers, the people who govern the island of Antigua, who are also citizens of Antigua, are legal residents of the United States, a place they visit frequently' (*ASP* 68). Vere Cornwall Bird's political roots were in labor politics: he founded the Antigua Trades and Labour Union in 1939 and then created the Antigua Labour Party in

1951. Like Guyana's Forbes Burnham, however, and Grenada's Eric Gairy, his political career was dedicated to serving very different class interests. He became minister of trade in 1956, chief minister in 1961, and after Antigua became an associated state of Great Britain in 1966 he became the first premier; he thwarted a march for recognition by the Antigua Workers Union in 1968 by calling a state of emergency and commanding the police to tear gas the protestors. After a brief interlude when George Walter replaced him, Bird headed the government from 1976 to 1994 and was then succeeded by his first-born son, Vere Jr. (His son Lester was also in government.) Among other achievements, during the 1980s Bird made illegal weapons deals with South Africa and Israel. As part of the cold war strategy of ensuring friendly regional regimes, the U.S. supported Bird, maintaining a large military installation on the island.[12] In 1980 Bird agreed to allow transmission of the Voice of America radio station from the island, over the objection of the Deputy Prime Minister that '"every Caribbean government whether right, left or center in political orientation would feel that Antigua had become a bastion of US metropolitan presence in the Caribbean'" (qtd. in Pearce 156). The Bird government continued to serve the interests of neoliberalism, privatizing national assets and borrowing money in order to encourage foreign investment and orient the economy towards tourism. In Robert Coram's words: 'No other English-speaking island in the Eastern Caribbean has had a greater U.S. presence or received more U.S. dollars than Antigua' (6–7).[13] This record is presented to us repeatedly through anecdote, sometimes in general terms that echo the critique of postindependence governments launched by other Caribbean writers. When Kincaid writes in a parenthetical aside 'in places where there is a Minister of Culture it means there is no culture' (*ASP* 49), we recall Roger McTair in his 1970 poem 'Politics Kaiso:' 'Men widout education/Is Minister of Education,/Men widout culture/Run de Ministry of Culture.'

At other times we get sketches of Antigua's particular idiosyncrasies: the Redonda stamp scandal, which the narrator remembers hearing about as a child; shady government profiteering from foreign car dealerships, cable companies, drug trafficking, prostitution, and off shore banking (58–9). The postindependence government's corruption gives fuel to apologists for British colonialism, like the woman whose ancestors established the racist private Mill Reef Club, 'notorious for liking Antiguans only if they are servants,' and now working to restore the old library:

> She said to me then what everybody in Antigua says sooner or later: The government is for sale; anybody from anywhere can come to Antigua and for a sum of money can get what he wants. And I had to ask myself, What exactly should I feel toward the people who robbed me of the right to make a reply to this woman? For I could see the pleasure she took in pointing out to me the gutter into which a self-governing—black—Antigua had placed itself. (47)

A Small Place answers by revealing the continuation of imperialism in a new guise: the economic foreign domination that maintains and is maintained by the

Antiguan ruling class. The neoliberal priorities of this regime ensure that social services—schools, hospitals, libraries—are starved of funds while money is poured into the coffers of foreign corporations and domestic government officials. This is why 'there is no proper sewage-disposal system' (14), the school could be mistaken for latrines (7), the library has not been repaired since an earthquake in 1974 (8–9), and the hospitals are so substandard that 'the ministers in the government go overseas for medical treatment. Not one of them would stay in the hospital here' (66).[14] In short, the nation is run by 'corrupt men (who) have given their country away to corrupt foreigners' (55) along the lines of a nepotistic corporation: 'people say that the man who has headed the government for twenty-five years perhaps by now thinks that the government of Antigua is his own business, for two of his sons are members of this cabinet' (72).

The book's critique of tourism is within this broader economic frame: tourism does not simply resemble slavery because (black) Antiguans are serving (white) tourists, but the nation's reliance on tourism is also symptomatic of a relationship to the global economy that remains subordinate and ensures the poverty of the majority of Antiguans while enriching a foreign and domestic minority. The IMF and World Bank often prescribe tourism for Caribbean nations, but the perils of this route are writ large in Antigua where one of the biggest tourism booms in the region was accompanied by accumulation of the largest debt burden. By 1979 a full 36 percent of Antigua's GDP came from tourism. Over the next decade a full 80 cents of every dollar made in the tourist industry went to foreign operations, not to Antiguans.[15] By the end of the decade World Bank officials were fearful that tourism was creating its own demise:

> Environmental problems could also become a deterrent to future tourism. Marine pollution, beach pollution, land degradation, beach mining, inadequate sewerage facilities, together with household, industrial, and municipal waste, lack of or deterioration of forest cover, and improper siting of beach front facilities are major environmental problems affecting Caribbean countries. Oil spills could damage tourism activity. (qtd. in McAfee 28)

When tourism does create jobs within the host country they tend to be low waged and seasonal, and, of course, they are mainly within the service industry and therefore require servitude:

> An institution that is often celebrated in Antigua is the Hotel Training School, a school that teaches Antiguans how to be good servants, how to be a good nobody, which is what a servant is. In Antigua, people cannot see a relationship between their obsession with slavery and emancipation and their celebration of the Hotel Training School. (*ASP* 55)

Kincaid's account of tourism is reminiscent of that of V.S. Naipaul in *The Middle Passage*, written more than two decades earlier. Naipaul, like Kincaid, flies in to Antigua (en route to Jamaica), and describes his taxi journey to St Johns. In this passage he is responding to news reports of Americans buying land in Tobago, Barbados, Antigua, Dominica, and Montserrat:[16]

> These islands were small, poor and overpopulated. Once, because of their wealth, a people had been enslaved; now, because of their beauty, a people were being dispossessed. Land values had risen steeply; in some islands peasant farmers could no longer afford to buy land; and emigration to the un-welcoming slums of London, Birmingham and half a dozen other English cities was increasing. Every poor country accepts tourism as an unavoidable degradation. None has gone as far as some of these West Indian islands, which, in the name of tourism, are selling themselves into a new slavery. The elite of the islands, whose pleasures, revealingly, are tourist's pleasures, ask no more than to be permitted to mix with the white tourists and the governments make feeble stipulations about the colour bar. (191)

Naipaul assembles the various ingredients of Kincaid's analysis: economic compulsion driven by lack of other sources of economic productivity; dispossession of peasants and the theft of the best land for tourism; subsequent migration. Naipaul's infamous tendency towards scornful attacks on West Indians is also recognizable here, in the singling out of the region for failings that seem to go beyond those driven by poverty—'None has gone as far as some of these West Indian islands'—and in their implication in their own enslavement—'selling themselves into a new slavery.' This attitude is encapsulated earlier in the text: 'The history of the islands can never be satisfactorily told. Brutality is not the only difficulty. History is built around achievement and creation; and nothing was created in the West Indies' (29). A not dissimilar tone can be heard in *A Small Place*:

> And it is in that strange voice, then—the voice that suggests innocence, art, lunacy— that they say these things, pausing to take breath before this monument to rottenness, that monument to rottenness, as if they were tour guides; as if, having observed the event of tourism, they have absorbed it so completely that they have made the degradation and humiliation of their daily lives into their own tourist attraction. (68–9)

While this passage follows a lengthy discussion of the corruption of Antiguan government officials and so would seem to be indicting them, the start of the sentence actually refers back to a passage several pages earlier discussing Antiguans in general: 'I look at these people (Antiguans), and I cannot tell whether I was brought up by, and so come from, children, eternal innocents, or artists who have not yet found eminence in a world too stupid to understand, or lunatics who have made their own lunatic asylum, or an exquisite combination of all three' (57). The distinct separation between speaker and Antiguans (West Indians), and the attitude of scorn and disgust expressed by the former for the latter, connect Kincaid's account to Naipaul's, and bespeak the conflicted subject position of the narrator that I will be exploring in more depth.

First, though, it is important to note that towards the end of the third section of *A Small Place* Antigua's political and economic crises are associated with those of other countries in the region, and, crucially, with American imperialist interventions. First Antigua's military dependence is compared to Grenada's defenselessness against U.S. intervention, and we are told that Antigua

> has an army of sorts, an army that can only stand around as a decoration, the way it did in Grenada when the United States invaded that island; an army, then, that can only lend legitimacy to illegitimate acts. And though this army cannot really fight a war, is not trained to really fight a war—Antigua, after all, has no enemies—the men in this army can shoot at people, and if they cannot fight a war but can shoot at people, what people will they shoot at? (73)

Then quickly we move from Grenada to Haiti, and the Bird regime is likened to that of the Duvaliers: 'And so people see anchored to this father and his two sons who have wielded power in Antigua for so many years, and who might find it hard to quietly relinquish this power and sit in New York spending the contents of their enormous bank accounts, the event of Haiti and the Duvaliers' (73). The U.S. government supported both regimes, as part of its post war strategy of securing interests through client regimes, and doubtless would give the Birds refuge if, like the Duvaliers, they were forced out of power by a mass movement. Anticipating the pattern followed by Aristide, we then are given an imaginary scenario in which a popular leader emerges as an alternative to the Birds: 'And so they imagine another event, the event of Maurice Bishop in Grenada, and they imagine that such a man will materialize in Antigua and he'll do Maurice Bishop-like things and say Maurice Bishop-like things and come to a Maurice Bishop-like end—death, only this time at the hands of the Americans' (74). The Americans opposed Bishop, as they had already opposed Manley and would soon oppose Aristide, and would feasibly remove such a figure were he to emerge in Antigua. This connection takes on even greater significance when one considers that the U.S. State Department chose Antigua as 'an American satellite, a bastion of democracy whose role would be an anchor against what Washington saw as the insidious, pervasive, and dangerous spread of communism' (Coram 117) soon after the invasion of Grenada. This led to the construction of a new U.S. consulate and the erection of a Voice of America transmitter 'to convince people of the region that democracy had many advantages over the leftist theories espoused by Maurice Bishop' (Coram 117–18):

> Three months after the Grenada invasion, on January 13, 1984, a State Department paper was issued as a rationale for the close relationship between Antigua and America. The document said Antigua is 'strategically placed in the Leeward Islands, thus a potentially dangerous hazard would be posed for the region if it falls to a hostile power.' Despite the pervasive corruption of the Bird government, this would continue as State Department policy even after the Soviet Union and communism collapsed in the early 1990s. (Coram 120)

A Small Place's reference to Bishop at the conclusion of the third section of the book highlights the role of U.S. imperialism in the political fates of Caribbean nations; it also underscores—and accounts for—the overwhelming sense of pessimism that pervades this and so much contemporary literature by Caribbean women:

> The invasion was a watershed in U.S.-Caribbean relations. Never again would the small islands of the region look on America in the same fashion. They were independent nations, but after October 1983, they knew that America was the colossus to the north, the behemoth that, like a sleeping elephant, should not be disturbed or angered. (Coram 119)

Colonialism was replaced by corrupt domestic regimes complicit with U.S. imperialism; alternatives would be removed by political destabilization, sponsored coups, or military interventions. There is little reason to be hopeful for a different future.[17]

With Feet in Two Worlds

From its first page, *A Small Place* presents a speaking voice that is (at least) dual; this is the 'undecidablity' explored by Isabel Hoving in 'Jamaica Kincaid is Getting Angry.' While the narrator addresses a very specific persona—the hypothetical tourist—she at the same time is describing what *she* sees as she approaches the island. She is, in the first section at least, occupying the subject position of the tourist, and is more closely identified with the 'you' of the address than with 'them'—resident or returning Antiguans. At moments the difference between tourist and nontourist is delineated more clearly in racial terms: 'you are a tourist, a North American or European—to be frank, white—and not an Antiguan black returning to Antigua from Europe or North America with cardboard boxes of much needed cheap clothes and food for relatives' (4), but at such times the speaker still seems more of an observer than a participant. For most of the first section tourists are 'you,' Antiguans are 'they,' and the speaker is indeterminate: 'Antiguans hate them' (11); 'the people who inhabit the place in which you have just paused cannot stand you . . . behind their closed doors they laugh at your strangeness' (17). And occasionally a distinct personal voice intervenes: 'we Antiguans, for I am one' (8); 'people like me you see walking around you in Antigua' (10).

The final passage of the first section presents a different opposition, one that again implies a shift in how we perceive the subject position of the narrator:

> That the native does not like the tourist is not hard to explain. For every native of every place is a potential tourist, and every tourist is a native of somewhere. Every native everywhere lives a life of overwhelming and crushing banality and boredom and desperation and depression, and every deed, good and bad, is an attempt to forget this. Every native would like to find a way out, every native would like a rest, every native would like a tour. But some natives—most natives in the world—cannot go anywhere. They are too poor. They are too poor to go anywhere. They are too poor to live properly in the place where they live, which is the very place you, the tourist, want to go—so

when the natives see you, the tourist, they envy you, they envy your ability to leave your own banality and boredom, they envy your ability to turn their own banality and boredom into a source of pleasure for yourself. (18–19)

This passage encapsulates the preoccupations, tensions, and contradictions that pervade the broader body of literature considered here. It clearly expresses the class inequality that is determinant globally—the world is divided into those who are poor and immobile and those who are wealthy and mobile—while capturing the tone of alienated cynicism that is familiar especially in Jamaican fiction about the 1980s.[18] The very fact of the narrator's subject position—one who leaves and returns with ease—again places her in the category of 'tourist' (mobile) more aptly than that of 'native' (immobile/constrained). At the same time the suppressed fury that runs throughout the passage (and the book) is an expression of protest against the world's inequalities and injustices that, in drawing attention to these realities, implicitly posits the possibility of an alternative, even though none is available in any explicit way. In other words even while expressing the absence of any model of mass social movement akin to those that animate the literature of national liberation, the text names and decries the new forms of imperialism that continue to delimit people's potential and necessitate substantive social change.

As the above passage also reveals, just as *A Small Place* discloses the class divisions that are definitive in Antigua and the globe, so does it demonstrate the contradictory class position of the writer, who is removed from the poor and working class whose interests are nonetheless championed in the text (which was also the case for the earlier generation of writers) and also isolated from movements for social change (which was not the case during the period of national liberation). The gulf between writer and subject is often made explicit in the works of the 'pioneer' writers. C.L.R James inhabits the role of anthropologist in his explanatory note about the barrack-yards of Trinidad:

Where people in England and America say slums, Trinidadians say barrack-yards . . . Every street in Port-of-Spain can show you numerous examples of the type: a narrow gateway leading into a fairly big yard, on either side of which run long low buildings, consisting of anything from four to eighteen rooms, each about twelve feet square. In these live, and have always lived, the porters, prostitutes, carter-men, washerwomen, and domestic servants of the city. ('Triumph' 108)

This evinces the metropolitan audience that (especially expatriate) Caribbean writers are bound to: no barrack-yard resident would need the supplement in order to understand the sociological origins of the fictional world. It furthermore demonstrates the extent to which the (Caribbean) writer is also an 'outsider' to the world of the poor: the narrator is separate from 'people in England and America,' but also from 'Trinidadians,' and is clearly not one of those living in these familiar environs. The introductory note further emphasizes the gap between writer and subject through language and allusion: 'In the centre of the yard is a heap of stones. . . . Not only to Minerva have these stones been dedicated. Time was when they would have had an honoured shrine in a local temple to Mars, for they were the major source of ammunition for the homicidal strife which in times past so often flared up in barrack-yards' (108). James here uses high burlesque: References to classical figures serve to elevate (humorously) the banal to the mythical, and also to underscore the disparity between the highly educated discourse of the writer from the vernacular of his subjects. This opposition is maintained in the dialogue:

> Yet Celestine was grieved that she could do nothing to help Mamitz in her troubles, which she attributed to the evil and supernatural machinations of Irene, their common enemy.
> 'Take it from me, that woman do you something. I's she put Nathan against you. When was the quarrel again?'
> 'It was two or three days after Nathan gave me the first beating.'
> Nathan then had started on his evil courses before the quarrel with Irene took place, but Celestine brushed away that objection.
> 'She must 'a' had it in her mind for you from before.' (111)

The marked separation is maintained through the ironic juxtaposition of the wry, polished narrative voice with the rough colloquialisms of the characters. While the barrack-yards stories pay tribute to those whose lives have been skipped over by the official histories of the region, it does so at times with the amused and condescending tone of the observer used by Alec Waugh, or James Anthony Froude, Anthony Trollope, or others cited in Naipaul's *Middle Passage*:

> At midnight with the necessary rites and ceremonies, Ave Marias and Pater Nosters, she bathed Mamitz in a large bath-pan full of water prepared with gully-root, fever-grass, lime leaves, guérir tout, herbe à femmes, and other roots, leaves and grasses noted for their efficacy (when properly applied), against malign plots and influences. (James 114)

The self-conscious parenthetical comment ensures the ironic comic distance between narration and actions. While some of this is reminiscent of Waugh's 'they still retain the fetishes of the bush,' clearly James's project is very different. He has talked in interview about the anthropological field work that preceded his fictional rendition of the barrack yards: "'I went to live there, the people fascinated me, and I wrote about them from the point of view of an educated youthful member of the black middle class'" (qtd. in *The West Indian Novel* Gilkes 29). Waugh may have been 'fascinated' by the 'natives' but never did he consider living among them; his entire depiction of the region's inhabitants serves to bolster the myth of the white man's burden and to establish the manichean oppositions of colonial racism. James is separate from but allied with 'the people:' he and his contemporaries understood their important role in national liberation struggles as middle class intellectuals but they looked to the working class as the key motor force of social change.

In the postcolonial world inhabited by Kincaid, though, while the distance between writer and masses remains, such faith in the revolutionary potential of the latter has been eroded by the bitter disappointments of independence. One of the symptoms of this is an extremely ambiguous attitude towards ordinary Antiguans, which can be seen in *A Small Place* in the sometimes exasperated and scornful tone—that evokes Naipaul at his most patronizing—and in the famed 'undecidability' of the speaking voice: the narrator sometimes speaks as an Antiguan and sometimes speaks of Antiguans as 'they;' she refers to herself as a 'native' and yet elsewhere defines 'native' as those who cannot leave, while she has clearly left and returned.[19] Part one of *A Small Place* reverses the objectifying gaze used by the colonizer and tourist against the native and in so doing it champions the native. It sees the world primarily in terms of rich and poor, rather than west and nonwest or white and black; here 'you' refers to the rich and 'they' to the poor. The narrative voice clearly *identifies* not with 'you' but with 'they,' but to which group it *belongs* is not clear. In the second section 'they' and 'you' are white colonialists; 'I' and 'we' (significantly the first person pronoun is as often plural as it is singular) is/are clearly identified as black and Antiguan; the fact that the narrative is now back in the preindependence period, before the narrator left, removes much of the ambiguity of the previous section. Again the binary oppositions of colonial discourse are reversed; now the antagonism between tourist/native is replaced by that of colonizer/colonized, and now instead of 'you' (tourist) and 'they' (natives) the key pronouns are 'we' (Antiguans) and 'they' (British), as in these typical lines: 'We thought they were un-Christian-like; we thought they were small-minded; we thought they were like animals, a bit below human standards as we understood those standards to be' (29); 'We felt superior, for we were so much better behaved and we were full of grace, and these people were so badly behaved and they were so completely empty of grace' (30). The text thus exhibits in condensed form the entire spectrum of contradictory impulses, from identification with to scorn for the oppressed, as they are inscribed and reinscribed across Kincaid's oeuvre.

Different texts bring in to sharp focus distinct points on the spectrum. In *Lucy* the narrative voice consistently identifies with the working class. Antiguans per se are occasionally represented in memories, but the narrator sees herself as one of the countless immigrant workers in the U.S.A. and therefore of a different world than her employers. In one scene Mariah introduces Lucy to a museum, which becomes one of her favorite places. She there learns of one of the artists,

> a French man, who had gone halfway across the world to live and had painted pictures of the people he found living there. He had been a banker living a comfortable life with his wife and children, but that did not make him happy . . . immediately I identified with the yearnings of this man; I understood finding the place you are born in an unbearable prison and wanting something completely different from what you are familiar with, knowing it represents a haven. I wondered about the details of his despair, for I felt it would comfort me to know. (95)

Even as she identifies with this figure, who is surely one of those 'who can leave,' Lucy recognizes what differentiates him from her:

> Of course his life could be found in the pages of a book; I had just begun to notice that the lives of men always are. He was shown to be a man rebelling against an established

order he had found corrupt; and even though he was doomed to defeat—he died an early death—he had the perfume of the hero about him. I was not a man; I was a young woman from the fringes of the world, and when I left my home I had wrapped around my shoulders the mantle of a servant. (*L* 95)

The moment demonstrates other important elements of this novel, including its feminism—the artist is canonized because he is male—and its third-worldism—he is from the center of the world rather than 'the fringes.' It also clearly emphasizes the extent to which this novel sees the world through the lens of class: leaving your home to become an artist is in a different category than doing so as a servant. Soon after, the same themes are elaborated. Lucy attends a party with Peggy, the working-class Irish nanny she befriends for a time, where she meets some artists who 'seemed to take for granted that everything they said mattered' and cause her to reflect on different categories of people:

I thought of all the people in the world I had known who went insane and died, and who drank too much rum and then died, and who were paupers and died, and I wondered if there were any artists among them. Who would have known? And I thought, I am not an artist, but I shall always like to be with the people who stand apart. I had just begun to notice that people who knew the correct way to do things such as hold a teacup, put food on a fork and bring it to their mouth without making a mess on the front of their dress—they were the people responsible for the most misery, the people least likely to end up insane or paupers. (98–9)

This encapsulates the narrative's primary points of identification: with the paupers, the prematurely dead, those whose lives go unrecognized and are excluded from the world of those 'who knew the correct way to do things;' but also 'with the people who stand apart.'

The strongest voice in *My Brother* is also one of protest against inequality from the perspective of the workers and poor. Focusing as it does on the experience of her brother dying of AIDS, the book confronts the horrors of inadequate health care provision: squalid hospitals, insufficient medicines, overworked doctors and nurses. The narrative constantly moves out to generalize from the specific experience of Devon:

It is felt in general, so I am told, that since there is no cure for AIDS it is useless to spend money on a medicine that will only slow the progress of the disease; the afflicted will die no matter what; there are limited resources to be spent on health care and these should be spent where they will do some good, not where it is known that the outcome is death. This was the reason why there was no AZT in the hospital; but even if a doctor had wanted to write a prescription for AZT for a patient, that prescription could not be filled at a chemist's; there was no AZT on the island, it was too expensive to be stocked, most people suffering from the disease could not afford to buy this medicine; most people suffering from the disease are poor or young, not too far away from being children; in a society like the one I am from, being a child is one of the definitions of vulnerability and powerlessness. (31–2)

The narrator is from this country; she also has moved away but is acutely conscious of the possible alternate trajectory of her life had she stayed there with her brother. Just as in *A Small Place* the narrator is neither 'you' nor 'they,' in *My Brother* she is both part of and separate from the life of her family who remained. The book resonates with a passion that is part grief and part rage against the painful inequities of the world. The emotional intensity of the narrative is generated by the combination of deeply personal introspection, relentlessly graphic depictions of Devon's decaying body, and the constant pan out to the bigger picture:

> On that last visit that I made to see my brother, the visit where I quarreled with him (not him with me) and I did not kiss or hug him goodbye, and even told him that I did not want to kiss or hug him and did not tell him that I loved him (and he did not say that he loved me, something he had said many times before), I spent one day trying to find Dr. Prince Ramsey. My brother was in great pain. A stream of yellow pus flowed out of his anus constantly; the inside of his mouth and all around his lips were covered with a white glistening substance, thrush. (138)

One barely has time to absorb the poignant shock of learning that this quarrel was to be the last exchange between the siblings before grasping the extent of Devon's physical suffering. Then, in the account of her search for the doctor, this most intimate of moments is followed by a reminder that his is not an exceptional story:

> I joined a group of people sitting in chairs waiting and waiting for the doctor, and we waited not in joy, not in anger, but more as if we were in a state of contemplation, as if we were seeing the whole panorama of life, from its ancient beginnings in the past to its inevitable end in some future, and we accepted it with indifference, for what else could we do? And this is the way people wait, people all over the world wait in this way, when they are powerless or poor, or both at the same time. (139)

This is the dominant voice of the book, and clearly resembles that of *A Small Place*: 'most natives in the world . . . are too poor to go anywhere. They are too poor to escape the reality of their lives; and they are too poor to live properly in the place where they live' (*ASP* 18–19).

If *A Small Place* contains the strongest expression of solidarity with the oppressed, *My Garden Book* enunciates from a position of privilege. In the section describing her trip to China with a botanical group to collect rare specimens, the voice is that of the tourist looking at the natives—poor peasants in a huge country characterized by extreme uneven development—with scorn and disgust worthy of a Waugh in the Caribbean. The most striking theme of this section is horror at the pervasive filth and excrement. Rather than seeing these as symptoms of poverty, the narrative discusses them in cultural terms as evidence of different standards of personal hygiene peculiar to the Chinese character:

> As we drove through the villages that were in the mountains and the hills and the valleys, there was that strange, rotting, fetid, unpleasant smell of other people, their shit;

human feces is such a valuable commodity in China, it is why all the vegetables were so vigorous-looking in cultivation, it is why people were so able to feed themselves. In all the time I was in China . . . the thing I noticed people doing most frequently was growing food and eating food. (196)

It is impossible not to hear behind such passages the distinction, made earlier in this text and in other works, between the gardener who gardens for pleasure and the laborer who gardens for subsistence.[20] The relationship is complicated by the presence of another member of the tour, John, the liberal multiculturalist who chides the narrator for her lack of tolerant cultural pluralism and sees every encounter with filth in terms of the 'authentic' Chinese experience. Things come to a head in Judian, where the narrator has a breakdown and confronts their Chinese guide with these words: "'The rooms are the filthiest rooms I have ever been in; there is blood on the walls, there is shit on the walls, there are the remains of vomit on the walls'" (206). John responds (according to the narrator, of course, whose version of events is the only one we have), 'that the whole experience of the unsanitariness of everything, the preparation of our food, the places in which we ate and slept . . . that all of this made our experience in China more authentic' (207), and the narrator mentally formulates but does not verbalize her response to him: 'I did not say to John, I like the Chinese, I like the way they grow food (I would then be thinking of how those terraces and terraces were cultivated), I like the way they eat food, it is the things they do in between growing and eating I don't like, the things they do after eating the food, I don't understand' (207). Thus the only available positions are culturalist: there is no materialist explanation for the conditions the group is encountering, only tolerance or intolerance for 'Chinese ways.'

The Chinese peasants are represented in isolation from the world of connections portrayed so powerfully elsewhere in Kincaid's work: they seem fixed in the moment of observation, unchanging, inherently and inexplicably unhygenic and tolerant of their own and others' filth. The attitude recalls many a colonial report of the West Indies, such as Dr. Howard Coleman's 1917 observation of Grenadians:

[p]eople with little responsiblity, few desires, and practically no wants, they get along quite contentedly in a small thatched house with a minimum of household furniture. Breadfruit and plantains are too easily obtainable to make real hunger possible. There is no home life. Scant obedience to parents by children; a variable interest in cleanliness; no conception of sanitation. (qtd. in Steele 291)

Or this 1938 account also of Grenada:

It is doubtful if one peasant's house in a hundred is provided with latrine accommodation. Soil pollution was therefore gross and the struggle against flies, flyborne and intestinal infections, such as the enteric and dysenteric group of diseases and helminthic infections such as Ankylostomiasis and round worms, is rendered infinitely more difficult. (qtd. in Steele 291–2)

Naipaul writing about India, discussed and quoted here by Michael Gilkes, repeats such horror of dirt and defecation:

> Naipaul's disillusionment with India is in direct proportion to his longing for an 'unsullied' cultural heritage: his reaction to the Indians' apparently casual attitude to defecation is therefore almost frenzied:
> 'Indians defecate everywhere . . . beside railway tracks . . . on the beaches; they defecate on the hills . . . on the streets. . . . These squatting figures are never spoken of . . . never written about; they are not mentioned in novels or stories; they do not appear in feature films or documentaries. . . . But the truth is that *Indians do not see these squatters.*' (*The West Indian Novel* 99–100)

Gilkes places this exaggerated 'personal alarm' in the context of the 'cultural elitism . . . which produces in Naipaul an instinctive respect for "purity," pedigree, tradition. Even in his journalism there is this fastidiousness of reaction, a respect for the elitist, sybaritic quality in others' (99). While nothing like this generalization can be made of Kincaid's oeuvre, there are elements of elitism scattered through the texts, and certainly traces of something Gilkes identifies in Naipaul's depiction of British photographer David Hockney, 'as successful not only because his work is popular and fetches high prices, but also, more significantly, because the Bradford-born artist has escaped his unimaginative, narrow, working-class background; from his own "Miguel Street"' (Gilkes 99).

My Garden Book offers its own, comparable, explanation for this tone when it acknowledges the distance between the narrator's roots (poor resident of a third world country) and current location (wealthy gardener touring a third world country). As she contemplates her garden and thinks about the history of conquest and its relation to the power to name, the narrator reflects on her own position: 'I thought how I had crossed a line; but at whose expense? I cannot begin to look, because what if it is someone I know? I have joined the conquering class: who else could afford this garden—a garden in which I grow things that it would be much cheaper to buy at the store? My feet are (so to speak) in two worlds' (123). While *A Small Place* suggests a definition of class as a relationship, between those who own and control and those have to work to make a living, here class is understood as identity: moving from a position of want to one of comfort is conceptualized as joining the 'conquering class,' even though the speaker, whether considered as a narrative persona or as Kincaid, in Marxist terms is hardly ruling class but someone who produces literature for a living, albeit a prosperous one. However, her accumulated wealth certainly places her in the privileged minority of the globe's population, with the mobility and leisure time denied to the majority. Here we can see very clearly the conflict that is beneath the surface in so much contemporary Caribbean women's literature: the sense of having one's 'feet in two worlds' not only geographically but also socioeconomically.

Mr. Potter is closer to *My Garden Book* than *A Small Place*, although there are certainly many points of connection with the latter: the use of repetition and stream of consciousness; the combination of autobiography and fictionalization (more of this in *Mr. Potter* than in the more grounded personal voice of *My Brother*); the pervasive sense of interpenetration of individual and social, local, and global forces. At moments this work expresses a worldview that is very close to *A Small Place*, especially in its powerful overview of the global system determining lives and events everywhere.   Early on Mr. Potter, who is a chauffeur, waits for passengers from a newly arrived boat: 'a large steamer coming from some benighted place in the world, someplace far away where there had been upheavals and displacements and murder and terror. Mr. Potter was not unfamiliar with upheavals and displacements and murder and terror; his very existence in the world in which he lived had been made possible by such things' (7). Mr. Potter is the product of centuries of violent expropriation, colonialism, and exploitation, and we are frequently reminded that he is the descendant of slaves. At several points in the narrative we are presented with the material sources of the violence and exploitation: the raw materials and manufactured products over which wars are waged. The beautiful island of Antigua, and all aspects of the natural world itself, cannot be extricated from this history of human and economic relationships:

> Oh, the beautiful blue of the seawater lap-lapping against the shores of Five Islands Bay, hugging the village of Grays Farm, hovering near the open tract that was Greene Bay, a place where people of no account lived, the beautiful blue sea that could be seen from the village of Crab Hill and the village of Freetown and the village of Urlings, that was not something Mr. Potter thought about as he walked to Mr. Shoul's garage. And the fields of sugarcane, stilled now but with their history of horror unspeakable imprisoned in each stray blade, each stray stalk; and so too the fields of cotton and the rows of sweet potatoes and the rows of Irish potatoes and the rows of tomatoes and the rows of carrots . . . (121)

These moments recall the powerful contrasts of *A Small Place*—the juxtaposition of images of natural beauty, 'the beautiful blue of the seawater lap-lapping,' with those of surprising violence, 'their history of horror unspeakable imprisoned in each stray blade,'—and like the earlier work serve as a constant reminder of the machinations of a violent world system that leaves nothing and nobody untouched. The book is populated by refugees from wars and disasters, displaced by seemingly impersonal forces that serve the interests of the powerful and wealthy. The global production line creates the very clothes worn by Mr. Potter— 'even his body was mixed up with the world and he could not extricate himself from it'—and exists in a dialectical relationship with him (46):

> He could not imagine or know of his importance to all the turbulence in the world, how necessary he was to the world of silks and gems and fields of cotton and fields of sugarcane and displacement and longing for places from which mere people had been displaced and the flourishing centers of cities and the peaceable outlay of villages . . . And Mr. Potter had no inkling of the turbulence: silks, gems, fields of cotton, fields of sugarcane, and centers of power and villages that lay in peace because of the violence perpetuated by those in faraway centers of power. (116)

The passage describes the reification that obscures the interconnected processes and relationships of the capitalist system of production based on exploitation, recapitulated here by Lukács:

> For the commodity *is* produced and even the worker in his quality as commodity, as an immediate producer is at best a mechanical driving wheel in the machine. But if the reification of capital is dissolved into an unbroken process of its production and reproduction, it is possible for the proletariat to discover that it is itself the subject of this process even though it is in chains and is for the time being unconscious of the fact. As soon, therefore, as the ready-made, immediate reality is abandoned the question arises: 'Does a worker in a cotton factory produce merely cotton textiles? No, he produces capital. He produces values which serve afresh to command his labour and by means of it to create new values.' (180–81)

Mr. Potter does not see 'how necessary he was,' how thoroughly a part of this 'world of silks and gems and fields of cotton and fields of sugarcane and displacement'—this 'process of capital production and reproduction.' He 'had no inkling of the turbulence'—he is 'for the time being unconscious of the fact.'

But whereas in Lukács the proletariat has the capacity to become aware of these processes and so achieve a revolutionary consciousness, Mr. Potter remains 'in chains and . . . unconscious of the fact:' ignorant, myopic, uncurious, and, as we are told again and again, illiterate. Furthermore, his illiteracy is seen as the *cause* of his inability to understand the world and himself: 'because Mr. Potter could neither read nor write, he could not understand himself, he could not make himself known to others, he did not know himself' (21); 'he did not seek to interrogate the past to give meaning to the present and the future' (25). Literacy is equated with self awareness and the capacity to see things clearly: the author is the one with the power to create, name, define, and give meaning: 'I can write it down and make clear how all this came to be' (94); 'he was my father but he could not read or write, he only made me and I can read and I am also writing all of this at this very moment . . . and I can place my thoughts about him and all that he was and all that he could have been into words' (48); 'I am the one who can write the narrative that is his life, the only one really' (87); 'I can write it down and make clear how all this came to be' (94); 'I still managed to acquire the ability to read and the ability to write and in this way I make Mr. Potter and in this way I unmake Mr. Potter' (158).

In part all of this is generated by one of the text's main feminist themes: the abandoned daughter taking revenge on her father by redefining his life through her writing. One of the most symbolically significant events in the narrator's remembered childhood is when she approaches her father, at the mother's request (after the parents' separation), to ask for money for some writing paper, and the father slams the door in her face. Despite this, not only does the child learn to read and write, but she grows up to be a prolific, cosmopolitan author with the capacity to define the once powerful provincial patriarch. Throughout Kincaid's work this act of authority through inscription is repeated: *Lucy* ends with the narrator writing her name on a blank page; *Autobiography of My Mother* with the declaration that '[t]his account of my life has been an account of my mother's life. As much as it has been an account of mine' (227); At the close of *My Brother* the narrator promises to rectify her mother's past book burning by spending 'the rest of my life trying to bring those books back to my life by writing them again and again until they were perfect, unscathed by fire of any kind' (197–8). Seen in terms of the larger body of writing, and the broad issues surrounding the relationship between the (Caribbean woman) writer and the people (of the Caribbean) who are her narrative subjects, these dynamics are also expressive of a contradictory class location—and multiple, conflicting points of class affiliation—and a historical moment when the writer ultimately is an individual severed from any collective, social, action. The composite perspective understands history as 'an open wound, each breath I take in and expel healing and opening the wound again, over and over' (*MGB* 166) and yet is deeply inscribed with pessimism regarding the possibility of social transformation: 'Death is the only reality, for it is the only certainty, inevitable to all things' (*AMM* 228).[21]

Notes

1   The critical body of literature surrounding Kincaid is too large to cover here, but for samples of these approaches see the following: Laura Niesen de Abruna, 1999; Donna Perry, 1990; Diane Simmons, 1994; Moira Ferguson, 1994; Helen Tiffin, 1993; Isabel Hoving, 2001. See also *Callaloo* 25.3 (Summer 2002), the special issue on Jamaica Kincaid, and Harold Bloom's edited anthology, *Jamaica Kincaid*.
2   For a survey of criticism representing these tendencies see my '"Dem tief, dem a dam tief:" Jamaica Kincaid's Literature of Protest.' *Callaloo* 25.3 (Summer 2002) 977–989.
3   Michael Gilkes of the University of the West Indies uses this term to describe the generation of writers who came of age in the 1920s and 1930s and were to have a profound impact on the development of West Indian literature: H.G. De Lisser, C.L.R James, Roger Mais, and Edgar Mittelhölzer.
4   This color consciousness is exemplified in Claude McKay's 'Mattie and her Sweetman.' The scene is a party in New York City and every character is described in terms of their skin tone to such a degree that color references form a subtext to the narrative. References to color and colorism pervade contemporary Caribbean women's literature and are routinely explicitly acknowledged and challenged.
5   See footnote 2.
6   See for example, Margaret Cezair-Thompson, *The True History of Paradise*, Elean Thomas, *The Last Room*, Vanessa Spence, *The Roads are Down*.
7   Like most of the region's islands, Antigua was densely wooded prior to its colonization by Britain in 1632. Plantation economies necessitated deforestation, and intensive monoculture furthered the process of soil erosion. Today, droughts of serious proportions occur every few years (Coram 10).
8   James Loewen uses the term 'heroification' to describe the processes of euphemization and sanitization inherent in representations of famous people in high-school textbooks and other mainstream historical discourses.
9   Devon's attitude is reminiscent of that described by Jan Carew, speaking in interview about the impact of Ben Yisu Das in Guyana's Berbice High School in the 1930s: 'We

did the history of the British empire for the Cambridge exams. We were identifying with Drake and Hawkins and Frobisher and so on, when Yisu Das gave us, in translation, Spanish histories of the same period to read. The heroes of English history were no different from the heroes of Spanish history. He did not say anything. He left it like that. It stunned us . . . that gave me a clear insight on how subjective this imperialist business was' (Birbalsingh, 'Jan Carew: the wild coast' *Frontiers* 43). In this case British colonialism is denaturalized by the comparative context provided by Yisu Das.

10 Williams demonstrates the immense profitability of Barbados: 'The tiny sugar island was more valuable to Britain than Carolina, New England, New York and Pennsylvania together. "Go ahead, England, Barbados is behind you" is today a stock joke in the British West Indies of the Barbadian's view of his own importance' (141–2).

11 Poet Benjamin Zephaniah caused a stir recently in Britain when he rejected an OBE on similar grounds. As the British *Guardian* reported: 'The Rastafarian poet argues that the very name of the Order of the British Empire reminds him of "thousands of years of brutality—it reminds me of how my foremothers were raped and my forefathers brutalised." The poet writes: "Me? I thought, OBE me? Up yours, I thought. . . . You can't fool me, Mr. Blair. You want to privatise us all; you want to send us to war; you stay silent when we need you to speak for us, preferring the voice of the USA"'(*Guardian* December 2003).

12 In 1981 Jenny Pearce described it as a 'large US military installation . . . which houses both a naval and an air force base; the naval base is the major "secret" underwater listening post for the Eastern Caribbean. . . . According to sources interviewed by *Covert Action* both bases are "being beefed up because of Grenada"' (156).

13 In the decade before publication of *A Small Place* (the first decade of formal independence) external debt levels in Antigua increased from US$19.8 million to US$266.9 million (McAfee 18).

14 Kincaid does not exaggerate, as Robert Coram's account of postcolonial Antigua confirms: 'Because Antigua has no central sewage system, each hotel is supposed to have a sewage treatment facility. But when those treatment plants break down, as they often do, the sewage is pumped into McKinnon Swamp.' For three years the sewage plant at the government-owned Halcyon Cove hotel was broken and 'the waste from tourists in 127 rooms and 16 suites, along with the waste from the hotel's restaurants, was drained into McKinnon Swamp. Other hotels along Dickenson Bay and Runaway Bay did the same thing. . . . Today McKinnon Swamp continues to overflow across two of the most popular beaches on Antigua, dispersing its offal among the tourists, who are so happy to be in the sun they do not notice what else they are in' (Coram 164–6).

15 World Bank, *The Caribbean Region*, April 1990. Clive Thomas explains that the tourist industry is dominated by TNCs (transnational corporations) in every area—airlines, hotels, tour-guides, food production—and the expected generation of scarce foreign exchange has seldom materialized due to the 'high foreign-exchange content of the original investment in the hotel and infrastructure, caused largely by the incapacity of local industries to supply the various construction materials, furnishings, heavy-duty equipment and other machinery needed for building the hotels, airports, harbours and telephone systems' and the 'high import content' of transport, food and drink, and advertising. Yet 'TNC-controlled hotels have taken over some of the best beaches and scenic locations in these territories' and have had a region wide negative impact on the environment (*Poor and the Powerless* 161–6).

16 Birbalsingh makes this comparison in his 1991 interview with Jamaica Kincaid: '*A Small Place* seems to reproduce many of the insights of *The Middle Passage* which is

still considered to be a destructive book' (*Frontiers* 140). Kincaid replies that 'the difference between Naipaul and myself is that I am not ashamed either of anything that has happened in the place I come from, or of the things that have been done by the people I come from' (140).

17 At the start of the decade the Antigua-Caribbean Liberation movement, which had achieved some support through public exposes of government corruption, was trounced by the Bird government. In the early 1980s right-wing regimes were supported by the U.S. in Antigua, Dominica, Jamaica, St. Lucia, and St. Vincent (McAfee 35; Pearce 158).

18 While this opposition (between the mobile and immobile) makes sense in the context of a discussion of Caribbean tourism, it actually rests upon a false premise: the poor of this region, and indeed of most of the world, are forced to relocate constantly in search of work; it could more accurately be said that 'most natives of the world are too poor to stay where they are.' This is confirmed by the exploration in *Nations Unbound*, edited by Linda Basch et al, of the consequences of 'the migration that is "forced" on . . . transmigrants by their nation states' marginalization in the global political economy' (92).

19 While many critics, including Isabel Hoving and Susan Sniader Lanser, have addressed the ambiguities of the narrative's pronouns, none I have come across analyzes them as they are inflected by the contradictory class location of the writer.

20 While China is an emergent economic global power, combined and uneven development means new wealth is accompanied by pervasive poverty: 'Nowadays peasants fall into such deep poverty that, to the best of my reckoning, some 70 percent of the rural population cannot afford to see a doctor and about 25 percent have not money even to buy seeds and fertilizer to plant their lands' (Li Changping 199–200).

21 In the 1991 interview with Birbalsingh referred to above Kincaid makes an interesting comment on this shift in describing an exchange she had with George Lamming who was championing Cuba. After pointing out those aspects of the regime that cannot warrant support, Kincaid adds these comments about Lamming's frame of reference as opposed to her own: 'It was the old language of rebellion. But that is finished, you know—rebelling against the great United States. The rebellion is not against the United States, it is about the things that the powerful United States can do and does do: that is what one is against. Lamming was still fighting that battle of Independence' (142).

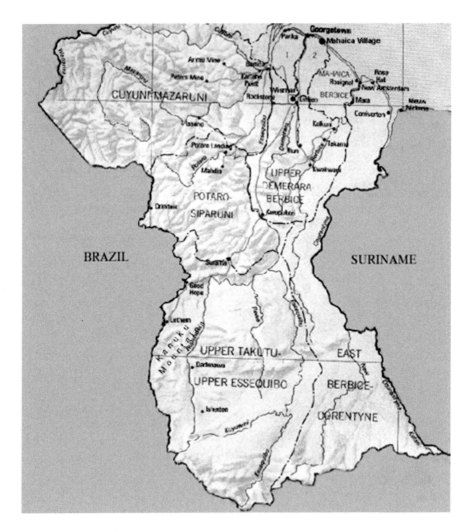

Figure 3   **Map of Guyana**

Chapter 3

Land of Waters

Events within the past decade bear out the necessity for an imaginative relativizing agency within neighbouring though separate peoples whose promise lies in gateway conceptions of community.

The predicament of the Indian continues to deepen with new uncertainties as to the authority which governs him. Such authority has been at stake for centuries within the decimation of the tribes. And a political scale is still lacking: the land under his feet is disputed by economic interests and national interests. It is within this background that the theme of the decoy seems to me pertinent to the whole continent of South America. For not only does it reflect the ruses of imperialism which make game of men's lives, but it occupies a curious ground of primitive oracle as well, whose horizons of sensibility we may need at this time to unravel within ourselves as an original creation.

Wilson Harris, Note to 'The Laughter of the Wapishanas' 1971

'Sermon of the Leaf' (part of Wilson Harris's 'The Laughter of the Wapishanas') tells of the quest of Wapishana, a girl belonging to the tribe she is named for, 'in search of the colour and nature of laughter—the source of laughter—which she was determined to restore to the lips of her people' (4). She dreams that she 'now cradled the dry mourning leaf of the elder tree of laughter' and sets out with it on a staircase that opens out into many branches representing her people and their origins with the 'elder branches of fate:'

> Wapishana held their flesh or leaf, stamped irresistibly into the root of her senses, to her lips afresh and blew along its stiff razor-like edge as if to share something of the mingling of the sharpest blow of sorrow in the strings of laughter. It was as if the withered sliced lips of her people had become the sculpture of a song—an ancient feast of the bone which sometimes turned the tables of the tree on hunter by hunted in order to memorialize a silent debt of creation—creature to creature. (4)

As she reaches the end of her journey she tries to grasp the source of laughter but it eludes her:

> However she looked at it it became senseless and faint except as the source of laughter—the first or the last model of man made in advance of the woman of the soil— in advance of bog or bed. As such it seemed to possess no authentic subsidence which could be verified—no sunrise, no sunset, no blood—but merely an unconscious plea that in its extremity it was the enduring laughter of the tribe which all would come to wear in

death standing against drought—within another folded maiden light as veil or sap out of which the first stitch of rain would fall from the elder tree of god to tie a leaf to unfleshed wood. (5)

This short piece of prose contains in condensed form many of the historical and cultural issues pertaining to Guyanese literature and the broader concerns of this book. 'Sermon of the Leaf' turns to Amerindian mythology to tell the tale of colonial expropriation and violence, replaces conventional narrative with successive imagistic moments, undermines definite meaning by juxtaposing opposites, and offers only paradox and suggestion in place of solution. It can be read as exemplar of postmodernist postcolonial writing, shunning as it does the certainty of historical or political statement in favor of mythic contradiction and the intangible. But while such a reading remains generic, 'Sermon of the Leaf' can be read also as emblematically Guyanese, product of a very specific history and a cultural tradition that shares much with the West Indies but is also part of and strongly connected to Latin America.[1]

The 'Wild Coast' of South America is site of the legend of El Dorado, that describes the quest up river into the interior in search of gold epitomized by Walter Raleigh's 1595 narrative, 'The Discovery of the Large, Rich and Beautiful Empire of Guiana, with a relation of The Great and Golden City of Manoa (which the Spaniards call El Dorado).' More than gold, the region provided immense wealth for Europeans through plantations exploiting first African slave, and later, after abolition, East Indian indentured, labor. What would become modern Guyana consists of 80 percent rain forest and only 4 percent coastal land suitable for cultivation, but nonetheless the Dutch colonized and established plantations in the seventeenth and eighteenth centuries, and the British fought for possession of the region and created British Guiana in 1831. Sugar and rice production continued into the twentieth century, when bauxite was also discovered and exploited by North American companies.[2] Unlike much of the West Indies, the Amerindian populations of Guiana, 'land of waters,' were not entirely erased by European colonization; today their descendants make up an estimated five per cent of Guyana's population: the Wapishanas are one of the seven tribes of the interior; three other tribes live in the coastal plains (Premdas 11, 15; Spinner xii; *Stains on My Name, War in My Veins* Williams 133–7). Guyana has a particularly sharp history of ethnic and racial divisions which have been perennially exploited to divide and control the laboring class: Amerindians were used by European planters to police African slaves; after abolition 10,000 Indians were imported and strategically placed to forestall the bargaining power of former slaves. In the twentieth century the sugar industry depended primarily on Afro-Guyanese labor and the rice industry on Indo-Guyanese labor. The government of Forbes Burnham (about which more later) fostered racial divisions to his own end: As George Lamming puts it, 'the long survival of Mr. Burnham as Prime Minister and President of Guyana depended on the manipulation of race as a device' (qtd. in *From Pillar to Post* Birbalsingh 11).

Harris, born in 1921 with European, African, Indian, and Amerindian ancestry, embodies the ethnic/racial intermixture that is the reality of modern Guyana. Before settling in England in 1959 he worked for some years as a surveyor in British Guiana's interior, an experience that furnished fertile material for his literature. Harris' note to *Laughter of the Wapishanas* places imperialist conquest of land at the center of Guyana's past and present: 'the land . . . is disputed by economic interests and national interests,' 'the ruses of imperialism . . . make game of men's lives' (Harris 3). In 'Sermon of the Leaf' we see the brutality of colonization in images of aridity and bodily violence—'years of drought when the source of laughter itself appeared to wither on the lips of the Wapishanas,' 'the withered sliced lips of her people'—and also the survival of 'the tribe' despite its dispossession. But the Note also points us specifically to the 1960s: 'Events within the past decade bear out the necessity for an imaginative relativizing agency within neighbouring though separate peoples whose promise lies in gateway conceptions of community' (3). The tumultuous years of transition from British colonial rule to independent government under Forbes Burnham also featured devastating racial and ethnic rivalries that destroyed the historic hope for unity many had found in Cheddi Jagan's People's Progressive Party (PPP). This period also saw the emergence of a generation of writers, including Harris, who were deeply invested in the anti-colonial movement around Jagan, and profoundly impacted by its defeat. Seen in the light of this nexus of events, Harris' literary and philosophical moorings form a very specific expression of mass political mobilization followed by profound defeat and disillusionment. *Laughter of the Wapishanas* decries colonial expropriation and violence, but retains no hope for collective political struggle. Barbara Webb reads Harris alongside the Marvellous Realists Alejo Carpentier and Edouard Glissant, and while finding many points of similarity between the three argues that Harris, unlike the other two, rejects both historical investigation and collective struggle for social change. Webb concludes that 'although all his novels express the need for change, it is only realized . . . in individual consciousness and art' (151).

While in isolation this assessment could equally be applied to any number of Caribbean writers, Guyana's specific history—both social and literary—generates a unique nexus of concerns and conditions that shapes both its earlier and later generations of writers. In Guyana the general forces discussed in my introduction take a particularly intense form: middle class involvement in national liberation struggles, hopes for interethnic unity against colonial domination, and the interrelation between cultural and political movements all reached a highly developed state. Naked conspiracy between old colonial and new imperial forces shattered hopes for national liberation, and the resultant spiraling economic and social crises rapidly transformed one of the most prosperous Caribbean nations into one of the poorest and least stable.[3] One of the consequences has been an extraordinarily high (even by Caribbean measures) level of out migration including among writers.[4] This particular history also shaped the women writers who came after the great wave of (mostly) male writers in the middle decades of the twentieth century, and as I shall show, the disastrous transition from colonial to postcolonial regimes figures highly in their literature. Before a closer investigation of the impact of the 1950s and 1960s on contemporaneous and subsequent writers I want first to consider the roots and distinctive characteristics of the Guyanese literary tradition, which are indelibly stamped on the pages of the women novelists considered in this chapter: Beryl Gilroy, Oonya Kempadoo, Pauline Melville, Grace Nichols, and Janice Shinebourne.

Guyana boasts an impressive roster of writers including some of the region's most famous international figures, many of whom were born within a few years of one another: Jan Carew (born 1925); Martin Carter (1927); Cyril Dabydeen (1945); David Dabydeen (1957); Wilson Harris (1921); Roy Heath (1926); Peter Kempadoo, known as Lauchmonen (1926). The significant literary journal *Kyk-Over-Al*[5] was published in Georgetown between 1945 and 1961, as was the cultural and arts journal *Kaie* between 1965 and 1973. Even before this explosive period a considerable body of work had emerged from British Guiana: Edgar Mittelhölzer (1909–65) had already published several of his two dozen novels by the early 1950s; Eric Walrond's (1898–1966) short story collection *Tropic Death* was published in 1926; and A.J. Seymour (1914–89), editor of *Kyk-Over-Al*, was already an established poet, critic and publisher by the 1940s, when he formed the British Guiana Union of Cultural Clubs (BGUCC). Notable foreign literature set in Guiana include the novels of William Henry Hudson, Arthur Conan Doyle's *The Lost World*, and numerous renditions of the legend of El Dorado dating back to Walter Raleigh's travel narrative.

The motif of the voyage into the forested interior recurs, often becoming, as Hena Maes-Jelinek says with reference to the work of Wilson Harris, 'a metaphor for the Guyanese psyche' (Preface). The association between the landscape and sexuality, and particularly the trope of Guyana as a woman's body, is pervasive. According to Mark McWatt, both 'sexual inscription of landscape' and correlation of landscape with text are widespread and 'while they may be used to reinforce or reify imperialist or sexist readings of landscape and sexuality, they can also be exploited by the creative imagination to bring about a subtle erasure of such entrenched attitudes and prejudices' (82).[6] Edgar Mittelhölzer's Kaywana novels seem to fit the first category, with their obsessive racial biological determinism and depiction of erotic sexual conquests against the violent backdrop of mercantile trade, colonization and slavery. Mittelhölzer's novels are, despite their obvious flaws and what some see as pornographic tendencies, influential, and some of his themes and figures— the legacy of a brutal history of expropriation, the ruthless powerful matriarch, psychic conflict stemming from ethnic divisions, eroticized violence—recur more broadly. Michael Gilkes draws out the significance: 'The Kaywana trilogy is an epic, imaginative record of the peculiar social and historical reality of Guyana, a national novel, but it is also a prodigious, pioneering attempt to examine the cultural and emotional ambivalence which is a heritage of the West Indian past' (*The West Indian Novel* 84).[7] The attempt clearly influences later women writers, even as they variously confront the objectification of the Guyanese woman that is so central to its sexualization of the landscape. Both Jan Shinebourne and Beryl Gilroy have spoken positively of reading Mittelhölzer for the first time and finding in his novels affirming depictions of their homeland. Shinebourne tells Birbalsingh, 'Mittelhölzer's *CorentyneThunder* hit me for six. I felt so thrilled when I opened it and found that somebody had described the same landscape, climate, rivers, trees, people, speech—everything that I wanted to do' (*Pillar* 148). Sandra, the protagonist of *Timepiece*, defends Mittelhölzer against a co-worker's snide dismissal (*TP* 73). Gilroy also identifies *Corentyne Thunder* as the first 'novel set in British Guiana' that she read (Condé 13).

The prolific and vibrant literary tradition that developed in British Guiana was closely connected to broader social conditions extant by mid century: relative economic prosperity; a working class with a 'tradition of militant anti-colonialism and . . . trade unionism . . . in which large sections of the work force were influenced by Marxist ideas' (Thomas 252); a large and successful middle class which in turn spawned ethnically based political and cultural associations. Many of the writers born in the 1920s had careers in the public sector—Carew was a customs officer in the Civil Service, Heath worked in the District Commissioner's Office, Harris was a government surveyor—attended Berbice High School in New Amsterdam and/or Queens College in Georgetown, and knew each other.[8] Birbalsingh's interviews with Carew and Heath reveal an intimate network of politically engaged and intellectually stimulated writers. Carew describes his association with Wilson Harris: 'I knew Wilson very well because he was courting my sister in Georgetown. He married my sister. Wilson and I became very close— night and day, shouting, arguing, discussing, reading—Marx, Spengler, Nietzsche, anything' (*Frontiers of Caribbean English in Literature* 44). Heath describes a similar camaraderie with Martin Carter: 'The first time I did any reading apart from school tests, was shortly before I left Guyana, when Martin Carter and I became interested in Marxism and got hold of a book called *A Treasury of Russian Literature*' (75). Carew explains the profound interconnection between politics and literature:

> The criticism of our literature, which is fundamentally anti-colonial and aims at liberating a colonial imagination, has never caught up with that nexus or upsurge. They are putting it into contexts that are askew. Criticism has to understand the eruptive force of the anti-colonial movement. 'The anti-colonial movement' almost sounds like a cliché. This is not exactly what I mean. I mean this awakening of the human spirit, this feeling when I went with Cheddi into the countryside of Guyana, when we were setting up the Youth Movement for the PPP, and I could hear the peasants talking poetry to me, or I could hear Martin Carter reading his poems in the car, by lamp, at night in the Canje, while the people talked back to him in poetry . . .
>
> Q: Do you think literature gave expression to the political feelings of the period in the early fifties?
>
> A: Yes, it has some apprehension of the power of this upsurge through Wilson Harris, and through Martin Carter. It does not matter what direction they go in now. It was the times which spewed them out. (Birbalsingh, *Frontiers* 49–50)

Significant political events made their way in to literary works, and many of these writers were personally involved in organized anticolonial politics.[9] Jan Carew describes his return to Guyana in 1949 after a period abroad:

> My mother was there, and Wilson was there. Cheddi Jagan had just come back from America. I heard him speaking at a street-corner one night in Georgetown. He was analyzing the role of the peasant in Guyanese life, and his relationship to the big estates; how they steal his own land and only cultivate small portions of it, how they control water and land and penalize the independent peasant. No one had ever done that kind of analysis. It had a tremendous effect on me. (Birbalsingh, *Frontiers* 46)

Carew met and became close to Martin Carter (the latter was arrested in 1953 during the period of direct rule from Britain) and, with Wilson Harris, joined the movement around Jagan:

> It was tremendously important and stimulating. Wilson and I took Martin up to Canje. All day long and at night as well, we talked about books and poetry. The creative thing was really getting us. The political aspect was profoundly affecting the creative part. There was a symbiotic relationship. (Birbalsingh, *Frontiers* 47)

Given the centrality of 'the political aspect' it is worth spending some time characterizing the movement, what it represented, and how it was defeated.[10]

Cheddi Jagan, born in 1918, was son of East Indian sugar cane workers—his father became a supervisor—who invested in his education by sending him to Queen's College and then to the U.S.A. where he trained to become a dentist. While there, between 1936 and 1943, he met and then married Janet Rosenberg (who was related to Ethel and Julius Rosenberg, executed for their communist affiliations during the height of McCarthyism), and with her became involved in Marxist politics before returning to Georgetown to set up a dental practice. Engaged with the labor upsurge of the time, they organized the Political Affairs Committee (PAC) in 1946, the politics of which 'crossed ethnic lines by basing itself upon a class analysis aimed at unifying the largest body of people in British Guiana, the working class of urban blacks and rural East Indians. Self-government and adult suffrage were the immediate political aims, and once achieved, would provide the means through which economic and social justice could be obtained' (Spinner 24). The PAC ran candidates, and in 1947 Jagan took office:

> Hammering away at the sugar interests and the foreign owned bauxite mines, Cheddi Jagan became an immensely appealing figure to a large number of dispossessed Guyanese. He demanded adequate taxation of sugar and bauxite, better housing for the worker, improved health standards, redistribution of the excess land owned by the sugar plantations, government-sponsored drainage and irrigation schemes . . . and universal adult suffrage. (Spinner 25)

In 1948 the Jagans formed the People's Progressive Party (PPP). The chairman was to be Forbes Burnham, born in 1923 to a black middle class Georgetown family, educated at Queens's College and then at a British university from 1945–49. In 1953, a prolonged struggle against British colonialism culminated in internal self-government: free elections under colonial rule. Cheddi Jagan as leader of the PPP won 18 of 24 seats and headed up a popular democratic socialist government.

The limits of 'internal self-government' became very clear 133 days later when Churchill's government sent in troops, suspended the constitution, and removed the entire elected administration. The U.S. government gave support to these measures and denied Jagan permission to pass in transit through the U.S.A. In a remarkable example of collaboration between two imperialist powers, the British colonial office and the U.S. government (largely via the CIA[11]) waged a campaign against Jagan over the next decade, during which time he nonetheless won elections in 1957 (after four years of interim British colonial rule) and 1961. The struggle against colonialism had forged unity among East Indians and Africans, and now the imperialist powers again used 'divide and rule' policies to split these populations. In an attempt to weaken the PPP, a new party was formed in 1957, the People's National Congress (PNC). With Forbes Burnham as its leader, the PNC was projected as the African counterpart to Jagan's PPP, now cast as the East Indian party. At the same time the CIA ran a generalized destabilization campaign, provoking internal unrest through riots, violent attacks, and political murders, pouring money in to unions, financing Burnham's campaign, and pursuing a propaganda operation against Jagan. The U.S. information service, for example, showed anti-Cuba films on street corners, and warned that Jagan would bring Castro in to Guyana. The U.S. also placed an economic embargo on the country, corporations withdrew, and Britain refused to grant independence. Eventually in 1964, following changes in the constitution to obstruct majority rule, Burnham took power as head of the PNC in a coalition government with the right-wing party of business, the United Force; two years later Guyana became an independent nation.

British and U.S. hostility to Jagan stemmed from his reformist platform, which included levies on foreign corporations, investment in domestic social spending, land redistribution, and pro-labor legislation (Spinner 36), and, in the cold war context, his links with Communist Parties and to the Cuban and Soviet regimes (Manley 8). While the PPP formally affiliated with the USSR in 1969, Burnham's PNC pledged allegiance to the U.S. Jagan further represented the 'threat of a good example:' a genuinely independent government in a region over which the U.S. was determined to exert its control. Arthur Schlesinger Jr. in 1965 described the position of Washington: '"an independent British Guiana under Burnham . . . would cause us many fewer problems than an independent British Guiana under Jagan"' (qtd. in Manley 57). The class character of Burnham's PNC was also compatible with the needs of U.S. imperialism: The key leadership consisted of 'a group of lawyers, teachers, professionals and small businessmen' who sought power through consolidation of the state and garnered support from the newly cohering Guyanese capitalist class, who were eager to work with foreign corporations (*Stains on My Name, War in My Veins* Williams 36). In the early years of his regime Burnham pursued the Puerto Rican Model of development, also known as 'industrialization by invitation,' which emphasizes incentives for private foreign investment. This did not materialize: in fact private investment fell between 1966 and 1972 even while Guyana remained dependent on colonial-style export production. Burnham's regime from the 1970s embarked instead on a campaign of nationalization and even made overtures (favorably received) to Jagan. Because of Guyana's history of broad popular support for militant labor and anticolonial politics, Burnham consistently used the rhetoric of socialism and populism, and in 1970 declared Guyana a cooperative republic.

This did not unduly worry Washington: rhetoric notwithstanding, Burnham's government functioned, as did other repressive regimes in the region, to suppress the social unrest that inevitably accompanies extreme class inequalities. Furthermore, the gulf between the regime's articulated position and its actual practice was immense: while pledging to 'feed, cloth and house the nation' through nationalization of industry, Burnham purchased the sugar, rice, and bauxite industries on terms favorable to the transnational corporations that owned them, saddling the nation with massive debt just in time for the economic world crisis of the early 1970s, and attendant falling prices of sugar, rice, and bauxite. In collaboration with the IMF and World Bank his government pushed through structural adjustment that slashed wages, downsized the public sector, and removed food subsidies. To manage the social instability and protest provoked by these conditions Burnham's regime became increasingly militarized, suppressing civil and human rights, taking control of the media, cracking down on any political opposition, and securing its own survival through blatant electoral fraud and the use of paramilitary groups to terrorize the population.

The mobilization of communalism led to violent attacks on ethnic communities in the early 1960s, most infamously the massacre at Wismar (fictionalized by Kempadoo, Nichols, and Shinebourne), and was to leave a devastating legacy. Brackette Williams' sociological study of a Guyanese community he calls 'Cockalorum,' finds insidious ethnic stereotypes about African, East Indian, Portuguese, and Amerindian Guyanese. His conclusions concur with the overview provided by Premdas:

> Even though objectively there exists a wide array of racial mixtures, a person is soon stereotyped into one of the existing social categories to which both 'blood' and 'culture' are assigned a defining role. From this, a society of ethno-cultural compartments has emerged with various forms of inter-communal antagonisms of which the African-Indian dichotomy dominates all dimensions of daily life. (12)

These ethnic stereotypes are pervasive in the Guyanese literature discussed below, as is the condition of generalized socioeconomic crisis reached by the end of the 1970s: more than 50 percent of the population were living in poverty, unemployment was at 25 (and with underemployment 40) percent, and the infrastructure—electricity and water supply, sewage systems, education, and public health—was in a shambles (Apena 108–9; Spinner 183–5).

All of this reverberated adversely on social life. Unable to make ends meet, those who could not migrate faced personal and family degradation. Family life for all communal sections was thrown into turmoil as a new neurotic modality of 'hustle' developed. It marginalized many, but above all, it led to the fall in self-esteem. Personal ambitions and career structures for improvement were no longer entertained. The loss of hope, compounded by a sense of powerlessness, bred a population of cynics who could not change their government. In this ocean of despair, ethnic antipathies did not die. (Premdas 163)

In this context, throughout Burnham's tenure his base of Afro-Guyanese support gradually eroded while opposition grew in all populations. In 1974 the Working People's Alliance was formed from a coalition of Afro- and Indo-Guyanese left-wing groups opposed to the PNC government—one of its members was the socialist historian Walter Rodney—and it increasingly drew working-class support. The government responded with more repression: arrests, beatings, and even assassinations of opposition leaders, firing or reassignment of public sector workers, and direct censorship of dissenting newspapers such as the *Catholic Standard*. In 1980 Walter Rodney was killed: 'The vast majority of Guyanese and most impartial observers were convinced Rodney was murdered by the PNC' (Spinner 185). But despite widespread discontent, the government held on to power through a combination of violence and corruption. The immense hopes of the 1940s and 1950s, when Carter, Harris, Carew, and Heath combined activism and art with a vision of unity and liberation, had been destroyed. Three of the four, like the majority of writers born in Guyana, emigrated, only to return for short spells.

The impact of the Burnham years on women was harsh on many fronts. Adeline Apena explains that the three prongs of structural adjustment—layoffs in the public sector, removal of food subsidies, and reallotment of money from social services to debt servicing—disproportionately hurt women, who 'face the high cost of living, decline in real earnings, and have to cope with the increasing gap between real earnings and expenditures' (110). As more men migrated, the burden of maintaining households fell on women. The emphasis on communal 'traditionalism' only heightened repressive ideas about women's role, while the generalized climate of violence, begun in the campaign against Jagan and systematized under Burnham in what Premdas calls a 'quagmire of government terror . . . formal and informal state-sponsored thuggery, harassment, inhuman treatment, assassination, terror, and violence' (138), increased rape and violence against women. State violence was of course used against women who protested: Soon after the murder of Walter Rodney, PNC thugs attacked a meeting of 'women against terror' (Spinner 187), and women protesting against food shortages also met state repression: 'Tear gas was now being employed not only against striking bauxite workers, but also upon angry housewives in a food line' (Spinner 176). Gita Sen identifies persistent correlations between neoliberalism, militarism, and violence against women: She describes the 'growing number of military controlled governments, most of which have as their main *raison d'être* the suppression of internal dissent, (this must be seen in the particular context of widespread popular resistance to IMF-backed programmes for "structural adjustment" through domestic austerity)' and shows their connection to 'the mushrooming of a culture of violence against women in which "macho-ness" and brutality are dominant: its flip-side is contempt for women expressed through reactionary notions of women's proper place in society' (67).

Guyanese Women Writers

Women played a role in all the important political movements, from the labor struggles at the turn of the century (Peake 110), the Enmore strike of 1948 (Poynting 98), to the anticolonial formations of the postwar period. The Women's Political and Economic Organization, which in 1953 became the Women's Progressive Organization, was crucial to the activism that led to formation of the PPP, and Janet Jagan played a highly visible leadership role in the PPP.[12] Women also actively opposed Burnham's military state, both in protests against food shortages and state terror and in formal political groupings such as the Working Peoples' Alliance (WPA). But with just a few notable exceptions (such as Rajkumari Singh [1923–79], leader of the Messenger Group and a mentor of many Guyanese artists, and novelist Beryl Gilroy [1924–2001]), women writers emerged a generation after the major wave of male writers: most who published in the 1980s and 1990s were born between the late 1940s and the late 1960s. The emergence of larger numbers of women writers after the 1970s was at least in part a result of the postwar educational reforms that increased access to schools and colleges.[13] Beryl Gilroy taught in British Guiana before moving to London, where she formed friendships with other West Indian writers in Britain—such as E.R. Braithwaite, George Lamming, Andrew Salkey, and Samuel Selvon—and later became Britain's first black head teacher. In an essay of 1990 she describes the reformist post-war climate of her home country:

> Teaching in British Guiana during the fifties allowed teachers to be innovative. Children were keen and when there weren't books in the schools, they could be bought in the shops. There was a culture of reading as the gateway to learning. Scholarship was valued. Throughout the society there was a vibrancy—a mix of cultures, that stood me in good stead when I came to Britain. ('Reflections' 14)

The world she found when she returned for a visit in 1968, and captured in her 1986 novel, *Frangipani House,* was shockingly different.

Some of these Guyanese writers have drawn little attention from American academic postcolonial and feminist literary critics. Oonya Kempadoo, for example, has not yet given rise to any substantial critical analysis. One reviewer suggests that this is because her works do not easily lend themselves to the preoccupations of postcolonialism: 'there may not be sufficient density of text for (post-colonial) theorists to sink their "meaning" into' (Wyck Williams). Certainly many critical responses to Shinebourne, Gilroy, Nichols, and Melville exemplify the critical patterns described in my introduction. Veronique Bragard draws on Homi Bhabha and Simon Slemon to argue that Janice Shinebourne reflects recent 'doubts in relation to the historical discourse'

> . . . the very western concept of history, a discourse that is still very much centered around glorious male deeds, movements, peace and war, political and economic conflicts, written records and linear progress. Janice Shinebourne's fiction challenges this conceptualization of history in many ways by focusing on women, ordinary and poor people, 'unhistoric acts' (*Timepiece* 3) and daily life. (13)

Claiming that 'most literary works from the coolie diaspora are concerned with the poetic retrieving and imaginative re-exploration of the past' (14), Bragard uses Torabully's concept of 'coolitude'— a reclaiming of the racist term as 'a means of palliating what history, in its western conceptualization, has not been able to do' (15)—to describe Shinebourne's 're-membering of the past, of Indian values and rituals . . . as a healing process' that uncovers 'an identity that is plural and migratory' (21). The same analytical frameworks often used to describe Kincaid are employed here: Shinebourne is found to embody 'coolie' multiplicity, uncertainty, and polyphony in contrast to 'western' singularity, objectivity, and linearity: Shinebourne's 'polyphony of voices allows her to break the linearity of her text and echo the working of memory' (22) and thereby 'rethink western conceptualizations of history and politics' in a way that 'defies the monolithic idea of History' (23).

Some of these traits are undeniable. They could also be found in works by male writers such as Wilson Harris, as Barbara Webb finds: 'rather than plot as such [*Palace of the Peacock*] develops in a series of psychic illuminations' (74); 'Harris rejects any interpretation of history that consolidates the victor/victim conflict' (76); 'for Harris myth or the mythic imagination is tantamount to deliverance from the alienating effects of the historical process' (80). Webb also provides a convincing ideological and historical explanation for these characteristics that also could be applied to many women writers:

> since he has little faith in the possibility of human progress within the framework of any existing social system, for him history is still the nightmare from which Caribbean writers are trying to awake. His strategy is therefore to subvert the role of history, which he considers all too dominant in Caribbean fiction, by subordinating it to that of the mythic imagination. (150)[14]

It is impossible to correlate generic and political categories: a Harrisonian literary model, as much as a realist one, may be employed for politically conservative or revolutionary ends. I would argue that *Timepiece* and *The Last English Plantation* are much more securely within the framework of social realism, a literary tradition that Shinebourne sees herself as part of and contributing to, as is suggested by her epigrammatic use of George Eliot in *Timepiece* (from which Bragard cites the phrase 'unhistoric acts' as evidence of Shinebourne's mistrust of history). The literature—especially the realist novel—seen by Bragard as oppressively 'western' is understood much more dialectically by Shinebourne in this 1992 interview: 'Later I went to Berbice High School and discovered Dickens, George Eliot and Shakespeare. I was especially interested in George Eliot. I was fascinated by the scope of the novel in being able to portray not only characters but a whole society. I remember loving Dickens for that' (Birbalsingh, *Pillar* 148). Shinebourne's novels struggle to articulate a clearer understanding of the past and to counter dominant ideology. Furthermore, while Bragard gestures towards 'an identity that is plural and migratory' it remains unclear how the assertion of 'coolitude' as a preferable alternative to 'western' values achieves this end, and arguably runs counter to these novels' rejection of communalism and ethnic separatism. Shinebourne has Chinese and Indian heritage, her protagonists are ethnically and racially mixed, and the village life captured in *Last English Plantation* is as multicultural as the world of her own childhood:

> I am portraying an extraordinary society in which the races in Guyana, especially the African and Indian races, experience more unity between them than they have ever done. . . . When I go back to Guyana now and tell people about this unity, they look at me blankly, because today the races are more separate than they have ever been in Guyana. . . . I moved very easily among European, Indian, Chinese and African friends and family who were all equally important to me. (Shinebourne in Birbalsingh, *Pillar* 152–3)

In her discussion of fiction by Janice Shinebourne and Trinidadian writer Lakshmi Persaud, Brinda Mehta rejects 'coolitude' as an essentialist concept without any politically oppositional weight.

Mehta also calls for more specificity in critical responses to Caribbean literature, which she sees as too inclined toward unsustainable generalization and homogenization. As a corrective she reads Shinebourne's *Last English Plantation* within the context of 'the impact of colonial schools on Indo-Caribbean girls,' which she calls 'a relatively underdeveloped area of literary analysis in Caribbean studies' (112), although the relationship between colonial curricula and subject interpellation has received much attention within postcolonial criticism, especially since the publication of Gauri Viswanathan's much cited *Masks of Conquest* in 1989. Taking Foucault and Bhabha as points of reference, Mehta develops an account of the 'linguistic dependency' generated by colonial education, citing especially the act of naming and renaming, valorisation of 'proper' English, devaluing of creole, imposition of western culture and frameworks. Her account is reminiscent of critical analyses of the schoolroom and daffodil scenes in Kincaid's *Annie John* and *Lucy*, and similarly suggests that discursive structures are determinant: 'Colonial misappropriation inscribed cooliehood within a double displacement, characterized by the physicality of cooliehood, as demonstrated by the indentured slave trade, as well as a *more pervasive (and invasive)* attitudinal or psychological coolie-ness' (125; bold in original, italics mine). Mehta's critique thus remains idealist, as does the idea that coolitude currently maintains 'cultural stereotypes and racism against Indians' but could function differently in the future:

'as each diasporic location begins to negotiate its own tryst with "coolie" culture, the necessary politicized deconstructions of meaning will give new agency to the term as a locus of post-colonial identity' (126).

Isabel Hoving reads Nichols' *Whole of a Morning Sky* for its 'thematics of orality, visuality, isolation and belonging' (161), and in relation to Kristeva's notion of female focalization: 'every girl has to enter an adult semiotic system that is structured by lack' (172). Hoving sees the novel challenging some tenets of postcolonial studies: 'What is innovative in *Morning Sky* is its refusal to situate standard English outside the realm of address and sensuality, thus implicitly criticizing [Bill] Ashcroft's proposal to differentiate the ideal norm of Standard English from the englishes of the colonies' (176); 'the postcolonial theoretical tendency to follow poststructuralist theories of language and subjectivity to read the body as text, and the text as body, is problematic when it comes to texts that do not wish to be read as texts alone' (182). Hoving finds in Nichols' novel—and Merle Collins' *Angel*—rejection of 'western scriptocentrism' in favor of 'an auditory art' (182). Of Gilroy's *Frangipani House* Hoving says it 'displaces the destructive linear and cyclical times it also presents' and demonstrates that 'all languages are hybrid' (17–18).[15]

Sarah Lawson Welsh reads Pauline Melville's short stories in analogous terms, finding that they 'challenge or blur the conceptual boundaries between the natural and the supernatural, the artist and audience, the magicians' agency and the effects of magic' and 'undermine any single dominant interpretation and defer any final reading' (145). She quotes Evelyn O'Callaghan: '"With Kincaid and Brodber, [Melville] blurs the boundaries of time and space and narrative centrality . . . she deconstructs the easy adversarial status that too often informs political rhetoric"'(145–6) and agrees that '*Shape-Shifter* is a collection that crosses "borders" . . . in order to challenge received boundary demarcations and to unsettle certain assumptions' (146). Welsh is attentive to the specificity of the Guyanese context, citing, for example, the 'particular "geo-psyche" of coastal "exterior" versus unmapped "interior"' (148) as one of the collection's structuring paradigms. That her primary interest is in the text's self-reflexivity can be seen in the choice of 'You Left the Door Open' (a tale explicitly concerned with unstable identity and narrative unreliability) as the 'central story' rather than, for example, 'The Iron and the Radio Have Gone' (one that is grounded in the material conditions of poverty and political chaos in postindependence Georgetown). The latter choice would understand Melville's explicit emphasis on 'breaking down preconceptions, stirring up doubt, rattling judgments, shifting boundaries and unfixing fixities' (Melville in Busby 740; qtd. also by Welsh 148) as a reaction against the repressive climate of Burnham's militarized regime and the absolutism of ethnic chauvinism as well as an expression of the ethnic and racial diversity that characterizes Guyana.

The Ventriloquist's Tale arguably offers an ironic parody of the postmodern sensibility and of academic postcolonial criticism. The Amerindian ventriloquist of the title is present for the prologue and epilogue, and initially sketches a critique of 'western scriptocentrism' while celebrating 'auditory art:' 'My grandmother distrusts writing. She says that all writing is fiction. . . . We, in this part of the world, have a special veneration for the lie and all its consequences and ramifications' (*VT* 2–3). But this is not a voice to take seriously, as we are reminded a few lines later when the narrator adds 'My grandmother is full of all that crap' (3). So too statements such as 'Where I come from, disguise is the only truth and desire the only true measure of time' (7) and, again paraphrasing his grandmother, 'history [is] only to be trusted when it coincides with myth' (9), are unceremoniously dumped when the narrator declares that the rest of the story will be both written and realist:

> In order to tell these tales of love and disaster, I must put away everything fantastical that my nature and the South American continent prescribe and become a realist . . . Why realism, you ask. Because hard-nosed, tough-minded realism is what is required these days. Facts are King. Fancy is in the dog-house. . . . Now, alas, fiction has to disguise itself as fact and I must bow to the trend and become a realist. (9)

There is of course further irony, because the 'realist' novel that follows contains much that is fantastical and fanciful, and the historical tale of incest at its heart does conform to an Amerindian myth—one of the many also being studied by a European anthropologist named Wormoal. But the idea that orality, undecidability, and ambiguity are somehow better suited to the South American personality than script, clarity, and definite assertion is lampooned.

In the critical analysis that follows I place these works in the context of Guyana's history—including that of imperialism and resistance—and literary tradition. Melville's biography, like most of this generation of women writers, was shaped by the rise and fall of Jagan followed by the long Burnham regime: some left the country with their parents during the great wave of migration, others left as young adults in search of professional opportunities no longer available in Guyana. Janice Shinebourne (nee Janice Lowe; also known as Jan Lo Shinebourne) was a child in Guyana in the 1950s, taught primary school in the mid 1960s, met and married an English man and went with him to Britain in 1970 where she published two novels—set in Guyana of the 1950s and 1960s—in the late 1980s. Before leaving her home country Shinebourne experienced some of the literary and political community enjoyed by the earlier generation of writers. The Georgetown literary magazine *Expression* published some of her short stories, she read Mittelhölzer and other local writers, met Martin Carter and A.J. Seymour, and was inspired by Jagan. Her description of this period of her life resonates with those of Carter, Harris, Heath, and the other male writers:

> We were encouraged by Martin Carter. I found this urban, Georgetown literary culture so stimulating that I came out of my sugar estate shell . . . . Cheddi Jagan was also very important. He gave us a different sense of reality by saying that the country was dominated by the sugar barons. No one, before him, had challenged the political authority in the country by saying this in public, loudly and clearly, and offering an alternative. He gave me the capacity to question things. He also gave me a sense of pride by saying that we were not just indentured immigrants or oppressed people: we

had contributed labour for which we should be rewarded. All these things created a certain outlook in me. (Birbalsingh *Pillar*, 148–9)

In addition, ironically, given the repressive nature of his regime and its routine denunciation by Guyanese fiction writers, Burnham hosted the first Caribbean cultural festival—Carifesta—in 1972. While Burnham intended the event to bolster nationalism and therefore shore up support for his regime, it had unintended consequences for artists. Jan Shinebourne describes Carifesta and her subsequent work:

> It brought together Caribbean writers, artists, and performers from a variety of art and folk forms, and it brought them together in a popular context. I met and heard and saw Caribbean writers and performers for the first time. No one in Guyana failed to be excited by Carifesta. . . . Forbes Burnham had authoritarian views about culture and literature. . . . Carifesta symbolized the strengthening of the bond between art, culture, and nationalism. . . .
>
> I began to write my first novel, *Timepiece*, during the late 1960s. I had a sense of being influenced by all this and of needing to come to grips with Guyana's political culture. I had a sense that it was a chaotic as well as a creative time. I felt it was important to know the roots of both the chaos and the creativity. In the process of doing that, it was necessary to uncover the contradictions, misguided sentimentality, corruption, psychotic violence, and anger that turned my country upside down, the neglect and betrayals—and also the immense worth, genuine morality, and intense commitment that had come to replace the old complacency about political culture. (Cudjoe, *CWW* 143)

She speaks of *Timepiece* and her second novel, *The Last English Plantation*, as attempts to explore the experiences of the 1960s and draw on 'a working people's awareness of their tradition of activism' while meeting new challenges, including '1980s American neo-colonialism' (144).

Even though they were not yet born, or were young children, and were absent or only partly present during those years, the mid-century turmoil is also the subject of novels by Grace Nichols, who was born in 1950, moved to England at the age of eight where she stayed and became an acclaimed writer, and Oonya Kempadoo, born in 1966 in England to Guyanese parents, returned to Guyana for much of her childhood and lived in Grenada at the time of her first novel's publication in 1998. The fiction of Pauline Melville, born in Guyana in 1948 and first published in Britain in 1990, repeats the major themes—politically repressive regimes, neoliberalism, the failures of nationalism, the continuity between colonial and postcolonial imperialism—and articulates the historical succession of hopes and disappointments. The sample of novels and short stories explored below (and it is by no means exhaustive of works or authors) suggests something of the range and flexibility of creative literature by Guyanese women published after 1980, in authors' location and circumstance as well as texts' style and form. They are distinctively Guyanese even as they are global, and they variously give voice to the specific historical and political conditions, and their fallout, discussed above.

While the explicit fusion of political activism with cultural work seen mid-century had evaporated by the time most of these writers came of age—and every text evinces the isolation of the middle-class individual—their fictional works nonetheless vocalize against both the postindependence domestic regime of Burnham and the ruses of imperialism.

Plantation, Savannah, Rainforest, and City

These novels are strikingly Guyanese: taken together they represent the nation in all its geographic diversity. Not surprisingly, given the demographics, the coastal strip of Demerara and Berbice counties, incorporating Georgetown, New Amsterdam and the plantations and villages between, forms the setting for most of the fiction, sometimes using invented and sometimes extant place names. *Whole of a Morning Sky* begins in the swampy village of Highdam, thirty miles outside of Georgetown, and then moves into the capital city. *Last English Plantation* and *Timepiece* both take place in the Canefields region around New Amsterdam: the former in New Dam village (created after Old Dam is razed by the plantation owners) and then New Amsterdam, and the latter in Pheasant. *Buxton Spice* is set in the coastal village of Tamarind Grove, one of the many 'all along the coast of Guyana to Mahaica' (*BS* 44).

The world of rice and sugarcane fields, dams, canals, bridges, rivers, and seawalls, is vividly and evocatively described, often nostalgically remembered from childhoods. *Whole of a Morning Sky* opens in 1960 as the young girl, Gem, and her family are about to leave their village home for Georgetown, and the child's sense of loss runs throughout the narrative, which moves between an omniscient voice in the past tense and Gem's first person present tense voice:

> Standing in sunlight water and watching the dark moving shapes of the fish below. Standing with your fishing rod at the edge of a dam, waiting for the cork to duck, then jumping like mad after catching a small patwa. Going to the backdam. Rowing with Dinah in Uncle Joe boat, past the courida trees with their bird eggs. . . . Things you'll miss about Highdam. (*WMS* 29)

The protagonist of *The Last English Plantation* is June, who at the novel's start is preparing for high school in New Amsterdam. June's life in New Dam is overshadowed by the factory, plantation, and memory of Old Dam before the plantation owners leveled it. As June travels across the region on her new bicycle, descriptions of the landscape are haunted by a sense of impending change even as they express a powerful connectedness:

> She stopped her thoughts, raising her eyes from the water and letting them follow the line of the horizon from north to south. There was so much space in what she saw and yet their lives were so fretful. The landscape before her was a solid wall of sky and land. You could walk and walk and the land would never end and the sky would stretch further and further away from you—that was how walking on the backdam felt; the land

was bigger than you and the smell of water followed you everywhere: creek, river and canal water. It was as if it was too big to hold people and they worked it until it turned into their grave. (*LP* 34)

Timepiece takes up the story of Sandra Yansen in the mid 1960s as she leaves her village to go to college in New Amsterdam. The novel opens, though, with a much older Sandra returning to the village, which is now practically deserted and in a state of advanced decay. This narrative frame lends a similar aura of loss to descriptions of the landscape, and colors the way we see Sandra's occasional flashbacks to her childhood:

> She saw the canefields as they were on a still, sunny Sunday when the children bathed and swam in the canal. The children were sitting in a group under the bridge which offered shade from the sun. Sometimes, one of them broke away from the group and dived into the water. The children were talking and laughing. The water tasted of ripe cane and the bed of the canal, laden with old cane, was springy to the touch of feet and hands. (*TP* 130)

Kempadoo's *Buxton Spice* ends with the family of the protagonist, the early adolescent Lula, fleeing Burnham's Guyana for Britain. This imminent departure again lends a poignant sense of loss to the sensual representation of Lula's encounters with the natural world, seen here through the eyes of the Buxton Spice mango tree, personified throughout the novel:

> It could see the fruits on the trees and the sharp green shine of the water-hyacinth leaves clogging the brown canals down there. . . .
> And on to where the red-mud banks of the big Broadie Canal was smooth from us sliding down into the milky-tea water. Saw us splashing and pushing each other into the deep part, where we not supposed to swim.
> Could even see over the roofs, between the tall swaying coconut trees, past the dome of the broken mosque, to the endless seawall and the distant brown sea. (29)

Frangipani House shifts perspective from the young to the old, telling the story of Mama King, placed in an old people's home by her adult children who now live abroad. Gilroy explains why she wrote this story: 'I returned to the West Indies in 1968 and visited a friend who ran a superior nursing home for the mothers of successful West Indian professionals in the USA. If there were men, I did not see any. I thought of myself in that situation and I told my friend I would run away. Thus *Frangipani House* took seed' (Condé, 16). The location is less specific, which is indicative of Mama King's institutionalized alienation from her surroundings: Frangipani House is located in an unnamed town, though references to airport, hospital, and fish market suggest that we are not far from Georgetown. Mama King's acute sense of loss as she reflects on her life creates a perspective that is very similar to the other works:

> She was a girl again—fishing with Aunty Lula on a sun-and-shadow day at Elmer creek. They were under some tall trees. Flies were plentiful and the fish jumped to catch those that had the effrontery to skim the surface of the water in their search for insects.
> 'Throw your line,' Aunty Lula said. 'Fish jumping!' You will catch! Jumping fish is hungry fish!' She sat expectant. After a while there was a gentle nibbling on the end then a tug. (*FH* 27)

The novels are thus saturated with the particular environment of Guyana's coastal plain, reclaimed from the water for cultivation: key events take place on bridges or the seawall; leisure time is spent in the waterways. They capture also the ubiquity of migration: from Guyana to Britain, Canada, or the U.S.; from rural to urban regions within the country; and, in the wake of ethnic violence, from one village to another in search of refuge. This generates what Roy Heath calls 'the power of evocation, of things remembered from long ago, from childhood, which have a strange mesmeric power' ('Criticism in Art' 69). Lula's older sisters have 'gone back to England' (*BS* 23) before the rest of the family follow at the end of the book; Archie's brother Lionel is 'thinking of moving to Canada' (*WMS* 145); Mama King's children have all settled in the U.S.A.; Sandra's lover Son leaves to study in Canada (*TP* 180) and we know that Sandra too ends up going 'abroad' (6). Both *Whole of a Morning Sky* and *Buxton Spice* end with the home of the young protagonist for sale and the family about to move away; the former also begins with a move from rural to urban residence. The humorous ventriloquist-narrator who opens and closes *Ventriloquist's Tale* moves all over the world, and Beatrice, one of the central characters from the historical narrative within the novel, ends up living in Montreal (*VT* 271–81).

These journeys, like those of the authors themselves, bear witness to the high levels of out-migration I have already noted: 'a migration rate conservatively estimated at over three-quarters the rate of natural increase of the population. Less conservatively, estimates indicate an absolute decline in the population since 1975' (Thomas, *Poor and the Powerless* 256). Just as pervasive is the movement from village to town. Urbanization accelerated from mid-century, as the sugar industry employed fewer people—from 1950 to 1960 employment fell by one fourth (Thomas, 'Bread' 40)—while the rural population expanded, forcing people out to the city in search of work. Again, characters in all the novels leave their villages for New Amsterdam, or more frequently Georgetown, and the impending sense of the end of an era explicitly dramatized in *The Last English Plantation* is echoed in every text.

The novels set in the coastal strip are aware of the forested interior and savannahs and mountains beyond—and of the significant body of literature representing the voyage to the interior: references to 'buckman,' 'Amerindian from up-river,' 'pork-knockers' (gold prospectors), and the 'bush' abound, and, especially in Shinebourne's works, the interior threatens to reclaim the cultivated land. Occasionally the coastal characters venture into the forests, as when Sandra and her village friend T paddle a canoe up river: 'They stroked the water faster, gathered speed, and moved further into the depths of the forest. . . . The forest roused sensation and feeling. The sky, the wilderness of thousands of huge, entangled trees, the river, all signified a vast, unchartable and infinite mystery' (*TP* 44). The interior is also often portrayed as an alternative to the coastal plain where colonialism and capitalism define individuals' fates. In *Timepiece* Sandra's father's friend Reuben goes not to the city like other former estate workers, but to the interior, which represents self-determination and independence (40).

The voyage to the interior and the parallel metaphorical psychic journey are at the heart of Melville's novel. *The Ventriloquist's Tale* takes place largely in the savannahs of Guyana's interior, north and south of the Kanaku Mountains, west of the Rupununi River and the rainforests, towards the western border with Brazil. The present of the novel focuses on Chofy McKinnon—Wapisiana with a Scottish grandfather—who scratches a living from the harsh landscape with his wife, Marietta, until sickness decimates their cattle and he is forced to go to Georgetown in search of paid work. While there he meets the English academic Rosa Mendelson (she introduces herself as daughter of 'Jewish communists of a certain period. . . . We are all called after people like Rosa Luxemburg or Leon Trotsky' [*VT* 40]) who is researching Evelyn Waugh's visit to British Guiana in the 1930s. The novel also tells a second narrative: that of Chofy's Uncle Danny and Aunt Beatrice, brother and sister, who as teenagers in 1919 journey together from their home in the Rupununi savannah in to the rain forests to conduct their love affair, only to be pursued and separated by the zealous Catholic priest, Father Napier. The novel describes several voyages across the interior in both directions: south/west from the coast to the rainforest and savannahs; from the savannahs south into the rainforests; and from the rainforests or savannahs north/east to Georgetown: Chofy's grandfather McKinnon makes the journey from the coast to 'escape civilization,' falls sick and nearly dies but survives to marry two Wapisiana sisters and settle in Waronawa; Beatrice and Danny leave the savannah and travel along the Kassikaityu River; father Napier voyages from Georgetown into the villages of the rainforest in order to convert the natives to Christianity, and later pursues Beatrice and Danny; Chofy leaves his village to seek work in Georgetown; Rosa and Chofy travel by bus to Pakuri village from Georgetown.

Behind these movements are echoes of many earlier literary depictions of the voyage into the interior; the perspective is that of the Macusi and Wapisiana who have long withstood the assault of colonialist expeditions that continue in new guises. In the earlier narrative McKinnon is despised by the Georgetown 'upper classes of the colony' who 'reserved for him that particular hatred which colonists have for one who they feel has betrayed his race and class' (100), but he also represents the mentality of the colonizer in his desire for capitalist accumulation, which is ridiculed by his wives, Maba and Zuna, and the other Wapisianas who settle with him: 'Nobody could understand what drove him to keep trying out new things or why he continually pottered about when he could have been lying in his hammock' (100); indeed his entrepreneurial efforts consistently fail and eventually 'he gave up the ideas he had once had of creating a flourishing business of one sort of another. The land seemed set against it' (98). The voracious Father Napier is not so easily deterred: 'Ignoring his presentiments and the oblique warning given to him by the wild coast, he made up his mind to pit himself against whatever befell him. It was his ambition to strike into the interior of the country as soon as possible, to evangelize the most remote regions of the empire' (107); he sets off up the Essequibo river, establishing missions and renaming villages along the way 'like a cancer virus mimicking the workings of a cell it has entered' (150).

Here and to a degree in all the novels the land is personified and placed in a hostile relationship to colonizers. The Guyanese characters have an ambiguous relationship with their environment, which is seen sometimes as a safe harbor and at other times as a threat. Especially throughout *Frangipani House, Whole of a Morning Sky,* and *Buxton Spice* the trees—mango, guenip or genip, greenheart, dungs, mangrove, coconut, flamboyant, jamoon, starapple, breadfruit, poinciana, jacaranda—bear witness, provide shade, shelter, and comfort, and sometimes also represent unnamed fears and ominous secrets. When Gem and her siblings flee the 1960 burning of Georgetown they go to Cousin Wilma's rural home 'almost hidden by a tremendous guenip tree which seemed to be guarding the house in its immense shadow' (*WMS* 109). Back in the Georgetown neighborhood the Ramsammys' rebellious daughter-in-law at times 'ran out of the house and from the safety of the paling, behind the bread-fruit tree, would hurl abuse at the entire family' (*WMS* 125). Mama King's friend Miss Ginchi remembers the night she helped kill Mama King's abusive husband Danny while '[t]he branches of the mangrove trees motionless, in the windless night, stood like an army spellbound at what it had seen' (*FH* 75). In *Buxton Spice* Lula has tangible relationships with the different trees and especially with the eponymous mango that knows but refuses to reveal the secrets of her confusing world.

In Shinebourne's novels, too, trees possess symbolic significance. June corrects Sarah, the spoiled English overseer's daughter, when she calls the Madam Yass tree 'Parkinsonia' and explains that it was 'named after the English botanist who discovered it, Parkinson' (*LP* 26). Before leaving for the city Sandra enjoys her bedroom that was once her grandmother's: 'with the guinep tree growing against one wall, and the mango tree near the other. Their branches grew and met, hugging the house' (*TP* 12). And she is at home in her environment even at night: 'the darkness outside did not hold a threat. She could close her eyes as the car drove through the familiar villages and by the alternating scents know exactly where she was: where the black sage grew; the canefields; the dank vegetation in a swampy village; the canals smelling of over-ripe and rotting cane and weeds; the sawmill; the jumbie tree in the graveyard' (*TP* 53). June enjoys equal familiarity: 'There was a skill to cycling over the earth road. She knew the rough and smooth of it, where the earth was worn and the stones and pot-holes exposed' (*LP* 50).

In *The Ventriloquist's Tale* both Dutch and English colonizers are at odds with the land, never quite able to subdue or understand it, prone to madness or early death; as the widow of Mynheer Nicklaus puts it 'the Europeans could not ever see what was really going on in the place' (*VT* 37). McKinnon is nearly killed by the perils of the interior, and Napier views both forest and savannah as foreign, immoral, hostile, wastelands to be conquered, while Danny and Beatrice easily adapt to the rainforest, finding shelter, food and means to prepare it, and reading the flora and fauna around them:

> Beatrice thought that she had never seen surroundings that were more alive. The river was about thirty feet across. The trees on either side shimmered, tingled and exploded with exuberant bird noise. . . . Danny himself seemed to come alive in the bush. He was more alert, vigilant and inventive. . . . There was an abundance of food. They lived well on fish, nuts, fruit and game. (*VT* 196)

In contrast Napier is perturbed as he travels along a tributary of the Essequibo:

> The trees nearly met overhead, forming a lofty fretwork of grey sky. On either side, dense banks of foliage, dripping with water, sloped down to the river. Giant green water lilies, their ridged sides turned up like pastry flans, nearly sank under the weight of the water. Father Napier felt chilled and damp. The seats in the boat were wet and uncomfortable. He suffered cramp in his buttocks. Something flapped over the surface of the river. The priest could not even recognize what species of creature it was. It could have been some sort of duck, a bird, a frog. (*VT* 187)

The land is portrayed as resisting colonial invasion:

> The region would not submit easily to measurement. The intentions of those who designed the canals and kokers—which looked like guillotines—and who attempted to measure the tidal gradation of rivers were insidiously confounded and the capital city seemed to have been stretched out beyond its ideal size to keep at bay the citizens' terror of the land mass at its back. (*VT* 36)

The physical environment's antagonism to colonial settlement figuratively represents anticolonial resistance past and present.

The protagonists often feel a connection to the natural world that is in stark contrast to the colonial attitude, but the allure of romanticization is counterbalanced by the unromantic experience of labor. In *Frangipani House* Mama King in her old age remembers a life of relentless hard work, including at one point brick-breaking for road repairs; *Last English Plantation* and *Timepiece* are dominated by the proximity of the canefields, and contain many descriptions of physically brutal and psychologically stultifying toil on the plantations and in the sugar factory. In *Whole of a Morning Sky* political events are grounded in the grievances of the laboring population, worn down by the monotony of their travails and proximity of unemployment; *Ventriloquist's Tale* reveals the different but equally alienating and demoralizing demands of subsistence farming in the savannah and wage labor in the city. In all the novels women are responsible for unpaid domestic labor while also participating in waged work on the plantations and in factories.

But while all these novels are acutely conscious of class exploitation, and generally champion the laboring classes, the overall narrative perspective is middle class. In fact much of the dramatic tension stems from the often contradictory and torn class position of the female protagonist. In *Frangipani House* Mama King's children have left the country and escaped the precarious poverty of their mother. In the process, the novel suggests, they have cut themselves off from their past and lost the communal and familial loyalties and camaraderie that Mama King remembers and yearns for—and instead of caring for their elderly mother themselves, they pay for institutional care. When they come back to visit their hospitalized mother they feel alienated from their native land, and the gulf is more than simply geographical. They encounter Carlton, a friend who stayed in Guyana: 'He overlooked the changes brought by time and money. He overlooked the differences caused by living in a more demanding society' (83), but Mama King's daughters 'looked at Carlton as if he was from the planet Mars. His barefootedness struck chords of poverty and distant times. His lack of sophistication epitomized all they had left behind' (83). At the hospital Token and Cyclette confront their mother with pent up rage:

> 'This place is the past—the painful past. Mama never wanted more than this. This is her life, not mine. I never never wanted to be like her—her altruism sickened me. Her patience—her low, low goals. Just look at her. Worn out—worked out for nothing.'
> Her words linked past and present so poignantly that Cyclette began to sob hysterically. 'There is nothing here for me either,' she blubbered. 'Nothing, nothing. Just pain and hatred of poverty, hardship and useless mud and dung, pain, mosquitoes and old age.' (*FH* 98)

All the books describe this severance, the protagonists either already one step removed from the working class majority or in the process of leaving. In *Whole of a Morning Sky* Archie Walcott is a schoolteacher with a paternalistic attitude towards the poor families who surround him, and Gem's sister Dinah gets a job in the Civil Service; In *Buxton Spice* Lula's mother was 'a convent schoolgirl when they met in Georgetown,' and her father was 'a young reporter' who now works for the United Nations and is involved in setting up a community co-op scheme; at one point he reminds his wife that 'the only reason we live here is to help improve the village' (*BS* 27). In *Last English Plantation* June's father Cyrus is son of a Chinese plantation laborer who 'worked his way up to a foremanship, earning himself a right to live in the junior staff compound where the standard of living was much higher than New Dam's, though much lower than the Senior Staff compound where the overseers lived' (11), and is himself a mechanic who mediates between the overseers and the laborers; in *Timepiece* Sandra's parents Ben and Helen own a shop, and Sandra becomes a newspaper reporter.

In every case education is the staircase of upward class mobility, and class is figured chronologically: the past symbolizes poverty but supportive collectivity; the future represents prosperity but dog-eat-dog individualism. In *Ventriloquist's Tale* this dynamic emerges in the earlier narrative: Beatrice goes to Georgetown to attend the elite school, and on her return no longer belongs to the savannah community: she 'felt jealous and dislocated' and 'had forgotten how to work'

(157–8). Shinebourne's novels explicitly name this process of removal from the working class, as in these two passages about Sandra and June respectively:

> After daybreak, the red lorries, loaded with men and women, passed up and down along the road, taking and bringing the labourers to and from the canefields.
> Five years ago, those lorries took away some of her poorest schoolfriends, Ralph Brijlall, Unis Ali, Joe Tiwari, to the canefields. Ralph went to cut cane, Unis to bale punts and Joe to catch rats in the canefields. The poorest girls left school earlier to help mind their family and do housework or to work the small farms in the savannah, or at the saw mill or become servants. (*TP* 13)

> All her old school friends were in their villages, working in their homes, at the saw mill, on farms in the Corentyne and some were even working in the fields and factory although they were legally too young. One day they were there playing and doing their best at primary school, the next it was over and while she was waiting to go to school in New Amsterdam, they were gone to work. (*LP* 31)

When June starts at her new school the headmaster Mr. Singh exhorts the students to 'conduct themselves like future leaders and superior citizens of this country' (*LP* 82). Sandra's co-workers have gone through an educational system that has left them aspiring to wealth and status while despising their origins. As Morgan says '"we all went to schools where you come out with a chip on your shoulder. . . . By the time those schools finished with you, you screwed up for life, especially if you were poor when you went there, like us. Nothing else is good enough for you after that"' (70). While some quit and some are fired, others remain focused on their own self-preservation: 'Stamp, most adept at intellectual and political slogans, saw his opportunity to join a new black elite' (71). Others, like Bradley, despise those who betray their origins:

> I know some of these fellows when they were shirt-tail in the nigger-yard. The first thing they doing when they get degree is buying big car, house, and getting wife and child. Setting up a comfortable, nouveau riche, bourgeois life style. No man, I couldn't be part of that. The poor people I come from still around. I would feel very schizophrenic in my big car, and seeing my friends and family hustling in the city, seeing my grandmother hobbling round on she big foot at Bourda market. (*TP* 127)

The subtext of all these stories is this movement into the middle class and the conflicts it produces between old loyalties and new contingencies.[16]

Parents often represent the duality of this process: June's mother Lucille is ambitious for her daughter, scornful of the workers, and eager to remove any trace of association with them. This is expressed in cultural terms: she constantly reminds June to speak 'proper English,' not Hindi or creole, associates with the Anglican Christian rather than Hindu religion, and despises Boysie, the militant Indian plantation worker. June's father Cyrus is less invested in these questions, but his class affiliations are apparent in his political positions: he is for 'self-help' rather than union solidarity, and tends to be generous in his assessments of the overseers. Sandra's parents Ben and Helen represent village and town, respectively, but both also the past—their deaths at the end signify the disintegration of the plantation economy. As shopkeepers they are impacted by the class conflict that erupts but they do not strongly identify with either side. When Helen is in hospital dying Ben says to Sandra 'the whole estate running down, with the strike, trouble with the union. The manager threatening to close everything down. All that break Helen spirit. All she could talk about is how she waste her life here with me' (164). June then pictures their home as 'a sinking desert of shifting sand, tottering with despondency' (165). After Helen's death Ben cannot withstand his bereavement and 'the problems on the estate, shut down every day, the men restless while the unions and management locked themselves away for talks' (*Timepiece* 185).

This conflicted ideological location—neither with worker nor management and often torn politically—is predominant even in the fiction that explicitly champions labor against colonial and domestic rulers. Often the climactic moments of the narrative involve conflagrations seen by observer rather than participant and featuring compromise rather than decisive victory or defeat. So at the end of the *Last English Plantation* during a spiraling clash between workers and overseers 'Cyrus cautioned Boysie to proceed slowly, to talk, not fight' (164), and ultimately the situation is defused when overseers and police reach a just resolution. This posture is pervasive in representations of the rise and fall of Jagan and consolidation of Burnham's rule. The novels are acutely aware of the class inflections of political loyalties: *The Last English Plantation* covers the 1950s and shows the British colonialists' and plantation owners' hostility to Jagan in the face of wide support for him among the plantation workers (though Boysie mistrusts Jagan and Burnham for being so removed from plantation labor); in *Whole of a Morning Sky* Archie identifies with property and business owners, mistrusts Mohabir (the fictionalized version of Jagan), and favors the United Force (National United Front); his daughter Dinah agrees with her Marxist co-worker when he defends Mohabir and declares that 'Indian sugar workers, black bauxite workers, rice farmers, they all have to come together in a united front. . . . you can't fight the capitalists with a divided labour force' (81); *Buxton Spice* portrays the considerable popular hatred of Burnham in the 1970s, and Lula's parents are persecuted by the state for supporting the opposition.

In all the novels social class and status are metonymically figured by houses, which have distinctive construction features in the Guyanese coastal strip due to the constant threat of floods.[17] In *Ventriloquist's Tale* the Guyanese musician Arthur Singh, who stays in the Mynheer Nicklaus Lodge (itself symbolizing both old and new wealth) where Rosa is also living, expresses one interpretation of the customary abode: 'Sometimes I feel that it is because we Guyanese live in houses on stilts that we do not quite have our feet on the ground as a nation' (43). Throughout the novels individuals' material security (or lack thereof) is embodied in their homes, which offer varying defense against floods and other perils, and broadly signify social hierarchy. The estates in *Last English Plantation* and *Timepiece* are physically divided into compounds for overseers, foremen, and workers: the manager has the biggest house, and members of each stratum on the descending scale live in houses appropriate to their status, all the way down to the small plots and flimsy shelters of the casual laborers (*LP* 19–20). When her mother visits the home of overseer Sampson, June plays with his daughter Louise in the spacious bottomhouse:

> The flooring was so high under these houses you could hold big weddings and wakes here. The bottomhouses in New Dam were a quarter of the size of this one. The old logies in Old Dam hardly had a bottom house. . . . People in the overseers' houses had nothing to fear from floods, rodents and crawling creatures from the mud, bush and canefields. The concrete pillars here were very tall and exposed to the driving rain, hot sun and strong breeze which would blow or wash or dry such creatures away before they could reach the tophouse. . . . The overseers were safe in their houses here. (*LP* 100)

Social hierarchy is similarly mapped on to the topography of Tamarind Grove in *Buxton Spice*: as Lula walks out towards the creek she observes 'the rumshop. . . the only concrete building from Mainroad til Scheme. Mrs Boila was proud of that. . . . Miss Isaac's house—so new the wood wasn't silver yet, still dark brown. She didn't have no empty bottom-house like most people. It was half enclosed and she kept her best cows in there' (20), and 'the house with the longest front yard' was lived in by 'people rich so—with car and Lawngrass' (21). The prostitute Cockroach and her man Clinton, in contrast, 'lived in a small wooden house behind the shed across the road. It had no trees around it, no outside bathroom or latrine. Just the closed-up weathered shell stood in the lot' (70). The beggars with whom Mama King runs away in *Frangipani House* live in 'a bothy which the road-builders had abandoned. The walls were made of wooden slats and the floor cold underfoot, and smelling of cow-dung' (*FH* 59).

The protagonists do not inhabit anything like the overseers' mansions, but neither do they live in the lowliest abodes. Lula's parents have 'the biggest bottom-house around' (*BS* 27), with more than two bedrooms, a living room and an extra room for the live-in 'house-help' (*BS* 3–4). Sandra tells Son that

> [h]ers was the tallest house in Pheasant, that the bottom storey was not open since the shop took up the bottom half, that the top-half was encircled by closed windows, the roof cutting the skyline in different shapes, with one side a downturned V-shape and the other sloping at an angle nearly vertical with the horizon: green corrugated zinc topped by the dome of the blue sky. (*TP* 41)

The Georgetown home that Archie buys is of similar dimensions:

> A simple white house, oblong in shape, with a roof slanting downwards from front to back. . . . It was a house with many windows, giving it a well-ventilated appearance, and it stood on long wooden pillars like so many of the other houses. The house had two bedrooms, fairly large, and two flights of stairs, back and front. The doors and bannisters were painted in rust-red and there was ample yard space. . . . The house . . . gave the appearance of being quiet and aloof. (*WMS* 40)

The relative security of the central characters is thus contrasted with the radical insecurity of the slum dwellers. Archie is dismayed by the proximity of 'the tenement yard behind his house. . . . the sight of tumbledown buildings and range rooms all huddled together, and a teeming humanity, was both unpleasant and disturbing. This blending of contrast in Georgetown, of the old and dilapidated beside the new and elegant, never ceased to amaze him' (*WMS* 41). In Georgetown Sandra lodges with the wealthy Daphne, and when she returns to Pheasant she reflects that '[i]f Daphne's cottage and the houses in Bel Air Park were narrow islands of comfort, then this house was a sinking desert of shifting sand, tottering with despondency' (*TP* 165). The exorbitant significance of housing is repeatedly apparent: as when the workers in Canefields burn the home of the overseer (*LP* 135); or when the older Sandra returns to Pheasant to find her old home, like those surrounding it, 'in total decay' (*TP* 6).

The physical environment also bears the marks of ethnic and racial divisions, which are shown to be socially constructed and neither intrinsic nor inevitable. While the present of all the novels is overwhelmed by deep-seated ethnic consciousness and violence, all remember the past as a time when ethnicity neither defined nor divided people. In *Buxton Spice* the 1970s landscape is segregated: 'Black people lived in one village, Indians the next. Blacks, Indians. So it went, all along the coast of Guyana to Mahaica. Even if you didn't see people, you could tell which village was black, which was coolie' (*BS* 44). But it wasn't always like that: 'Mums said it was Riots made it so. Race Riots before we moved in. Fires and bombs chasing Indians out. Now Tamarind Grove was black race people, strong PNC party people. Dads, Bunty family and Aunty Babe was the only East Indians. And my family was mixed—Indian, black and white' (*BS* 43). *Last English Plantation* similarly describes the gap between the ethnically integrated past and segregated present:

> Half the families in Old Dam had been African, living in cottages set a little way from the logies where the Indian families lived. Yet they had lived like one large family in spite of their differences, the women sharing childminding and attending each other's birth, marriage and funeral rituals. They all, men and women, used to gossip and talk work and politics. She missed the feeling of belonging to that kind of village. Now they lived in separate African and Indian villages. (37)

And in *Timepiece* we hear of times past along the Canje when 'Africans and Indians shared each other's customs in a way that would be unthinkable elsewhere, and that was probably no longer possible after the race riots' (*TP* 54–5).

The novels describe the encroachment of racist ideology and ethnic cleansing that transformed village and city alike from connected sites of racial integration to isolated islands of ethnic communalism. Yet even afterwards the reality is that the different ethnic groups cannot be wholly separated. The protagonists themselves embody the ethnic intermixture within individuals and the broader society. Sandra is 'mixed race . . . My mother is part-Indian, part Chinese, my father is Chinese' (*TP* 152); June explains that '"My mother . . . is Indian. My father is not whole

Indian, he is Chinese too but he was brought up as a Hindu"' (*LP* 80); Lula calls herself 'part coolie' (*BS* 53). Archie's father was African and his mother 'had a little East Indian blood in her, maybe a little Amerindian too' (*WMS* 15) and this admixture is reflected in Georgetown where 'he watched the jostling move of people going by, a *mélange* of people of different races and different shades and mixtures of races. Africans, East Indians, Portuguese, Chinese, a few Amerindians and, of course, the growing numbers of Mixed' (*WMS* 52). Clara's cooking represents the principal of cultural fusion:

> While the pieces of meat soaked up the lemon juice and garlic and curry paste and eschalot and wiri-wiri peppers, Clara would pound the fufu in her sturdy wooden mortar. She kept up the rhythm with the long, smooth, thick pestle, up and down, round and round, getting the bits from the sides of the mortar. . . . Moist and magical, embodying at once all the diverse ingredients of her culture in this act of pounding fufu, Clara would pause to sip from a cup of imported English Red Rose tea. (*WMS* 84)

While the novels all contain descriptions of ethnic violence and hostility, they also include moments of interethnic solidarity. In *Whole of a Morning Sky* Lula's predominantly African neighborhood defends the Ramsammy family from the marauding mob looking for East Indian houses to burn. In *Frangipani House* Mama King, who is ethnically African, escapes the sterile world of the institution and takes refuge with the ethnically Indian beggars. During the final confrontation in *Last English Plantation* Boysie tells the police sergeant "'that the PPP under Cheddi Jagan, African, Indian, all races was united behind him in 1951, and that is how come we get we first legally elected government for the workers in 1953. But people hate fo' see poor people win an' from the time it happen all kind people workin' mischief"' (*LP* 167–8).

The novels all present multiculturalism as a positive attribute that has been tragically threatened by the creed at one point expressed by June in an argument with her mother: 'People should stay where they belong, with their own kind, especially when other people don' want us around them' (*LP* 92). These conflicting ideological positions are dramatized in *Ventriloquist's Tale* in the debate between Rosa, who says 'I'm an internationalist. . . . I believe in a mixture of the races' and the anthropologist Wormoal who replies 'People want to be with their own kind. Everyone nowadays is retreating into their own homogeneous group. Black with black. Serb with Serb. Muslim with Muslim. . . . I believe in the purity of the nation' (*VT* 78). When he adds that 'you Jews also choose to stick together now in Israel' Rosa counters with 'I am not a Zionist . . . I support the Palestinians on most issues' (*VT* 78–9). In the epilogue the narrator returns to the question: 'It was while I was in Europe that I nearly became fatally infected by the epidemic of separatism that was raging there. The virus transmutes. Sometimes it appears as nationalism, sometimes as racism, sometimes as religious orthodoxy. My experience in the rain forests of South America provided me with no immunity to it. . . . I saw that the desire to be with your own kind exerts a powerful attraction' (355).

But while this advocacy for internationalism and ethnic/racial integration remains the dominant voice, the narratives all turn upon a racial war that does indeed descend on the country like a virus, reeking havoc and fostering a generalized climate of violence: 'No one knew how the beatings and killings started or who really started them first' (*WMS* 137); 'Mums said it was Riots made it so. Race Riots before we moved in' (*BS* 43); 'the racial disturbances which began in Georgetown in 1961, spread to many other parts of the country and did not end until 1964, by which time fifteen thousand people, mostly Indo-Guyanese, had been forced to move their homes and settle elsewhere' (*TP* 12). The extent of the trauma is conveyed in shocking scenes of bodily violation inflicted by mobs transformed from individuals to animals: 'All the grisly details splashed across the pages: The body of a black man who was dragged from a hire-car and hacked to death in some East Indian village. The body of an Indian man floating in a trench in the city' (*WMS* 139); '"All them poor people were beating up each other and looting left, right and centre. Men on East Coast chop up each other. Women get raped all over the place"' (*TP* 126). Lula watches as a mob punishes a man accused of theft:

> Blows falling like rain on something I couldn't see. Greenheart staves thudding on flesh and bone. Loud above the shouts from men's bellies and the women's screams . . . women flying out from pale homes in the moonlight. Tearing paling staves out of their fences. Nylon nighties ripping, skin gleaming, bare feet thrashing through drains and knees grating on gravel to get at the thing . . . Miss Harper bawling. . . .
>
> 'All! All!' spurred her sister, plunging through the backs of men dragging and beating the thing. 'Kill him!'
>
> A paling point rammed through the thick bodies and stopped dead on bone. The bent backs dipped down and pulled up a head and an arm that dangled a wet hand from somewhere between the elbow and wrist. It flopped about for a minute or so, carried slowly forward before dropping back into the writhing caterpillar of bodies. . . .
>
> They mash-up both legs by the time he reach Mainroad. Now everything must be broken, crushed. . . .
>
> No human sound came from the centre of the squirming caterpillar. Just dull thuds. The sound of shoes hitting stomach.
>
> Three policemen came half trotting down the road. . . .
>
> As they neared the mass, batons out, the flesh and legs of the caterpillar fell away and the guts lay bare. The purple-black twitching pile glistened. (*BS* 47–9)

The same ingredients, the observer horrified and confused by what she is witnessing, the mob transformed to animals, the objectified victim described with visceral detail, are found in the violent incidents at the heart of *Whole of a Morning Sky*:

> Clara remembered the distinct foreboding she felt that morning when she picked up the newspapers and read about the unidentified body of a black man who was found at the back of the ricefields near Skeldon. . . . it set her imagination working—returning again and again to a vision of a slightly swollen, mud-dried corpse. . . . The woman ran as if all the devils of hell pursued her, her long black hair dancing like fine shreds of

elastic about her face . . . running in desperation . . . they pursued her like a pack of hounds, bicycle wheels in unison, pressing hard, doubled over the bicycle handles—a gang of twelve, fourteen, young men, shirts knotted at navels to expose hard, shiny black chests, faces gleaming with sweat and glee . . . They'll frighten the life out of this coolie bitch.   . . . ' Take her boys. Take her,' they cry hoarsely . . . laughing, 'Take her boys, take her.' (*WMS* 138)

While sometimes women are complicit in the mob violence, they are more likely to be victims. Immediately after the scene above from *Buxton Spice* comes a similar description, this time witnessed by Lula with three other children:

People were buzzing around on the bridge, then pushing round the huge concrete base. . . . Flowing like ants, down along the top of the stone wall and on to the mud . . . we followed the line of people struggling . . . The line turned sharply around something lying there. Then snaked back, scattering people to the seawall. . . . We held hands instinctively, the four a'we, struggling forward, mouths gummed up, blood screaming. A Face. The Pastor's wife. It was her face. Dead. Half in the mud, mouth open, stuffed with muddy grass. Her bare body twisted, just a piece of red shirt on one shoulder. Dull black skin in the sun. A gash on her neck glinted and between her legs more grass stuck out that had been stuffed into her bunge. (51)

As is the case here, the 'racial' violence is often sexualized, with rape figuring highly. *Timepiece* gives this account of the ethnic violence in 1963: 'They said that at Wismar women had held down women to be raped—Afro-Guianese women held down Indo-Guianese women to be raped in revenge for their men preferring them, revenge against their men too. Violence was always a weapon used by one sex against the other sex, so it was inevitable it would be used by one race against another.' (*TP* 16–17). There are two explanatory threads here that run through the books: the ethnic wars provoked in the early 1950s spiraled into generalized violence which was then exacerbated and institutionalized by the militarization of the state under Burnham; the racial and ethnic violence was closely related to a violent, misogynist sexuality.

Later in *Buxton Spice* comes another deeply disturbing scene with obvious parallels to the one describing the beating of the thief. A crowd is drawn to the house of Cockroach and Clinton by sounds of violence. As the four children move toward the house it becomes increasingly obvious that Cockroach is silently enduring a severe beating from Clinton:

The sound of flesh hitting flesh came from the closed-up house. The four a'we lined up inside the fence across the road, squatting, faces pressing between the staves of rough greenheart. A loud crash from inside sounded like a body falling. No screams, no crying, no shouting. And then a crack. He must'a broken off a leg of a chair or something. Sound of it hitting flesh and a high-pitched wail came seeping out the cracks of that house. . . . Then deep grunts started, between the thumping. The choked sobs got more frequent and took on a new tone. (72)

The crowd disperses as it becomes increasingly obvious that, as Lula's friend Judy puts it "'He fucking she now'" (71). This scene makes explicit what is never far from the surface of any of the novels: that the generalized climate of violence pervades domestic and sexual relations. [18]

The violence of the state pervades all areas of life: in the schools children are routinely beaten, and in the family and workplace children and women also are vulnerable to physical abuse. Mama King's old friend Ben reminds her that her husband Danny 'bumped, bruised and boxed your face and kick you about worse than football. He was the cruelest, most ignorant man in God's world' (*FH* 33); Mrs. Ramsammy's new daughter-in-law is a disappointment to the family because 'whenever her husband tried to beat her, Zabeeda would fight back, her wiry body clawing and scratching' (*WMS* 124); it is generally accepted that the overseers in Canefields routinely rape the estate's women (*LP* 83); prostitutes have the least status of all, and women who show signs of independence are labeled as prostitutes (*BS* 64; *WMS* 57; *TP* 32). One of the defining moments in *Frangipani House* is the violent mugging of Mama King at the fish market: the liming youth leave her looking 'like debris often seen along the shore when the tide was out' ironically while Gil Scott Heron's tribute to 'Grandma's Hands' plays in the background (*FH* 66–7). The final act of violence in *Buxton Spice* is against Lula's teenage friend Judy DeAbro: caught out at night (due to a police raid nearby that alerts everyone) with her black boyfriend she is indiscriminately caned by her furious mother who also strips off her underwear to check for signs of sexual activity (*BS* 164–8).

Sex and violence are thus indelibly linked, and the landscape too is sexualized. Yet women are also figured as desiring subjects negotiating the perils of sexual pleasure and danger. *Buxton Spice* dramatizes this the most clearly: the narrative centers around Lula's emergent sexuality, following her fascination with her own and other peoples' bodies, sex games with girlfriends, discovery of masturbation and orgasm, and frightening erotic encounters with the virile Iggy DeAbro. This novel and *Whole of a Morning Sky* contain similar scenes of 'playing husband and wife' where the young girls experience a safe area of sexuality focused on mutuality, pleasure, and joy:

> Sometimes you play ole higue. You like being the ole higue, glad for the chance to come hobbling along in an old sheet, then quietly pulling back the covers off Lurleena and nibbling at her neck. She would start shrieking and laughing the moment you reach the bed.
> Sometimes you play husband and wife, spreading ricebags under the steps, shutting off the sides with pieces of boards and boxes so no one could see. Lying quietly together in a tangle of legs. (*WMS* 90–91)

The scene in *Buxton Spice* where Lula and Rachel 'play husband and wife' along with Sammy and Judy is much longer and more detailed, but the atmosphere is similar:

> I stuck my head under the sheet and stared at the lovely swirl of light brown goldeny hair on the back of her neck just below the big neckbone. She knew it was time. Under the sheet she turned on to her back and wriggled an arm past my neck. . . . I put my nose in and smelt her ear . . . She was trying hard not to laugh, we rocking still . . . Pelting back the sheet we snuffed and skin-up our lips in the air, giggling and squeaking, feeling the little electric shivers raising hair. (*BS* 87–9)

Both scenes are unlike the 'playing house' scene in Rooplall Monar's 1989 novel, *Janjhat*: in his story the boy 'chooses' a girl to be his wife and is the active initiator of 'fumblings which both excited and made him feel he was doing something shameful and forbidden' (*Janjhat* 18). These games are prohibited after the elder sister of one of the girls finds them out, subjects the girls to a quick physical examination, and threatens to expose them. This episode makes the protagonist, Big-Bye, associate sexual desire with shame, which later colors his interaction with his wife Data. The games in Nichols' and Kempadoo's stories, in contrast, take place in a zone that seems unscathed by the brutality that surrounds most of the heterosexual encounters around them, even though the terms of the relationships are set by dominant gender frameworks (the girls take turns in adopting the role of active husbands and passive wives). In contrast Lula's charged encounters with Iggy are all framed by imagined or real violence, as when the two exchange erotic glances while his father beats him. In *Ventriloquist's Tale* the children's sex games, which are closer to those of *Janjhat*, do not interest Beatrice but she independently discovers the pleasures of orgasm (*VT* 127).

More broadly the women experience sexual pleasure in Guyana's natural environment, following in the long tradition of literary associations between the landscape and women's bodies. Here, again, the women become active desiring subjects rather than the passive recipients of male fantasies. In *Buxton Spice* Lula's emergent sexuality is projected onto trees, animals, the weather, every aspect of the physical world, and she reaches orgasm with the help of the powerful jet of water in the shower. In *Ventriloquist's Tale* Beatrice's 'first sexual experiences had not come about through human agency' (*VT* 125–6), but from the sun (to which she is linked through the recurring incest myth), and later from trees or the creek (126–7). The forest is particularly associated with her sexual desire:

> There, Beatrice discovered that the intense colours of certain flowers had the same effect on her as the sun. Branching off on her own to look for bark . . . she came across some scarlet flowers under a ceiba tree. . . . these flowers seemed to burn the air around them. She stared, fascinated. The flowers blazed like sores. She could not take her eyes off them. First came the familiar tingling in her nipples and then the other feeling started up in the bottom of her belly. . . . Later, Beatrice discovered that the vivid, electric blue of jacaranda petals started her nipples tingling in the same way. (*VT* 128)

The scenes of Beatrice and Danny in the forest read like rejoinders to books like Hudson's *Green Mansions*, closely linking the woman's body with the landscape but representing the female as subject (Beatrice) rather than object (Rima) on to which male desire is projected. Though not explicit, the same association of forest and sexuality, and the same reversal of the gaze, can be seen in the sequence in *Timepiece* when Sandra goes up river with her childhood friend, T:

> Sakiwinkis burst leaves off branches in their flight through the forest and the pheasants, strange, ancient-looking birds, curved a dipping path in and out of the trees. There were large intervals of silence here; you could feel the space open and shut round you. When it opened, it took you into its silence and snuffed out the life you brought with you; when it shut itself, it was like a flower closing, keeping the secret of its beauty. Then, it left you without comfort, feeling apprehension, so the sudden bursts of noise that broke like shrieks from its still, closed centre shattered and shredded any sense of calmness. (*TP* 45)

This passage resembles the dream Beatrice has some time after she has left Guyana to settle in Montreal:

> Her thighs had become immovably heavy and turned into the banks of the Potaro River, covered in vegetation in which herds of peccary scurried and swerved. She turned into her own sexual landscape. The silent silver stream of the river between her legs carried in it the reflections of clouds and a flight of macaws. The river flowed on through the steep escarpments. She felt tugging undercurrents beneath its surface. Still the smooth stream of silver gathered momentum, racing towards the great falls where it dropped, thundering into the ravine below. (*VT* 280)

Melville makes a sharper self-conscious allusion to the long tradition of depicting the rainforest as a woman's body, but both passages combine latent sexuality with a sense of hidden, alluring depths and disturbing danger.

This assertion of female desire is part of the struggle for autonomy and independence in a militarized authoritarian state that constrains the lives of all men and women but is fraught with particular hazards for women. In all the books adults take out their frustrations on children, and men on women. In *Last English Plantation* the authoritarian teachers pick on the boys from the poorest backgrounds:

> It was Rabindranauth Jekir, who was from New Amsterdam, and who was dressed poorly in cheap cottons . . . His hair was slicked down and he smelt of coconut oil. . . . Mrs. Farley squeezed his ear until he was bent double against her, the blood filling his face, and he groaned in pain, unashamedly, begging her to stop. She let go of him abruptly and he held his ear and wept in pain and shame. That seemed to get rid of some of Mrs. Farley's anger. . . . June felt sure Mrs. Farley would not dare lay a hand on children . . . whose parents were above Mrs. Farley's station. (*LP* 110)

The next student to feel the brunt of Mrs. Farley's wrath is Frank Hussein, son of a chauffer:

She lifted the cane and brought it down on his thigh. His right hand flew to shield his thigh and she brought the cane down on the hand. When he rubbed his right hand with his left hand she thrashed his left hand twice. He shrunk from her and she whipped him across his back freely. . . . . Frank took a few steps along the queue, backing away from Mrs. Farley but she pursued him, and whipped him with surprising strength and vigour, with a practiced rhythm. Frank decided not to run and stood his ground, taking the lashes, his body jumping each time the cane made contact with his flesh. When she finished with him she strode to the front of the queue where Rabindranauth was still standing, took hold of his right wrist firmly and began to whip him as hard as she had whipped Frank. Rabindranauth was not as brave as Frank and his degradation was painful to watch. . . . . he sounded like a man, half-man, half-animal, in his agony. (*LP* 111)

Schools are usually sites of frustrated violence vented on the most vulnerable children. In *Ventriloquist's Tale* Chofy's son Bla-Bla is punished for speaking Wapisiana to his mother when she visits his class room one day:

The blow took Bla-Bla utterly by surprise. It stunned and cut. The strap caught him on the side of the head but the blow seemed to coil round the root of his tongue. The teacher was asking him something angrily and telling him to speak English. But his English deserted him and he was unable to answer: the strap whistled and landed on the other side of his head and the top of his left shoulder. (*VT* 317)

In *Buxton Spice* the link between this institution and the larger society is made explicit. First we learn about former school friends who have signed up for Burnham's armed forces (138–9), then comes a generalized portrait of the militarized state: 'The power of the PNC was everywhere and Burnham's face was everywhere' (151), and soon after we get this account:

In our schoolworld Mr Brown the headmaster was Forbes Burnham. Had the same smirk too. . . . He made you aware of his power all the time. He smiled at me, sly, knowing I came from a non-PNC home—maybe even WPA. I looked right back at him like my body didn't exist, refused to show any signs of being scared or intimidated by his lecherous looks. He'd stand in one of the long corridors that ran the length of the school, just watching, making sure everything was going smoothly. And he'd watch you walk towards him, aware that the breeze was pressing the dress material against your body and that your thighs kept marching out against it, pointing to where your crotch is. . . . I'd seen him holding big girls' hands in his gold-ringed ones while telling them off softly or congratulating them. (*BS* 153–4)

In cases like these violence against women is a tool of those with power, but in most cases it is understood as a result of men's own powerlessness—and in the case of child abuse women's powerlessness—and a generalized climate of institutionalized brutality: men like Clinton take out their frustration on women, using them as punch bags; women in turn lash out at vulnerable children.

Men and women's political responses to the regime are circumscribed by class dynamics. Like their male counterparts, for the young women entering professions—Sandra as a journalist in *Timepiece* and Dinah in *Whole of a Morning Sky*—the question of political risk is paramount: they identify with oppositional politics but fear the consequences for their own material security. Both are threatened by their respective bosses with being fired if they follow their conscience: Dinah for not wanting to attend a march protesting Jagan's budget; Sandra for considering showing solidarity with her striking co-workers when one reporter is fired by the Burnhamite boss. Dinah avoids a direct confrontation with her employer by making an appearance at the march before sneaking off with Hartley. Sandra's friend Pat tells her "'You mustn't get involved. Once you become involved in politics, Daddy says, it spoils your life for all time'" (*TP* 172). But we often see working class women standing up against Burnham's regime. In *Buxton Spice* 'Aunt Ruth was the only woman in Tamarind Grove who dared disrespect Our Leader Comrade Linden Forbes Burnham' (78). Burnham makes a visit to the local food co-op:

> From afar, a wailing siren signaled Burnham's approach. . . . The black limousine stopped suddenly right in front of the Co-op, police bikes, with lights still flashing, circling it as Our Leader Comrade Burnham stepped out.
> . . . He wore the Well-off African Politician look—grey blue shirtjack over his paunch, black shoes glittering, gold band on his wrist. Escorts all around him, dressed the same, with dark shades on. (*BS* 80)

Fed up of long food lines and shortages, Aunt Ruth heckles Burnham from the crowd, and the scene ends with her defiance: "'Burn'am . . . '" Aunt Ruth rasped slowly, not moving, looking at him sideways, "you full'a shit. You know what you can do? You can kiss my black stinking arse'" (*BS* 82). Aunt Ruth is matched in Gilroy's novel by the defiant and irreverent Mama King.

Cities of Slums

While village life is impacted by Burnham's regime, it is the city that most graphically represents the generalized conditions of the postindependence nation, the impact of neoliberalism, and the continuity between the colonial past and the supposedly postcolonial present. In all the books characters arrive in Georgetown to scenes of urban poverty. In *Ventriloquist's Tale* Chofy rents a 'cramped and cheap' room in the Albouystown district. One morning he walks towards Stabroek market:

> He let himself through the broken gate on to the street, emerging into the raucous noise and the ramshackle, grey, sun-bleached, wooden slums of the neighbourhood. He picked his way over stinking trenches, piles of trash and junked tyres, holding his breath as much as possible against a variety of stomach-churning smells. The tingalinga tingalinga sound of a steel band fought to gain ascendancy over the tireless thump of reggae, tata toom, tata toom, bombarding his ears as people pushed past him and shouted to each other across the street. (*VT* 31)

Sandra's encounter with Georgetown on her first morning paints a similar scene:

> The smell and sight of the slums were never far away, the underbelly which occasionally turned urban Guiana upside down and rained down anarchy. Regent Street was lined mostly by stores and small eating houses, but people also lived there, in flats and houses squeezed into the alleyways. . . . Already, the tramps and beggars were out on the pavements, and porters were pushing their barrows along the sheltered pavements towards the wharves of Water Street. . . . the smell of rotting fruit wafted from Bourda market where dray carts and trucks were arriving from the country to deposit their goods. (*TP* 64)

Archie's walk around central Georgetown soon after his arrival echoes both descriptions:

> He crossed over on to the busy shopping junction in front of Bookers' Stores and made his way round into Water Street. As he walked along the narrow crowded pavement a stream of traffic moved sluggishly along with him. Yellow buses, cars and wobbling pedal cyclists, trucks, horses, pulling long, over-laden dray carts, huge sugarbulks. . . . He watched the hustle of the pavement vendors fastening on to prospective buyers. . . . He would never grow accustomed to the close proximity of the Georgetown houses. To the noise. The thieves. The hooligans. The slums. (*WMS* 51–3)

Each novel reconstructs the space of the city—naming streets and neighborhoods—depicts urban squalor, and portrays the bustle of people who to varying degrees pose a threat. The fish market in *Frangipani House* is very like these accounts, and Mama King's assault there brings to the surface the latent sense of danger in the others:

> The fish market was a rough and tumble cluster of stalls, roofed with interwoven coconut-palm fronds to keep out the sun and the rain. Before catching sight of the market one smelt its odors riding the breeze unashamedly. . . . They walked on until they came to the cake-shop, a lively little place full of noises, cheap cakes and a gaggle of young men standing around, or leaping and dancing to the music. (*FH* 65–6)

The urban scenes show a world without safety nets for the poor, the elderly, the unemployed: the old familial and communal structures have been removed, but nothing has been put in their place other than relentless individualism, privatization, and dog-eat-dog competition. This is seen in *Frangipani House* where the 'fortunate' old people have relatives who can pay for private care in soul-destroying institutions, and in *Ventriloquist's Tale* when Chofy's Aunt Wifreda gets medical care only through the religious charity of the St Francis of Assisi home, 'a city within a city, a city of the old, known as the City of Crones, consisting of a collection of one-room shacks run as a charity by the Catholic Church' (*VT* 69). It is seen also in *Ventriloquist's Tale* in the portrait of the run-down city university in Georgetown: 'The shoddily built university had a deserted feel to it. A lone cow cropped the campus grass. Instead of the revolutionary slogans that usually deck a university campus, the graffiti on the wall pleaded:

"TEXTS   NOW".   "SANITATION   NOW".   "WHERE   ARE   THE
FACILITIES???"'(306).

The poverty and decay of the city are connected to the pervasive force of
imperialism: in the narratives set prior to independence, Dutch and then British
colonialism; in the later scenarios, predominantly American economic and political
domination. *Last English Plantation* shows the confluence of both: June stops on
the Dolphin swingbridge—again symbolically significant as a transition point—
and watches 'a large foreign ship. . . . Perhaps it was a bauxite ship' (87), and soon
after asks herself, '"Was Guiana really just a big prison camp run by the British?"'
(*LP* 88). In *Timepiece*, set a decade later, the adjustment has advanced further: the
CIA funds right-wing unions and newspapers, and on the plantations 'the people
. . . were still fighting British domination while Georgetown was renewing its
relationship with the British, and entering into a new one with the government of
the United States, both anxious to prevent Guiana becoming another Cuba' (118–
19). *Whole of a Morning Sky* portrays American government and CIA agents
working behind the scenes to destabilize Mohabir's government (70, 71, 73, 89,
127). Cold war politics shape events in *Buxton Spice*, too, and impinge on Lula's
world when her home is raided by the military: Lula 'glanced at the piles of
Gramma newspapers from Cuba with their big red headlines. Mixed in between
them was WPA bulletins and the *Catholic Standard*. They wasn't opposition
papers? Propaganda? I had heard Dads saying something bout these Communist
papers. Redman [one of the police officers] was digging through the pile now'
(*BS*158). After the mother is imprisoned and then released, the family leaves
Guyana in fear of further persecution.

These novels thus reflect 'the ruses of imperialism which make game of men's
lives,' offer expanded 'horizons of sensibility' by refusing the logic of ethnic
communalism and racial divisions, and protest the paucity of conditions and
options for the majority of Guyanese. In each novel we meet a woman whose
struggle for self-determination mirrors, and sometimes is explicitly linked to, a
broader political struggle for real independence. In *Frangipani House* Mama King
is depicted as a rebel fighting to escape the constraints imposed by the institution's
dictatorial matron whose 'pervasive authority had touched everything' (*FH* 86). In
Whole of a Morning Sky Dinah befriends her Marxist co-worker, Hartley, and is
shown 'budding with a new revolutionary consciousness, showing a concern for
remoulding the world' (*WMS* 128). *Buxton Spice* gives us Aunt Ruth, defiantly
challenging Burnham, and in *Timepiece* and *Last English Plantation* the female
protagonists actively challenge the social inequities that surround them as they
struggle to become autonomous individuals. None of the political struggles
succeed: in each case ethnic divisions, an increasingly authoritarian state, and
pervasive foreign intervention stymie attempted progressive social change, and
those who are able leave the country they love.

In *Ventriloquist's Tale* the very structure of the novel highlights the continuity
of imperialism, through the juxtaposition of the two stories: the first is set in the
opening decades of the twentieth century, when life is circumscribed by European
landowners and missionaries; the second in the last decade, in a Guyana now

dominated by North American corporations and financial agencies. Early on Rosa visits the colonial club in Georgetown where Evelyn Waugh once stayed, and 'the unmistakable atmosphere of the country's colonial past rose up and enveloped her' (*VT* 44). While she waits to interview a former servant who met Waugh, '[a] group of businessmen drank and talked noisily at a table nearby' (45), and she ruefully remembers her communist father who, during Rosa's childhood in London, 'had mounted a bench in Dulwich Park and made a passionate speech about Paul Robeson and colonialism to which nobody listened' (45). The reference to Robeson of course evokes the cold war McCarthyite witch hunt which had such dire ramifications for the fate of Guyana, and points us towards the continuing omnipresence of American imperialism, which is emphasized again in the next paragraph:

> And now, her parents were dead and this colonial club still flourished smugly as if cocking a snook at her father's memory. Rosa was glad that both her parents had died before the collapse of the Soviet bloc. They would have been bewildered. All their adult lives had been spent working in the hope of a socialist world.
> A hearty guffaw of laughter from the next table made her look at her watch. Her interviewee was late. She wondered what her parents would have thought of the world turning into one enormous capitalist market. (*VT* 45)

Ventriloquist's Tale offers an explicit—if wry and sardonic—analysis of imperialism's continuity in the form of global capitalism, but it is implicit in the other texts: when Mama King's son tells his family, '"we have all been fouled up in this rat-racing world. All of us. Rat-racing has neutralised us all"' (*FH* 99); or in *Timepiece* when Son tells Sandra, '"[t]he only culture that matters now-a-days is American culture"' (*TP* 153).

During his trip to Pakuri village with Rosa, Chofy talks and drinks with his friend Tenga, who bitterly resents the incursions of outsiders searching for a taste of Amerindian culture without seeing 'what grows fastest here—the children's part of the burial ground' (*VT* 54). Tenga continues:

> We Amerindian people are fools. . . . We've been colonised twice. First by the Europeans and then by the coastlanders. I don't know which is worse. Big companies come to mine gold or cut timber. Scholars come and worm their way into our communities, studying us and grabbing our knowledge for their own benefit. Aid agencies come and interfere with us. Tourists stare at us. Politicians crawl round us at election times. (*VT* 54)

The most significant outside interference comes from Hawk Oil Company, whose representatives we first meet in the bar of the colonial club and who are soon after linked to the predatory anthropologist Wormoal who tells Rosa, '"[i]nformation is the new gold. . . . My knowledge of the Indians is a way of owning them—I admit it. We fight over the intellectual territory. But it's better than stealing their land, isn't it?"' (*VT* 80). Straight away we are reminded that the land theft, too, continues: 'As she stood up to go, a sparkling new Land Rover, with the words

"Hawk Oil" on the side, swung into the yard. Five burly, weather-beaten white men, all wearing baseball caps, got out' (80).

The Hawk Oil men who 'having been granted a two-million-acre concession to look for oil in the Rupununi' (327) are conducting seismic surveys near Chofy's village, dominate the end of the modern tale. Bla-Bla and two friends are walking to the post office, 14 miles away, and try to catch a lift with the oil men's truck, but the passengers only laugh at the boys while the driver calls out '"Walk, buck boys"' (*VT* 319). In a small act of resistance Bla-Bla and his friends set a trap for the men, and cause their truck to crash. The next scene is back in Georgetown where Rosa has taken Chofy to a dinner at the High Commission. The guests are local politicians and businessmen, the American Ambassador, and Hawk Oil executives. The Ambassador threatens the Guyanese finance minister, Olly Sampson: '"I think the IMF will probably refuse you any loan unless elections are supervised and a certain level of productivity guaranteed."' Sampson 'always sat through these dinners in smiling misery, hoping against all the odds that someone would say, "Look old chap, or buddy, or mein Freund, we think we'll just cancel the debt."' (*VT* 324). He dreams of 'turning the whole country into an enormous theme park for tourists. They would re-create their history as a spectacle. People could act being slaves. Ships full of indentured labourers would arrive in the docks' (324), and fantasizes about announcing to the world's rulers Guyana's resignation as a country: 'We are at the mercy of the rich countries. A team of management consultants from the United States could not find the answer, and for not finding the answer, we had to pay them an amount that substantially increased our national debt' (*VT* 325). In reality his reply to the American Ambassador is acquiescent: '"oh, the IMF is designed to keep the rich rich and make the poor even poorer. Last time they insisted we cut the sugar workers' wages. There were massive strikes. The whole economy deteriorated. What to do"' (325). Descriptions of lavish dishes are juxtaposed with the back-and-forth repartee of the diners (including Chofy, who tells a story that makes everyone laugh and counts as 'some sort of social triumph' [327] even though he feels like an imposter), such as the comment by the restaurateur Eric Chang that '"[i]n this country, a change of disaster is always refreshing. In Guyana it is always disaster that comes up trumps"'(328).

While the politicians and businessmen dine and joke, the people of the Rupununi are facing the consequences of the oil concession. The tragic event that dominates the end of the novel, bringing Chofy's relatives to Georgetown and ending his affair with Rosa, is the fatal injury of Bla-Bla in one of the company's explosions. Chofy's relatives go to the Amerindian Hostel, where the conditions are in marked contrast to the luxury of the High Commission: 'The warden opened the door of a hot, concrete cell with disintegrating plaster on the walls. He flashed his torch around the room to let them see what was there. The torchlight sent some cockroaches scurrying for the dark and illuminated two iron-frame beds, a geography of stains on the old mattresses' (340). Hawk Oil provides transport for the bereaved family, but no compensation because they have no insurance policy. Chofy experiences the loss of Bla-Bla as an accusation 'of abandoning his family, deserting his son, of not being able to keep the land safe for his children. With shock, he felt that he had lost not only a child but a whole continent' (345).

Lacking any concrete political alternative, each novel nonetheless struggles to articulate both the need for and possibility of such an alternative. One of the ways these contradictory pulls emerge is in the recurring trope of reality and illusion that is visible in different forms in each text. Running throughout *Ventriloquists Tale* is the idea, first explained to McKinnon by his Wapisiana father-in-law, 'that there was no point in trying to do anything about everyday life. It was an illusion behind which lay the unchanging reality of dream and myth' (99). This, and the related concept expressed by Beatrice in the rain forest as she contemplates the trees' reflections in the water, 'that it seemed impossible to know which was the real world' (144), is repeated many times, and is seemingly confirmed by the correspondence between myth and dream and the events taking place in the central narratives. In *Frangipani House* a version of this philosophy emerges from the ghosts Mama King converses with, who also represent lost hope and dreams; in *Buxton Spice* in the trees who converse with Lula, manifestations of the 'horrible dark-road secrets' lying behind her lived reality (*BS* 30). In *Whole of a Morning Sky* both Gem and Dinah experience 'a quality of unreality' after the outbreak of racial violence, and in *Last English Plantation* when Mariam is killed in a confrontation between the cane workers and the British troops June felt that '[i]t was too much like a dream' (*LP* 142). In *Timepiece* the trope is explicitly applied to Guyana's illusory independence: Georgetown 'was a place where people fought over and were driven by a power that they thought resided there. But it was a symbolic power, a power no-one here in Guiana really owned. . . . in Georgetown, the people were wholly enmeshed in the culture and values of those who had bequeathed them the symbolic power over which they fought' (*TP* 160). Even as the narratives turn on this negative equation—that reality is worse than the illusory surface suggests—they also offer positive alternate realities: a sexuality free from violence and the will to conquer; interaction between humans and land not based on exploitation; the possibility of different ethnicities and races living together in harmony. But the prospect of such a world not defined by oppression, power, and money is as yet only available as a dream.

Notes

1   Guyanese writer and contemporary of Harris Jan Carew emphasizes the significance of this location: 'One of the things is that, being from Guyana, we are in Latin America. The Latin American imagination feeds on exile without losing its kind of creative force. But in the English-speaking Caribbean, authors do not have the same umbilical binding to roots that the Latin American authors have' (*Frontiers of Caribbean English in Literature* Birbalsingh 50).

2   In 1966 two foreign-owned estates monopolized 90 per cent of sugar production. Rice had become an important export crop, mostly to the Caribbean. Bauxite production was

controlled by the Canadian Alcan and U.S. American Reynolds corporations (*The Poor and the Powerless* Thomas 251).

3   In a 1990 interview David Dabydeen notes the related disintegration of the education system: 'What saddens me is that under this PNC Government that we have had for so long, although we had the reputation of being the intellectuals and writers of the Caribbean, we Guyanese are now statistically at the very bottom of the examination leagues in the Caribbean' (Birbalsingh, *Frontiers* 169).

4   Spinner cites annual emigration figures of 5000 to 7000 people—mostly middle class Indo-Guyanese—in this period (142); by 1978 the figure reached 13,000. This in a country with a total population at that time of around 800,000 (Spinner xi; *Stains on My Name* Williams 33). Premdas, taking an overview of the impact of the crisis and Burnham regime refers to 'the mass migration of a third of the population overseas' (138).

5   Kyk-over-al is believed to be Guyana's first permanent European settlement, established in 1616 at the intersection between the Essequibo, Cuyuni and Mazaruni rivers (Manley 2). Early in Mittelhölzer's *Children of Kaywana* the colonial trader August Vyfuis explains to the half-English/half-Indian woman Kaywana the origins of the name: 'an island called Kyk-over-al . . . It lies in the river. They call it Kyk-over-al—see over all—because it commands a view of all the three great rivers—the Essequibo, the Cuyuni and the Mazaruni. The Portuguese discovered it a long time ago and built a fort there' (3).

6   He also argues that postcolonial uses of these tropes may 'suggest the inter-penetration of text and landscape as a means of subverting the confining "realistic biases" of creative writing in Guyana and the Caribbean' (82). This resonates with the ideological categorization of generic literary form—and specifically the idea that non-realist literature is subversive or anti-colonial—that is commonplace in criticism of Caribbean women's literature.

7   Jan Carew tells Birbalsingh that Mittelhölzer was expelled from Berbice High School for 'kicking a white (English) master at the school . . . (who) had made an insulting remark about the natives' (43). Such biographical details certainly throw into question a simplistic reading of his fiction as unambiguously pro-imperialist.

8   Even while half of British Guiana's population was non-Christian, 95 per cent of the schools were run by Christian denominations (Spinner 39). Berbice High School was established by the Canadian Presbyterian Mission; Port Mourant, Cheddi Jagan's school, was established by the Anglican church. Queens College, the 'outstanding secondary school' was the main government secondary school for boys in Georgetown, akin to Jamaica's Jamaica College (Spinner 18; *Frontiers of Caribbean English in Literature* Birbalsingh 13n9). Secularization of the schools was one of Jagan's platforms (Spinner 80).

9   Sometimes political events emerge through allegory, and sometimes through direct literary reconstruction. For example, Harris depicts the important 1948 sugar strike at Enmore in his *Genesis of the Clowns*. See Gilkes, *The West Indian Novel* (154).

10 This is not a common move in discussions of the women writers considered here. In her reading of Shinebourne's novels, for example, Veronique Bragard spends only a few sentences on the specific historical subject of the fiction—the political movements of the 1950s and their decimation in the 1960s—referring to the *Encyclopedia Britannica* as the single source. The contextual framework therefore leaves unexamined the central

myths of imperialist accounts of the period: that the communist leanings of Jagan's government forced the British to intervene and that 'ethnic rivalries' split the PPP.

11 Premdas, citing Sheehan (1967) and Pearson (1964) writes 'ample evidence was assembled by the *New York Times* and the *Washington Post* to show that the strikes in Guyana against the PPP were sponsored by the CIA' (107). Spinner quotes former CIA agent Philip Agee writing in 1964: 'Burnham's victory was "largely due to CIA operations over the past five years to strengthen the anti-Jagan trade unions, principally through the Public Services International which provided the cover for financing public employee strikes"' (116). See also *Stains on My Name*, Williams (185) on the role of the CIA in consolidating racial divisions, and Manley (7 and 57) on CIA manipulation of Guyanese labor unions and responsibility for the overthrow of Jagan's government.

12 See Rhoda Reddock's 'Feminism, Nationalism, and the Early Women's Movement' for a discussion of pan-Caribbean women's organization, including that of British Guiana.

13 While beyond the scope of this study, the geopolitics of publishing houses are worthy of consideration in any assessment of the greater visibility of Caribbean women writers. It is significant that many of these writers were first published by feminist presses—The Women's Press, Virago—as well as by international publishers of Caribbean literature such as Peepal Tree and Heinemann.

14 Webb here significantly uses the trope of history as nightmare that is so central to Danticat's *Dew Breaker* and before her Joyce and Marx, as discussed in Chapter One.

15 Hoving questions 'the assumption that the theoretical understanding of language and identity as always hybrid and plural is incompatible with straightforward political agency' and asserts that 'it is often important to differentiate between the practices of theorizing and those of political action, and to acknowledge the strategic force of clear, unambiguous and even essentialist statements.' Hoving's proposal is 'to deconstruct the Eurocentric dichotomy of theory/political action' (25).

16 Sometimes the characters are (in Marxist terms) petty bourgeois, in professional or managerial positions, or small business owners. At other times they are employed in working-class occupations, such as clerical or educational vocations, that bring more security and better wages than most waged jobs. In the latter case the characters sometimes identify with other workers, especially at times of strikes and protests, and at other times identify upwards with their employers.

17 Brackette Williams provides a useful overview: the 'house design is uniform. Houses are square or rectangular structures elevated on five- to seven-foot piles. Although the use of cinderblocks has increased recently, most houses are constructed of wood. . . . The interior of the house is divided into a living room and one or more bedrooms. . . . most have a detached kitchen shed or a kitchen area under the house. The latter (bottom-house) may be enclosed or left open when it is used as a kitchen. The typical roof is an inverted V. . . . Houses generally have two entrances—one at the front and another at the rear or side—with several steps leading up to them' (85). He goes on to analyze the extent to which houses express social status and class position (85–90).

18 The scene ends with 'the strong smell of greenheart,' again returning us to the specific physical environment of Guyana.

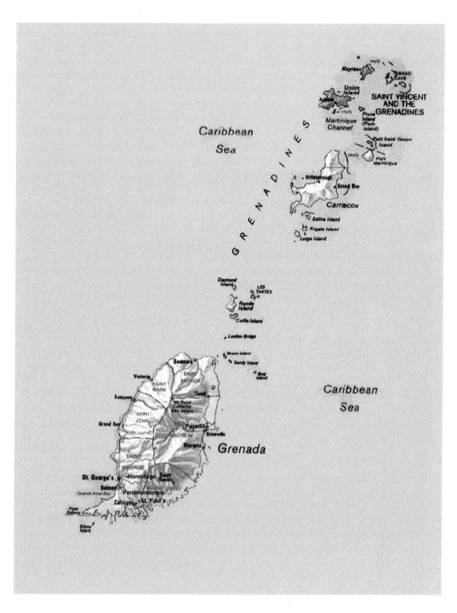

Figure 4   Map of Grenada

Chapter 4

The Spice Isle

Of all the fiction considered so far, Merle Collins's 1987 novel *Angel* most explicitly engages with the broad social forces identified in Chapter One, even while it departs most dramatically from the critical generalizations about Caribbean women writers' divergence from their literary predecessors. Merle Collins's experiences resemble those of the politically engaged writers of the earlier period more than most of her generation: she was a teacher who became an active participant in the political environment surrounding the New Jewel Movement, was a member of Grenada's National Women's Organization until 1983, and remained part of African Dawn, a group that fused performance poetry, African music, and radical politics, after she settled in England. The political movement in Grenada in the 1970s differed from the earlier period of national liberation in that it opposed not British colonialism but a corrupt postindependence regime, and because of this, class demands were fore fronted even while the language of national autonomy and economic development was prevalent. At the same time it resembled the era of national liberation elsewhere in the West Indies in that it forged middle class and working class alliances within a mass political movement, bringing writers and other artists in to the political realm. Women's rights were formally extended under Bishop's government and 'the self-conscious activism of women themselves . . . began to transform gender relations' (Marable 238–9).

Angel thus more closely resembles Fanon's 'literature of combat' than works by many other contemporaneous Caribbean women writers; its atypicality is evident in Belinda Edmondson's identification of it as 'the possible exception' when she describes Michelle Cliff's *No Telephone to Heaven* as 'perhaps the only female-authored West Indian narrative . . . that explicitly thematizes revolutionary political action through a female protagonist' (*Making Men* 126). Collins's depiction of Grenada's transition from colonialism to independence repeats the pattern anticipated by Fanon, as the new national bourgeoisie (under Eric Gairy's government) assumed the mantel of colonizer. A character says of Gairy late in the novel, '"way you ever hear leader of country lootin? He dat suppose to protec people dey, senin he people an dem to beat up people"' (226). This comment resonates both with Kincaid's *A Small Place* and McTair's 'Politics Kaiso:' 'Dey who was to save de nation/From foreign ministration . . . /Send for foreign ammunition/An automatic weapon/To show de Hooligan population/And children of de nation—just who/Is de Massa now.' *Angel* reconstructs a precise chronology of Grenada's history from 1951 to 1983, charting a people's extended struggle for self-determination, first, and successfully, against British colonialism, then again with success against the postindependence domestic regime, and finally, vainly, against neoliberal globalization.

Some of the explanation for the exceptionalism of Collins's novel lies in Grenada's particular socioeconomic trajectory: for various reasons the consolidation of an established middle class and an organized working class was delayed until after World War Two.[1] One of the consequences was a relatively underdeveloped literary tradition: Grenada has nothing equivalent to Guyana's early mid twentieth century cultural proliferation. *Angel* is very much a national novel, nonetheless, drawing on the oral folk tradition and cultural forms developed during the People's Revolutionary Government in order to tell a very specific tale. In her essays 'Grenada—Ten Years and More: Memory and Collective Responsibility' and 'Writing Fiction, Writing Reality' Merle Collins explains that she wrote *Angel* in an attempt to provide a historical record from the perspective of ordinary Grenadians:

> [*Angel* is] fiction drawing heavily on the reality of my existence, of the existence of those around me, reconstructing stories around images from the Grenada of the 1950s onwards. Using broad details rooted in lived experience, it dramatizes particular facets of existence, in an effort to understand, dynamically, how events in Grenada during the neo-colonial and post-independence period could have led to the 1980s and beyond. It focuses on the lives of people not in the headlines. ('Writing' 25)

The relationship between falsification of historical record and documentation of a community's experience generates one of the defining tropes of *Angel*, echoing the Guyanese fiction. Many of the proverbs that serve as section headings within chapters, and suggest particular readings of narrative events, pertain to the general notion of appearances belying reality: 'Not all skin-teet is good grin!' (8); 'Take win but you lose' (18); 'Not all wag-tail is promise not to bite' (19); 'Something boilin under de surface!' (245). Historical investigation, the novel tells us, is both possible and urgent. The novel also understands gender and racial oppression through the lens of class and vice versa: as men and women collectively organize around economic demands, they must challenge the prejudices and divisions they inherit from the past. The novel probes the rise and fall of the People's Revolutionary Government and the subsequent U.S. invasion, suggesting that the New Jewel Movement (fictionalized as 'Horizon') represented an incomplete break with a paternalistic paradigm of national 'revolution from above,' and that Grenada's location within the global capitalist system guaranteed the failure of this approach.

Angel is remarkable in its attempt to become what Helen Maria Lima calls 'the "collective novel" that Glissant almost believed could not be written' (n9 54). As it struggles to express the uncharted territory of revolutionary consciousness, it is formally innovative, and combines established literary modes in fresh ways. It makes broad and varied use of dialogue, most of it in the demotic, moving freely between Creole and Standard English, and although the narrative always uses the latter, Creole is the dominant voice.[2] As Isabel Hoving discusses in depth, the novel also makes extensive use of the epistolary form, and the letters are as likely to be in Creole as Standard English. Although named for the central character whose life we follow from babyhood through adulthood,[3] *Angel* is primarily a collective tale rather than a conventional *bildungsroman*.[4] Initially the novel is focused on Doodsie, Angel's mother, and the daughter only becomes central in the second third of the book; frequently important events are described from the perspective of minor characters or through the voice of a non-specific participant. The novel is an attempt to tell a collective tale, to reconstruct imaginatively a history from below; as Patrick Taylor writes, Collins 'dares to use narrative form to encode revolutionary experience, its tragic destruction, and its ever present possibilities' (14). While this produces exciting and compelling results, it also inevitably comes up against the contradictions of such a project: the gap between the author and her subjects and the subsequent problematic of middle class representation of the subaltern; the limitations of the novel form; the tension between political and artistic compulsions. My primary focus here is on *how* the novel tells three decades of Grenada's history through the imagined experiences of poor and working class women and men, and particularly how it speaks to the relationship between national and global forces; but I will return to these formal and aesthetic questions, which also have bearing on the broader concerns of this book.

'We can't all be the same in this worl. It mus have high and low' (*Angel* 28)

Grenada's history is punctuated by explosions of rebellion. Because of its location, Amerindians from the south settled early; aboriginal resistance, assisted by the island's mountainous topography, held European colonization at bay for longer than most of the region after Columbus' 'discovery' of 'Concepción' in 1498 (Steele 5; Sinclair 14).[5] The Kalinago, or Caribs, fought off the Spanish, French, and English for more than 150 years, and 'left more of a stamp on everyday Caribbean living than is traditionally presented' (Steele 46), before their decisive conquest in the massacre of 1654. Amerindian resistance is embodied by the legendary story of Caribs who in 1651 leapt to their death from the Northern bluff known to this day as 'Le Morne des Sauteurs'—Leapers' Hill—when stranded by armed French forces. Britain and France proceeded to fight each other for control of Grenada throughout the seventeenth and eighteenth centuries, Britain's superior military might being the final arbiter of the dispute. French language and culture are apparent today in the French Creole still spoken by some of the older generation, and the predominance of Catholicism.[6] In the 1790s a colored planter, Julien Fédon, led a rebellion against slavery, inspired by the French and Haitian revolutions, that persisted for well over a year before defeat by Britain and Spain.[7] In 1848, agricultural workers rose up en masse against the plantocracy.

As was typical of the region, Grenada as a sugar producing slave economy was 'an immensely valuable acquisition for Britain' at the height of the sugar trade (O'Shaughnessy 31). After emancipation, Grenada's extant system of slaves working their own plots of land in addition to laboring on the plantations was extended as planters sold off parcels of land (usually the least productive) to former slaves or 'allowed' them to remain as payment for agricultural labor. To a large extent the plantation economy was thus replaced by a sharecropping structure of small holders—former slaves and later indentured laborers from Malta, Madeira and India—who produced sugar, cocoa, nutmeg, and other spices (earning Grenada the title 'isle of spice') in the estates. The system known as 'metayage' was widespread: the individual laborer, or metayer, would be provided with tools and land in exchange for a share of the harvest. Grenada became a 'Crown Colony' in the second half of the nineteenth century, ruled directly from London (Brizan 133; O'Shaughnessy 33) and by the twentieth century was 'a semifeudal economy in which the merchants, the estate owners, and the middle-class civil servants ruled the inarticulate peasant and worker with an iron hand' (Lewis 8), and 'a dependent British colonial society, suffering from all of the ravages of colonialism' (Lewis 9). Even as more laborers were paid with currency, their wages were 'linked perilously to the world market prices of the export crops' (Searle 7) as the predominantly white absentee landlords sold the three main cash crops—bananas, nutmegs, and cocoa—and 'were allowed to siphon off almost all of the profits from agricultural exports . . . paying the workers just enough to keep body and soul together' (Steele 330).

Throughout *Angel* the estates, and the price of cocoa and other crops, dominate the lives of Grenadians, and possession of land is a necessity for survival in times of hardship. Two of the central characters, Angel's parents Doodsie and Allan, move from estate to estate—Lisle, Dunfermline, Delicia—wherever they can secure paid work. When unemployment is high they depend on their inherited land: early on Doodsie is thankful for the 'little piece her mother had given her, part of the family plot' (9). When Allan is away Doodsie 'went down by Tan Sase, Allan's mother, and got some things off the acre of land there. Thank God, she thought. Thank the Lord for the little piece o land and for the strength ah have so that ah could still plant the two grain o peas and corn, else ah don know how ah would make out' (49). This was a highly paternalistic system, and the ideology of patriarchal protection and provision, suffused with Christian forbearance, impeded organized opposition to its obvious injustices. One Grenadian historian describes it thus: 'Life for the rural peasant was wretched, but life was lived with a fatalism that provided no room for discontent or political action' (Steele 286). *Angel* conveys these circumstances early in the novel through a dialogue between Doodsie and her Cousin Maymay. The latter is expressing frustration and rage against the injustices inherent to the estate system:

'Well look non, ah pickin up nutmeg for the whole week, and at the end of it ah could barely manage to buy de poun o saltfish, you know! Ay! Is so we have to work out we soul case all the time never to have nutting! Ay! . . . Then after you work you piece of ground, put all you labour in it, when the cocoa they ask you to plant in between well in its growth now, they takin away the piece of land from you and give you a new piece to do the same thing. . . . five to six years later, when cocoa in that first piece of ground you work in in full bearing, you harvesting it for the boss for one shilling an sixpence a day' (11)

Doodsie at this point personifies the 'fatalism' identified by Steele when she answers Maymay: "'Is the same story all over. Is vyé nèg on the ground an bakra béké on top. We always startin, always in the beginning. . . . Bad how it is, this is the corner that is ours, so we just have to make the best of it until. . . . Is not you always tellin me to have faith?'" (11).[8]

Mass resistance challenged passivity and indeed the entire system of patronage in the strikes and organized arson known as Sky Red that swept the estates in February 1951, and can be seen as a delayed manifestation of the social upheavals elsewhere in the region in the 1930s.[9] Employers had responded to a fall in the world price of cocoa by cutting wages and evicting workers who had long been 'squatting' on estate land (Marable 201; Searle 7). This is where the novel opens, and we are thrown into the action, as an estate burning is reported in a nonspecific narrative voice that seems to be that of a participant, with brief, quick sentences conveying immediacy and confusion: 'The yard in front of Paren Comesee's house was full of restless silence. Quick whispers, staring faces, the sound of an occasional "Sh-h-h-h!" Some people stood on straining tiptoe to see better. Eyes wide open, staring. Eyes narrowed, peering. Mouths half-open' (1). The first named individuals—Paren Comesee, Maisie, Joyce, Mano—are not significant characters in the rest of the novel; their presence reminds us that this is a story not only of one family, but of an entire population, made up of many personal histories. The novel further encourages the reader to experience events as a participant by focusing on sensory details:

> Feet shuffled. People brushed away the sandflies. You could hear the slap! slap! against face, feet, the quick brush against skirts. Toes scratched impatiently against shins; air was whistled in through teeth. People stamped their feet to send the flies away. They were so tiny and quick that they were gone by the time you felt the sting. (1)

This attention to the minutiae of noise, sensation, and atmosphere—in short, staccato, sentences—recurs throughout.

One beneficiary of Sky Red was Eric Gairy, represented in *Angel* as Leader, who began his political career as a union militant while working in the Aruba oil refineries in the world war two boom, and later 'presented himself as the popular champion against the white oligarchy and the brown middle class' (*The Jewel Despoiled* Lewis 11). Gairy's future role is discernible even at the height of his popularity as a labor leader: The colonial authorities detained him in Carriacou but later released him in return for his promise to reign in the protests and ensure peace. He then 'addressed several public meetings, calling for a cessation of hostile actions by the workers, and setting out a plan of action whereby the ills in the society were to be eradicated' (Steele 354). Beverley Steele describes Gairy's persona: 'He took to himself the role of commander, the President-General for life. And he always dressed the part, sometimes in top hat and tails, sometimes in the regalia of a general, sometimes in pure white. The Grenadian worker loved it. They created anthems and set them to the tunes of rousing marches to sing in his support' (357–8).

Gairy's paternalistic attitude to the working class is comparable to that of the planters and colonial government, yet he retained popular support through independence in 1974 because he symbolically stood for the landless black worker against the mostly white landowners even as he actually 'represented a thin stratum of black businessmen who gradually came into their own as Gairyism strengthened its hold on the state and economy' (Meeks 139). Gairy was the first public figure to echo the sentiments expressed by one of the characters in *Angel*, Doodsie's brother Regal: '"People like you an me so, the harder we work in people kitchen and in people lan, the more we kill weself out and bring riches, is the poorer we get while we sweat going in other people pocket. How much time you see Mr De Lisle down workin in de estate?"' (28). Leader initiates a union for estate workers and leads a strike against pay cuts, winning the support of many like Regal through securing compensation for sacked workers and fighting for better conditions and civil rights. One such speech is dramatized in *Angel*:

> 'My dear people,' he explained to the meeting . . . 'You should go back to work. Victory is ours. They had to give in. Wages will be wages whatever the price of cocoa. Victory is ours. You will get a fifty percent increase in wages. Not as much as we wanted, but one step at a time. Victory is ours! . . .
> If we find in the future that we have to fight again, we shall not hesitate to do it, but for now, from tomorrow, Tuesday, everybody is going back to work.'
> Murmurs
> 'Ah fine we shoulda hol out still an make dem leggo who dey arres!'
> 'Yes. Dat good. We fight it an we win!' . . .
> 'Well meself ah not so sure . . . '
> Leader held up his white cane, the gold of his ring glinting in the sunshine. Faces turned toward him.
> 'I have promised the governor that this violence will stop. We have been given a satisfactory solution now, so let us go back to work . . . We fought for a cause. We won! We know when it is time to stop. We show them who is boss!' (32–3)

Even as it portrays the anticolonial movement's successes, the novel anticipates and then depicts Leader's transformation from union activist to powerful head of a repressive, militarized regime that crushed workers' rights and protected the wealthy; the workers are not an undifferentiated mass uniformly accepting Leader's rule, rather we are shown debates and divisions within the community regarding how much he should be trusted. Doodsie suspects Leader's motives before most other characters, remembering his 'pappyshow' wedding in Aruba to 'that airess from the big family home' (15–17), and his penchant for socializing with the bosses. She thus sees through his populist rhetoric and identifies 'his new alliance with medium and large businessmen and various transnational Caribbean firms' (*Grenada* Searle 9).

Gairy's reputation could not indefinitely withstand the increasingly blatant corruption and brutality of his regime, and opposition forces coalesced around the New Jewel Movement (NJM).[10] The leadership of this 'multigroup united front' of disparate interests were beneficiaries of the expansion of secondary and higher education in the decades following World War Two that 'produced a body of educated young people predisposed to question the erratic irresponsibility of Gairyite behavior' (*The Jewel Despoiled* Lewis 18).[11] When Maurice Bishop, Bernard Coard, Kendrick Radix and other major figures of NJM 'returned from the United States and Britain, they came with new ideas influenced by a cumulative and available ideological context of the late sixties' but they were also 'occupants of high positions in the society, enhanced significantly by their travel and study abroad' (Meeks 143). Politically they were influenced by Trinidad's black power movement, African socialism, and C.L.R. James' trotskyism. Their platform 'concerned itself, in the main, with particular problems of housing, health, food, and education. It urged a program of land redistribution based on a scheme of cooperative farms, free education up to the secondary-school level, a national health plan, the nationalization of the banking and insurance sectors of the economy' (Lewis 19). Opposition was consolidated in the face of Gairy's growing unpopularity and his suppression of dissent. In 1970 nurses demonstrated with their supporters and were set on by Gairy's infamous 'Mongoose Gang'—an informal network of armed thugs akin to Haiti's Tonton Macoutes and satirized in *Angel* as the 'Rabies Gang.' By 1974 mass protests exploded into a 'revolutionary upsurge' (Meeks 142). Gairy again used his armed gangs to break up the protests, but by this time even business owners had turned against him, and on March 13, 1979 his regime was toppled and replaced by the NJM's People's Revolutionary Government (PRG).

The New Jewel Movement is represented in *Angel* as Horizon, its popular leader Maurice Bishop as Chief. The revolutionary upsurge of 1974 is joyfully depicted:

> The people walked four abreast, some ten thousand of them, a tenth of the island's population, singing, shouting, clapping, drumming
> . . .
> Singing the song of the carnival bands Leader had banned from the streets the year before, the bands in which people covered themselves completely in black grease and paint, clattered through the streets with cans, pans, horns, celebrating like their African ancestors had celebrated emancipation . . . From the windows and balconies, people looked down past the raised clenched fists on to plaits, curls, hats, moving bodies. (211–13)

The picture is of broad popular support for the revolutionary government. In a section of the novel that captures something of the excitement of the moment, Angel describes events to her brother Simon in America in a letter:

You ever see that! Revolution directed by radio! Tout moun out in the streets, Simon! Was like carnival. If people didn want that change, eh, nutting coulda happen, because is people dat go out and get dose police to put up white flag an ting! You should see Melda! Remember Melda dat uses to work under Delicia cocoa! You should see Melda leadin a side! Simon, was something else! Mammie all right. When I went up by her, she was actually crying real tears and saying, 'We win! We win!' Boy she something else you know.   (232–3)

The victory of Horizon is celebrated, and seen as the continuation of the movement against the white landowners of British colonial rule.

Collins's account inserts itself into a battleground of ideological distortions. Geoffrey Wagner's right-wing *Red Calypso* epitomizes the cold-war anti-Communist version: 'Grenada's first Marxists . . . drunk with dogma from their holy books, Marx a new testament for a zombie priesthood ministering to an inexistent entity called "the masses"' (57). Wagner depicts Grenada's majority as passive, stupid, perhaps initially duped into supporting the PRG but quickly disillusioned. All this is accompanied by a hefty dose of old-style colonial racism: University of the West Indies is 'wild and woolly' (51); 'West Indians have five-minute attention spans' (54); George Lamming is 'an indifferent novelist who looks like a Bajan bear after having lost a tussle with a lawn-mower' (121). Grenadian historian Beverley Steele portrays the PRG as an antidemocratic regime that garnered short-term support for its popular reforms, but quickly resorted to repression and indoctrination once economic crisis intervened. And at the other extreme Chris Searle uncritically celebrates the NJM leadership as committed visionaries able to channel mass opposition to Gairy and turn it in to 'the first revolution in the English-speaking Caribbean' (*Grenada* 32). *Angel's* version confirms O'Shaughnessy's testimony that 'the whole of the island was coming out into the streets to celebrate' (79) and that the immediate celebration was sustained as the PRG not only dismantled the Mongoose Gang but also implemented a series of reforms and projects, including free milk for children, better health care, new jobs, improvements to the social infrastructure, equal pay for women, that were beneficial to the workers and poor.

While initially able to pass reforms and maintain a stable economy, by 1982 financial and political pressures bore down on the government. Finance Minister Bernard Coard consolidated a faction opposed to the Prime Minister Maurice Bishop, and placed him and his closest supporters under house arrest, only to be foiled by a mass protest that forced the release of the still popular figurehead of revolution. The Coard faction sent armed soldiers to disperse the crowd, and, shockingly, murdered Bishop and his allies. The central division between Bishop and Coard is often characterized as one between democratic socialism and Leninism, but there is much to indicate that the fight was not waged on these or indeed any other political divisions, but rather was the result of both subjective contradictions and objective pressures: Brian Meeks argues that the loose structure and top-down method of NJM and PRG, and the inclusion within both of

conflicting interests—business owners, unions, reformists, Trotskyists, Stalinists—made the ensuing fissures almost inevitable. Marable similarly characterizes the NJM as 'essentially an eclectic social movement of national democratic, liberal and progressive forces . . . [that] attracted individuals who shared a common antipathy toward the Gairy regime, but disagreed over other political issues' (210), and explains the PRG's degeneration in terms of these inherited contradictions as well as new ones stemming from the 'general policy of a "strategic alliance" between the national bourgeoisie, middle strata, workers and farmers' (233). Basch et al point to the structural contradictions that precipitated crisis:

> [I]n the context of Grenada's sparse resource base, the NJM continued to rely on aid from the International Monetary Fund (IMF), the World Bank, and the Caribbean Development Bank (CDB). It allowed the bourgeoisie to retain many of its privileges and sought investments from private investors and tourism operators in the United States. At the same time, the Bishop government was developing strategies to empower the working and peasant classes, whose interests cut across those of the dominant strata. (70)

These contradictions, combined with a weakening economy, caused the government to implode as factions blamed each other for the problems and proposed incompatible solutions. Critically, the PRG's national strategy was unable to combat global geopolitical and socioeconomic forces. While the novel does not explicitly identify this problem, it can be seen nonetheless in the novel's structure and particularly its unsettled ending (I will return to these matters).

These devastating events then provided the pretext for a U.S. invasion. While Wagner and Steele deny prior antagonism, many others have documented that '[t]he attitude of Washington toward the PRG was overtly hostile from the beginning' (Marable 240).[12] In a military action officially named 'Operation Urgent Fury' and nicknamed 'the sledgehammer and the nutmeg,' in October 1983 U.S. forces led a 'multinational invasion' of the island, removed the government, replaced it with an interim administration under the British Commonwealth's Governor General, then forged, funded, and ran a right-wing coalition party that won elections the following year. Radio Free Grenada was replaced with American controlled Spice Island Radio, and media representatives were carefully vetted and guarded (O'Shaughnessy 205). The U.S. government removed 'filing cabinets filled with microfiches of documents' from Grenada, declaring them 'the property of the Government of the United States' (Collins 'Ten Years' 74).

'Operation Urgent Fury' was not accompanied by a formal declaration of war and violated many aspects of international law.[13] The outcome of the battle was predetermined by sheer scale: the defending forces were outnumbered ten to one and had none of the air support and heavy weapons of the invading army. The catalyst for the invasion was the assassination of Maurice Bishop, but the official rationales were fourfold: to rescue American medical students and protect innocent Grenadians; to restore order and democracy; to satisfy a request for military assistance from members of the Organization of Eastern Caribbean States (OECS); and to rescue Grenada from Cuba and the Soviet Union. Although these official justifications were subsequently discredited, at the time they garnered crucial support from much of the American public.[14]   Jeff McMahan, among others, argues that the invasion of Grenada thus struck a blow at the Vietnam Syndrome—public hostility to American involvement in foreign conflicts—and established a precedent for 'legitimate' American military intervention in the region. Small and economically insignificant though Grenada may seem, economic interests in the broader sense were far from irrelevant. Then president Reagan declared, somewhat disingenuously, that "'50 percent of everything we import comes through the Caribbean, the Panama Canal. . . . It is vital to us that democracy be allowed to succeed in these countries'" (qtd. in McMahan 23). While much was made of regional support for the invasion, less was said of the considerable regional opposition, from regimes friendly and hostile to the PRG.

Angel, through structure as well as plot, dramatizes the invasion as the final, military, stage of protracted foreign opposition to Bishop's government, and as the termination of a 30-year struggle by ordinary Grenadians for liberation. In the process, the novel offers an explanation of how social institutions mitigate against social change, but also how consciousness can expand exponentially in the course of political struggle. The novel keeps open the possibility for revolutionary transformation, even as it traces the degeneration of the most recent attempt, precipitated by internal weaknesses and external opposition. The central tension of the work stems from the push and pull between, on the one hand, its secure location within the politics of 'Horizon,' and, on the other, its nascent critique of a *national* strategy of liberation in the context of a *globalized* economy and imperialist hostility.

Christ is the Head of this House

One of the ways *Angel* signals the historical continuity between different forms of paternalistic control over the three-decade period is through its exploration of religious ideology, the dominance of which is emblematized by the 'outline of the map of Grenada framed in mahogany' hanging beside 'the glass-covered words proclaiming Christ the Head of the House' on the wall of Doodsie's house (123). The established churches perpetuate colonial ideology, inhibit political struggle, and naturalize inequality. The idea of 'faith' functions as a tranquilizer, encourages acceptance of the way things are, and postpones justice until the afterlife. Doodsie's mother, Ma Ettie, while at times providing wisdom and support, is also a conduit for this pious resignation: When Regal is ignited by Leader's movement against the landowning exploiting class, Ma Ettie counsels acceptance of the status quo, first defending the rights of planters like De Lisle and then attributing wealth and poverty to divine purpose (28). Doodsie also initially expresses the idea that mortals can but pray for divine guidance or intervention.

At the same time, Doodsie and others mistrust clerical institutions, while the gap between different organized religions—predominantly Catholicism and Anglicanism—draws attention to their contradictory teachings. Doodsie battles with Allan's Catholic priest over their daughter's name—she insists on 'Angel' against his proposal of a Saint's name—and godmother (18–19). The racism of established religions is also exposed and criticized by Doodsie and others. This emerges in particular around recurrent discussions of and references to the question of whether angels can be black or white, and also whether those who may appear to be angels may really be devils, and vice versa. When their friend Martin visits Allan and Doodsie from St Lucia he remarks on how dark skinned Angel has become, and how she takes after her father. He adds: 'One thing, though. She name did suit her better when she was a baby' (60), and a debate ensues, typical of the novel's use of extensive dialogue to work through the implications of particular issues. Eventually Martin concedes the point to Doodsie that there may be black angels, but quips that if Angel makes it to heaven 'she go well lonely up there wid all dem white people God have roun im' and asks 'when Angel reach in heaven wid all those white people, what she go do? Domestic?' (61). The humor of Martin's position is in the picture he paints of a heaven that looks a lot like the Estate. Doodsie wants to believe that Christianity is egalitarian, but her anger is stirred by the knowledge that the church displays all of the prejudices and exclusions of the secular world.

When confronted with the dogma of the convent school Angel starts attending, Doodsie maintains a critical distance and tries to challenge her daughter's indoctrination in racist and sexist values that undermine her sense of self. Fellow students (richer and paler) and the nuns tell Angel that she is too black to play an angel in the school play, that she should straighten her hair, and that her mother is living in sin with Allan (113). Doodsie responds with little patience for this moralism and expresses a decisive ownership of her own faith and moral compass (108). Her refusal to accept religious dogma echoes that of Regal earlier, who rejects his mother's counsel to accept God's world of rich and poor: "'So you trying to tell me that god siddown wey he siddown an decide I have to be low while Mr De Lisle stay high? Well if dat true, Mammie, I go really have to start to look for a God of me own, because dat one is theirs for sure'" (28).

The battle over the idea of divine will becomes a marker of Angel's developing ability to question the social structures that shape her life. The motto 'Man proposes; God disposes' opens a section of the narrative where Angel, now at university, hears that her friend Ann has died. When she visits the grieving mother Angel looks at the ubiquitous painting of 'Christ in a garden' above the mother's rocking chair (146). Angel finds herself offering platitudes of forbearance that provoke the mother to respond: "'Yes, yes, me chile. Ah know. Man proposes, yeh! But God disposes! What to do?'" (147). Later, when talking with her friend Janice, Angel learns that Ann's doctor gave her scant help when she went to him with worrying symptoms. Janice echoes the phrase used earlier, 'man proposes,' but this time Angel replies "'Ah believe God does kine o propose more in countries wid less medical care an ting'" (147). This same realization is echoed toward the end of the novel, after the invasion and Angel's hospitalization in the U.S.A., when Rupert remarks "'One ting wid de Lord, when you see you put im in countries like dese without facilities, he doesn perform to the bes at all!'" (282).

Angel gradually replaces an idealist vision of the world with a materialist one, and her nascent questioning of unswerving faith to an establishment god becomes tangible. When at her friend Joy's house in rural Jamaica she is struck by the prominence of Christian icons so like those in her own home. Joy's mother, like Ma Ettie before, challenges her younger visitors: "'You children trying to solve the problems of the world in one flash. . . . You young people should have some faith'" (162). On Angel's return home these conflicts rise to the surface, as Doodsie extols the Christian gratitude and humility that Angel now sees as anathema to justice and social change. Angel responds with an angry outburst that reflects her newly developed suspicion of Christian forbearance:

> 'leave me alone! Leave me alone! De pries know what people life like? He know what people sufferin? Everybody goin an give im dey little twopence dey work hard for so heself could live comfortable an tell dem dey go get dey reward in heaven. So help me God if Christ come tomorrow sayin he is king of poor people and talkin revolution, all like you pries so is de firs one to mark he door wid X to make sure dey kill im! What you tellin me bout church?' (173)

Here, as in Danticat's fiction, we are shown two versions of Christianity: one a model akin to liberation theology, conceptualizing a Jesus who represents the poor and oppressed against injustice and inequality; the other serving the status quo and advocating quiescence and resignation for the lower orders. A further connection is made later, when the Horizon movement is starting to challenge Leader, but faces resistance from those who cling to the image of him as their champion. Angel visits Eva, who even after being wrongly imprisoned by Leader's thugs continues to be loyal to him, and starts to understand false consciousness. Doodsie sardonically praises Angel: "'It good to see how in the struggle all you talkin about you understand how people could get fooled an support people who not really workin for them!'" (221), but wishes Angel would extend this understanding to her own father, whose loyalty to Leader has provoked angry encounters between the two. Later Eva's grandchild defends Leader for the wrongful arrest, and Angel makes an important association between Christian paternalism and the family (221). Thus through Angel's developing awareness, we see the correlation between unswerving Christian obedience, the patriarchal family structure, and blind allegiance to political leaders. Collins conveys this not didactically but rather by imaginatively *showing* how these questions impact characters' lives, and how consciousness, fluid rather than static, is shaped by changing circumstances.

'Suffer the children'

Generational shifts—from the ideological acquiescence of Ma Ettie to the activism of Angel and her siblings—are traced throughout, but the novel also explores different kinds and sources of knowledge, at times juxtaposing bankrupt formal education with folk wisdom, at others asserting the importance of schools for fostering independence. Doodsie from the beginning perceives education as a way to achieve upward mobility, guard against a life of manual labor, and pave the way to women's independence from unpaid domestic drudgery and dependence on male wages (101–3). Angel's education is contradictory, however, and while successive achievements allow her to move through to each next stage, she also has to unlearn much of what she was taught at the convent school before she can develop independent critical thought. The first proverbial heading of this chapter, 'suffer the little children,' exposes the complicity of colonial and Christian ideology in the classroom. The barrage, from students, nuns, and racist literature such as that of children's writer Enid Blyton, is for a time too much for Angel, who begins to see herself as inferior and wish she could change her identity:

> At night, sometimes, when Angel sat down to do her homework, she just stared at the maths book, seeing upon its dull pages herself transformed into one of the ladies in some love story, long blonde hair flying in the unruly wind, blue eyes sparkling, laughing up at some dark-haired young man of indeterminate colour. Or sometimes she dreamt that she was in fact really the child of some queen in a distant country, that she had been given a drug to change the colour of her skin so that her kidnappers could keep her hidden. (113)

The scene resembles many depictions of the colonial classroom, such as that in Merle Hodge's *Crick Crack Monkey,* when the protagonist Tee creates a white, English, double, called Helen, or Kincaid's *Annie John* when Annie wishes she was named Enid and daydreams of living in Belgium.

By the time she reaches university, education has become a vital tool for Angel, but like Maurice Bishop and his peers, Angel finds formal education to be a double-edged sword: it is designed to train the elite of the next generation to manage the system; yet it can become a weapon capable of overcoming colonialist ideology.[15] At the University of West Indies in Jamaica, Angel and her fellow students, inspired by the black power and anticolonial movements, initiate the Search project, which takes them into Kingston's poorest neighborhoods. The broader political climate, campus and community activism, and intellectual pursuits produce a heady mix of political and cultural awakening for Angel and her student friends:

> They talked about conditions in hall, about student loans, about the food, about the old women who came to the dining rooms to collect the food they left on their trays while they grumbled about the constant white rice. They talked about living conditions in the

villages around, about lack of student knowledge concerning the surrounding communities. (153–4)

During one of their visits to West Kingston they are playfully reminded of the limits of academic learning when one of their hosts tells them, "'most times oonoo dis a chat chat an na a say much!'" and another adds "'An we know dat oonoo a come, nyam up de ital, reason wid we good good an den move back up a palace fe continue de nice life! Is like ting different for oonoo, see?'" (160).[16] In this way attention is constantly drawn to the tension between higher education as a means of individual class advancement, and the students' aspirations for social equality and justice. Towards the end of her time at university Angel expresses these contradictions in a letter to her friend Janice back home, this time connecting her worries about her own future to the broader social crises she is now alert to: *'If things at home are as confused as I hear they are, am I going to get a job, you think? . . . I get so really angry about all of this poverty all around. It just have to be immoral that some have so much and others could barely drink hot water. And all of this study! And I get so angry when I think about church, and about school and everything'* (166–7). This section also draws attention to the contradictory class location of the leaders of the New Jewel Movement/Horizon.

When they return to Grenada the students, as Doodsie complains to her friend Ezra, are 'vex with the world' (171). Angel's university experiences collide with her mother's expectation that formal education will be her ticket out of a life of drudgery. Yet at the same time Angel finds herself drawing on her mother's knowledge and skepticism. Finding her voice during one late-night discussion about racial and economic oppression Angel surprises herself by echoing her mother when she responds to the comment that "'in the Caribbean we have Black Power'" with, "'it not doing us no damn good . . . Look at Leader'" (157). Doodsie consistently refutes the rhetoric of gender- and class-blind black nationalism, even when those around her, including her spouse Allan, cling to the image of Leader as savior and champion of the black worker. Her brother Regal later admits that she anticipated Leader's betrayal even while most 'take the ting at face value' (193).

The complicated and contradictory nature of Doodsie's consciousness is one of the more persuasive of the book's characterizations. One minute she deftly cuts through the obfuscation of the black ruling class; the next she chastises her daughter for not conforming, or not using her education for self-advancement. She tells Ezra, "'[a]h woulda give the last piece o rag off me back to see dat chile get an education. And de way how she turn out, it hurt me heart'" (170) and "'[t]he chile that come back to me is not the chile that go. She vex, vex with the world. You have to beg her to put on a decent piece of clothes. Is like she see nothing to please her at all'" (171). The uneasy tension between mother and daughter is resolved when both engage in the collective projects of Horizon: 'The rhetoric of Black nationalism gives way to the discourse of revolution as Horizon, which takes control of the state with the full support of the majority of the Grenadian population' (Lima 50).

After the victory of Horizon a different model of education develops. As a teacher, Angel participates in the radical pedagogy that contrasts sharply with her own indoctrination: 'Teaching became more difficult. The students questioned, argued, listened to political speeches and asked all sort of questions about other countries. Angel was in a constant fever of excitement' (236). The new climate pervades all walks of life: 'In the staffroom the battle raged. Some of the teachers said that there was too much politics in the school these days. Angel said that politics was never out of the school, never had been' (238). The milieu is of freely expressed conflict, at work, at home, and at the large public meetings that combine poetry readings with discussion of literacy programs and water policy. In the context of mass participation, for the first time the dominant mood is of confidence, hope and forward momentum, as people rapidly shed old prejudices. This enters in to even the most personal relationships, including those within the nuclear family: 'Allan and Angel talked to each other more now. And now that she talked to him, Angel was strangely surprised to find that he listened, even when he didn't agree. He didn't always accept her views and they sometimes had heated arguments. Still, they continued communicating' (252). In this climate Angel is able to make her father see connections between his exploitation as a worker and women's oppression:

'The thing is, eh, Daddy, you treatin her in a way like how you tell me the boss, Mr. Peter, used to treat you. It even worse in away. She workin on the land too, but she not even gettin paid because is you wife an she have no say in how the money spend. Mr. Peter used to pay you an not consul you an act as if all decision suppose to be his an all the money you make is really his alone. She not even getting paid!' (253)

This environment of fluid individual consciousness amid rapid social change soon gives way to the calamitous degeneration of the government, the American invasion, and the erasure of the newfound mood of popular self-determination.

'How we reach here?' (*Angel* 260)

In *Angel* neither Cuba nor the Soviet Union is a tangible presence: the revolution is understood as indigenous to Grenada. Official American antipathy is not fore-grounded but is certainly part of the common sense of the narrative and is taken for granted by Angel and other characters. As part of the general process of challenging dominant ideology and developing an independent critical consciousness, Angel is skeptical towards cold war anti-Soviet propaganda, but remains undecided about the Soviet system, too. A debate in the staffroom of her school rehearses the arguments raging in the wider society. After some back and forth with co-workers Angel asserts: "'We never even try to find out more about what Russia is, if they policies good, if they bad, or even if we could really make a change and still do things different to them'" (240). In this way the novel inserts itself into the cold war conflict insisting on Grenada's right to an essentially nonaligned independence; later in the novel the U.S. is explicitly figured as an imperialist force antithetical to genuine independence.

The invasion is bitterly contested in heated dialogues between characters, but overall is seen as a new stage of colonial domination and therefore a step backward for Grenadians. Just before the invasion, Angel dreams about sugar plantations and fleeing cane workers trying to communicate with her, associating imminent events with earlier struggles for liberation (271–2). When news comes of the American landing, Allan is grateful, but Angel insists that the Grenadian people must decide their own fate, not the foreign invaders, and again the reference point is slavery: "'Dese same people dat comin to 'save' us now did only too anxious to kill us yesterday! They don like us! They don like Chief! They just trying to control us. But slavery days done!'" (275). When asked what the alternative would look like, Angel responds:

> 'We go make it. We have to figure a way to make it. Is only us black people that does suppose some great white father suppose to come inside we country an put things right, you know. We learn so good how to be inferior, we forget how to be anything else. You tink dem like us better than who here like us? You think they like us better than we like weself? . . . I know. We wrong. But that don make dem right.' (275)

Following the dawn invasion, shaken by the murder of Bishop, and accepting the American claim that the invasion was to avenge his death and defend the people, Jessie and Doodsie both thank god, and Allan waxes nostalgic for Grenada's days as a British Crown Colony. Doodsie challenges him, and the ensuing exchange associates the invasion with the formal colonialism of old (283). Again characteristically using dialogue to explore the broader political questions, the novel places new and old imperialism in the same category as slavery. The shattering of recent expectations is captured figuratively by Allan's inability to see the obscured horizon.

While defending the revolution and condemning the U.S. invasion, *Angel* asks how the immense potential of the former ended in disaster. The novel indirectly illustrates the analysis offered by Manning Marable, that this was not a socialist revolution in the Marxist sense—the self-emancipation of, and seizure of the means of production by, the working class—rather it was a 'revolution from above' that sought to reform rather than replace capitalism. While Grenada in the 1970s was clearly in a revolutionary situation, and the 1974 rehearsal saw a 'popular, broad-based, mass-driven upsurge' (Meeks 143), March 1979 was 'a party-led pre-emptive strike in which the popular forces were at first passive and later entered the fray enthusiastically, but as followers . . . 1979 reinforced an inherited configuration of deeply-entrenched hierarchy and paternalism which was the Achilles' heel of the revolution and the underlying condition of its collapse' (Meeks 144). Although by the middle of the next day 3000 people were assisting, fewer than 50 men carried out the initial dawn action. Bishop explicitly used the language of paternalism to describe the relationship of the PRG to the masses: "'what we did we did in their interest, even though they did not necessarily understand why we were doing what we were doing'" (qtd. in Meeks156). What Jay Mandle called 'paternalistic socialism' thus failed to break with the historical relationship that is critiqued in Collins's novel.

The novel expresses this failure not through argument or symbol, but through structural correspondences. The struggle for self-determination repudiates the model of a powerful leader who acts on the behalf of the people and stymies self-activity. The figure of the saviour takes many forms: the white master of colonial rule; the white god of Christian ideology; the people's champion (Leader); the invading liberators of the U.S. army. Doodsie's skepticism toward Leader is confirmed when he initiates prayer at a rally: "'is like people thinkin he is saviour'" (6). Even after Leader has clearly betrayed the striking workers the people are resigned because they see no alternative: 'All agreed that if it wan for leader, tings never could reach this far. Is a truetrue sayin. When God caan come he does sen' (34). Horizon is meant to constitute a different model, based on mass activity and inclusion rather than passivity and exclusion. The formulation, 'without Leader we are nothing,' gives way to its opposite, 'without the people the leaders are nothing.' Yet the novel makes connections that suggest an incomplete break between the two: When Horizon first coalesces, Doodsie writes in a letter to Ezra, 'for years now was a half dead opposition we have so we been waitin on somebody who would do something to oppose that devil so perhaps the lord send them' (207). The phrase used during the segment on Leader, 'when God caan come he does sen,' is also the title of the section describing the events of March 13, 1979 (228); Bishop's fictional name, 'Chief,' is virtually indistinguishable from Gairy's pseudonym, 'Leader,' and they are both distant figures who never enter the everyday world of the novel. The opening, where major and minor characters gather in Paren Comesee's yard during Sky Red, is also echoed in the later section describing March 1979:

> In Hermitage, a crowd stood in Paren Comesee's yard. Maisie cradled her grandchild, thinking: Dis ting not good at all, non! . . . She watched her son leaning against the mango tree. He was blowing a conch shell. As she watched, he threw back his head and laughed. 'Is better times ahead!' he shouted. 'We slay de dragon wid we bare hands! Mammie girl, it go be better!' The people laughed, shifted their sticks, watching, waiting. They looked from him to Maisie. (231)

Even at this early stage, while the very land itself is celebrating, the novel harbors an uneasy feeling that this is a rerun of previous, incomplete, attempts at liberation.

Angel only provides reported impressions of the faction fights within Horizon that led to the murder of Chief and provided the rationale for the American invasion. An overwhelming sense of confusion pervades the last section of the novel, capturing the disorientation of the historical moment. The tight control of the media and seizure of records during and after the invasion exacerbated this problem, but the gap between leadership and the general population—which is repeatedly signaled in the novel—compounded it. Collins later contends that the leadership increasingly 'ignored the wishes of "the people" who were suddenly treated as an un-informed and unimportant mass' ('Ten Years' 77). The novel dramatizes this through a community meeting where people frustrated with the slow movement of reforms ask when long promised water installations and road repairs will materialize, and a government representative counsels patience:

> we have to be conscious . . . of the fact that a lot is being done in other areas and as de comrade say we not a rich country, so we have to wait a little bit for some things. We gettin free education now, houses gettin fixed, free milk for children an so on, and a lot of money spendin on airport which will bring money into the country. So we ha to take tings bit by bit. (250)

Angel's extended family furiously debates the state of the Party: Doodsie and Melda join the mass protest for the release of Chief; before and after Bishop is killed Angel and Rupert disagree about where their loyalties lie and who is responsible for the divisions; after the invasion they both argue, against Carl, for fighting with the government against the invaders, but they also acknowledge that the Party was in the wrong. Doodsie's is the voice that first anticipates the government's increasing isolation from the people:

> Dey not suppose to hide ting from us. Dey on top but is we dat make Revolution. Revolution counta make if weself din go out on de road and make Leader ban give up. Horizon din even have no big army as such! Is we dat do we ting! Widdout us, de Angel O, de Micey O, de Rupert O, de Chief O, and all other Co-Chief an who not else, none o dem din nutting! Like dey forgettin! (258)

These words reiterate the seminal role of mass mobilization in toppling Leader and maintaining the new regime: a minority may have acted on behalf of the people, but could not have succeeded had it not been for the immediate participation of ordinary Grenadians. With the initial achievements of the government at risk, the leaders' response—to close down communications while becoming more authoritarian—endangered the very support on which they depended. After Chief's arrest, the protest to release him, and the government's attack on the crowd, Doodsie is again the one who identifies the crisis in terms of the yawning gulf between leaders and people:

> Look eh, when ting just start all of us been speaking with one voice, so was all right then. Was all right because practically everybody was on same side. Now mos people on same side again, saying leggo Chief, but now some of allyou who fight wid us self sayin is because we stupid an we caan see de truth! Perhaps. I not sayin so. But den that is how it is. If a few of you see it an de res of us don see it, what you go do, tie us down? Is not so it is, Angel. Dat is not what we fight for. We moving together or if not, we jus not moving, ah suppose. (267)

The murder of Chief and the quarantining of the remaining government mark the end of the self-activity and achievements so recently celebrated. When Angel feebly defends the Party later, Rupert echoes Doodsie: "'Why any government should siddown dey an expec people to tink that they rulin so dey musbe right? . . . To blasted hell was de Party! Any Party dat in Mars while people on earth is not no party we want to know about anyway! Let it stay to ass in Mars.'" (270).

'We need you for nation-building, you hear!' (Angel 234)

Angel thus through its extended exploration of different characters' responses to Horizon, sketches the central internal fault lines of the PRG. When it comes to far-reaching questions of nationalist strategies in a global context, the novel is even more ambiguous. The PRG's approach was fundamentally contiguous with the politics of National Liberation: as we have seen, Grenada in 1979 did not undergo a mass socialist revolution, but rather the PRG took over the state and used it as a vehicle for national economic development and reform. As Lewis argues, it pursued 'an economics and a politics of "breaking away," that is to say, of challenging the assumption—which had been treated almost as natural law— that independent Grenada, like everybody else, should remain within the economic and geopolitical orbit of the "Western world," which really meant the United States' (Lewis 32). To this end the government managed to 'effectively mobilize its people in the task of national reconstruction' (*The Jewel Despoiled* Lewis 33). Yet this was a contradictory process: money for this infrastructural investment, both realized and projected, came from sources that only highlighted Grenada's dependent location within the global economy. 'A massive infusion of over $168 million from sources as diverse as Cuba, and the Soviet Union, Libya, Canada and the United Kingdom' funded initial 'social programmes in health, child care, education and housing' (Meeks 164). Agricultural diversification was hard to realize, and 'Grenadian agriculture was still tied to nutmeg, bananas and cocoa, dependent on Britain and the European market and subject to drastic price fluctuations' (164). The government ultimately looked to tourism, which depended on completion of the new airport, to fill the gap. Meeks, citing others before him, draws attention to the bitter ironies of this solution:

> Mandle effectively highlights the paradox in which a left-wing government had adopted a model of development which had been roundly condemned by the Caribbean left for its potential for reinforcing racial stereotypes and the questionable contribution which tourism could make to the economy with its limited multiplier effect. A further dilemma was raised by Clive Thomas who suggested that a small state engaged in an anti-imperialist project could not seriously hope to consistently attract tourists from Western hard currency areas in the face of adverse and damaging propaganda. This was supported by the steady decline of stop-over tourists between 1979, when 32.3 thousand arrived, and 1982 when only 22.7 thousand came. (163)

In late 1982 loans from the OPEC countries had dried up and 'the economy, upon which rested the credibility of the paternalist leadership, was for the first time facing a severe bottleneck' (Meeks 164). External destabilization efforts further weakened Grenada's fragile location in the global market, as the novel suggests: Angel writes to a friend about mysterious murders and rumors and other problems 'boiling under the surface' (246); Her friend Janice warns in a letter from Brooklyn that she hopes leaders of the revolution are 'sticking together in spite of what people up this side wishing' (251). On a more fundamental level, the novel both dramatizes the contradictions of the model of national development, but also itself assumes this to be the only available course.

The novel's contradictory relationship to nationalism can be seen in its representation of the land. Significantly, given Horizon's orientation on tourism, *Angel*, like many works of Caribbean fiction, self-consciously distances itself from the 'tourist' image of the island: Paule Marshall observes, in comments used for the novel's cover by the Seal Press, that Collins tells the 'story of the West Indies that exists behind the tourist hype of happy islands in the sun.' At times this is explicit, as when Angel and her fellow students return from the University of the West Indies in Jamaica:

> It was early morning when an excited Helen shouted.
>   'Land, allyou! Land!'
> 'Awright, Columbus! Who dere already could go to hell! Is who comin dat matter!' Joy leaned with the others against the railings, peering into the distance.
>   They looked at the outline of brown against the horizon. They looked at the rocks which seemed to guard the entrance to the island's waters. Overhead, a white bird hovered. Angel remembered something her mother had told her about understanding the tourist's point of view for the first time when she saw the birds as the boat came in from Aruba. (169)

This is echoed at the novel's end, when Doodsie watches a bird from her window:

> Her mind did a somersault in time to come up again years back, standing on the deck as the ship came in from Aruba. She remembered the birds, white birds dipping and graceful over a beautiful blue sea. Doodsie had stood transfixed, seeing this view of the land for the first time and suddenly understanding what the white people she worked for meant when they said to her that her island was 'extraordinarily beautiful, with the most fantastic harbour.' Even as they talked to her and she focused her mind on her country, her only real memory had been of the nutmeg trees, of her hurting back, of the white people's kitchens; but she had smiled sympathetically when they said it, feeling vaguely pleased. Seeing it from the boat, she had understood and agreed. (290)

While as can be seen here there is great pride in and love for the land, the environment is mostly figured as the reluctant terrain on which to eke out a living, through growing bluggoes, peas, corn, eddoes, breadfruit, yam, and dasheen to eat, and nutmeg and cocoa to sell for money (in turn to be sold on the world market) to buy milk or other necessities (49, 64, 78). In these references, and in the overbearing presence of the crop-producing estates, Grenada's raw materials are metonyms for the island; the very island itself becomes a product for foreign consumption both in its common sobriquet, 'isle of spice,' and also in the tourists' predatory attitude: white tourists, white kitchens.

This reification of the nation coexists with repeated personification of the land. The first of many such instances occurs in an early scene: 'Doodsie could hear the palm tree rustling gently in the breeze as it stood with its top outlined against the sky up there, looking close to where God stayed. When she looked up, the other trees around had started rustling too as the breeze got stronger. She lowered her eyes, left them to their conversation, and went on outside' (12). At this moment Doodsie's perspective is obviously shaped by her religious faith, but there is already an implicit parallel between the trees' stirring and the restive populace during the Sky Red protests. As the novel progresses, elements of the natural world increasingly become emblematic and premonitory of social events. In the heat-wave preceding a hurricane '[t]he trees wouldn even rustle. Huggin their breeze to themselves selfish selfish and not even movin when people screw up dey face, take off dey hat to fan and look up at the treetops' (30).[17] At the same time, Leader has consolidated his victory and the people have resigned themselves to his paternalism because '[a]ll agreed that if wan for Leader, tings never could reach this far' (34):

> Doodsie was worried. She didn't like the way the clouds behind the mountain kept gathering to whisper silently and frown down at them. She didn't like the sound of the distant rumble that came every so often . . . Doodsie looked back at the mountain and saw that the frown had spread. The face of the mountain was threatening, furrowed. She looked up at the trees along the road. They gave no reassuring rustle in answer to her questing look. She walked quickly, frightened by their strange, silent unfriendliness. (34–5)

When Angel moves to the fore of the narrative, after the family has moved to rural Delicia, each stage of her consciousness is projected on to the natural world. While battling with a school system riven by regional and linguistic hierarchies and a largely irrelevant curriculum, Angel as a child terrifies herself with fears of ghosts as she walks home in the evenings: 'there would be only darkness and cocoa . . . She walked quickly under the stinking-toe tree, covering her nose against the pungent smell of the fruit. . . . Angel was a living shiver of fear' (92). At other times the landscape appeals to her as a sanctuary, albeit one with distinctly human characteristics, as in the moment when, while studying, she is bored by the tales of Marco Polo and turns instead to the view:

> She put the book down and moved to the other window. . . . She pulled down the louvres a little bit, quietly. . . . The overgrown garden, a few white roses coming through, a few red roses; the morning glory folded on the side, the sunflower looking dejected, a tangled mass of fern. Angel looked sideways at the cocoa trees, her tongue out to catch the spray from the rain. Straight ahead, at the back, the guava tree looked

so wet she felt like bringing it a raincoat. The gospo tree which provided gospos for juice . . . looked washed and waiting. (96)

As the novel proceeds the land is more consistently associated with the struggle for political emancipation. After Horizon's victory while people celebrate, '[t]he cocoa trees rustled with unruly delight, the banana leaves moved in the breeze. The sea bashed itself up on the beaches. The sand glinted silvery white and welcomed the water into its depths' (234). And when Chief is arrested, the weather reflects the disquiet felt by Angel and the others, and reveals their lack of preparedness for such events: 'They hadn't even seen the rainclouds gathering behind the mountain. When they looked up questioningly at the sudden darkness, the curtain of blue sky was covered; the rain came tumbling down. Behind Doodsie, the dry clothes on the line flapped a protest in the rushing wind and rain' (259). The specificity of Grenada's environment is thus evoked in human and political, rather than purely natural, terms, and the novel's most nationalist voice is deeply embedded in the narrative description.

At the same time, the figuration of the land as product apprehends the nation's dependence on the world economy, while the naturalistic plot reveals the extent to which '[t]ransnationalism, the living of personal and political lives across geographic boundaries, has become for many Grenadians . . . woven into the very fabric of their lives' (Basch et al, 52). Throughout the narrative we see characters constantly relocating, within the region—to work in the oil refineries of Aruba, the estates of Trinidad, or to study at University of the West Indies Jamaica—and to the U.S.—to pick fruit in Wisconsin, cut sugar cane in Florida, or work in the service sector in New York City. Just as the Guyanese novels recreate the very specific landscape of the nation as home, so does this Grenadian work evoke the natural environment in sensual detail; like Kincaid's *Mr. Potter*, *Angel* also uncovers the global relations of production and consumption that appropriate the Caribbean's resources. It is clear that Grenada is inextricably linked to a global economy, which ultimately supersedes national attempts to overcome the injustice and inequality that form the backdrop of characters' lives.[18]

'dream is dead in these antilles'

The end of the novel, which contains the most emotionally powerful scenes, describes the impact of Horizon's disintegration and the invasion that follows. Doodsie prays for an end to the party divisions: 'Things lookin up so well and America just waitin for us to fall for dem to laugh' (257). And when the fall comes she is heartbroken: 'Angel couldn't remember when else she had seen her mother cry' (259). After the murders at the fort, where Melda is killed alongside Chief, the shock and grief are palpable:

For a while, Carl and his friends, looking from the top of the bank, stared out into the sudden silence. No sound of shots, that is. On the road below, people rushed by, screaming, hurtling along the road, bending forward, glancing back, mouths parted, eyes wide in faces frozen into silent masks of unbelieving terror. . . . People rushed home, fell inside their houses; they stood there and sat there shaking and sobbing and shaking their hands and moving their feet and looking over their shoulders as if to be sure the horror hadn't followed them home. (265)

Back home, the family are initially struck dumb by the implications of what has happened:

> [Angel] sat bent over double in the chair, cradling her shoulders from the cold inside, still, listening to Doodsie's sobs. Aunt Jessie paced. Allan turned around in one spot. Moved. Returned. Cleared his throat. Moved. Turned. Came back to the same spot and stood clearing his throat, his hand occasionally going up to touch the back of his head; he stood as if listening for something. Carl stood in the corner by the sewing-machine. He held the scissors; he was methodically snipping a bit of cloth on top of the machine. No one sad anything. (266)

Angel tries to reassure Doodsie that 'we go work it out' but as she watches her mother 'Angel was suddenly seeing her grandmother again; Ma Ettie, tired, disappointed, leaving to walk back to Hermitage' (266).

The emotional and physical wounds of the invasion are deep. Rupert's girlfriend Janine is killed, and Rupert interrogated, by American troops; Angel receives serious injuries and loses one of her eyes. At the end of the novel she returns from the U.S. where her injuries were treated [answering Rupert's query the nurse marks the irony of this: '"We don't have a choice, comrade. They have the money. They have the treatment"' (281)] and we see the household picking up the pieces of their shattered lives.

The ending exudes faith in human resilience, connection, and healing. The last proverb is 'We never get more dan we can handle.' One of the final scenes is of Doodsie, Rupert, Angel, Allan, Carl, and Jessie 'relaxed in the warmth of companionship' (287) still debating black angels and white saviors. We hear that when Angel was in hospital Kai, one of her close companions in Jamaica, visited her, and when Doodsie jokes about marriage and cohabitation, 'Angel chuckled, the first sound of fun they had heard since her return' (288). But the net result is not so much a concrete depiction of future hope for social transformation as a somber illustration of the loss of such hope. Natural symbolism suggests fatalism about human capacity for social progress: Doodsie is seen calling to her chickens to stay together and so fend off a predatory hawk; Doodsie, Angel, and Carl watch a heavy thunderstorm wash away young shoots and seeds. Doodsie advises Angel to go to church, and repeats Ma Ettie's earlier counsel against fighting losing battles: 'Look at the fingers of you han, chile. Some long, some short. You can't change the Lord world!' (286). The final scene is of Angel lighting a candle and singing a French Creole song used at wakes. Lima writes that this ritual 'functions as a symbol of past traditions which Angel must retain if she is to have an awareness of her community and her heritage' (52). Yet given the novel's repeated caution against religious passivity, this could also be read less as a social

act and more of an individual healing of wounds inflicted by historical failure. The 'past traditions' may be necessary for survival, but surely cannot break the political impasse. They will provide comfort and allow Angel and others to endure the present; they will not provide any way forward for collective attempts to change it.

The years after 1983 witnessed the ascension of the right-wing New National Party and the dismantling of the social programs put in place under Bishop. The broader impact of the invasion was overwhelmingly negative: 'A rising tide of radicalism . . . was stopped dead. . . . In its place came a more traditional assertion of US regional power, military and economic' (James Ferguson 301–2); 'it set back the cause of political democracy and long-term economic development in the region' (O'Shaughnessy 219). In a galling twist, Herbert Blaize, a former functionary in the American-owned oil refinery in Aruba where Gairy first organized, replaced Bishop as head of state (Basch et al, 69). By the end of the 1980s Grenada had a foreign debt of around $50 million and a trade deficit of $60 million; a growing budget crisis; an official unemployment rate of 20 percent; record levels of alcoholism and drug addiction; and myriad other social problems. In response to the growing crisis, in 1987 President Blaize passed the Emergency Powers Act, stripping civil liberties and giving broad powers to security forces (Chomsky, *Deterring* 162).

It is not surprising, then, that this 1987 novel, while unambiguous in its support for revolutionary movements for genuine independence, equality, and social justice, is unable to envisage the realization of this goal. Poet Dionne Brand, who went to Grenada in February 1983 with a group called CARIPADA (Caribbean Peoples' Development Agency) to assist in the revolutionary project, described in a 1991 interview the climate in early 1983:

> When I wrote *Winter Epigrams* I was much more hopeful of the possibilities for people overturning those kinds of systems. I had just seen the end of the fighting in Zimbabwe. The Sandinistas were in power in Nicaragua, and Bishop was in Grenada. The wings of the America eagle hadn't clamped themselves over so much of the world as they have today . . . I felt that it was quite possible for a whole population to have a vision of equality, to see the possibility of living without being dominated by the kind of patronizing and patriarchal governments that we have in the Caribbean. (Birbalsingh, *Frontiers* 126)

Her characterization of the postinvasion climate is radically different: 'Here I was in Grenada with the possibility of assuaging the past in some way; and it had fallen apart. I thought, what the hell do we have to do to get redress? So in writing *Chronicles of the Hostile Sun* I was incredibly angry and terribly despairing at some points. Mighty ideas are not the same as military might' (Birbalsingh, *Frontiers* 128). Collins's account of the events of October resonates with Brand's in 'Military Occupations:'

> It came as a 'special announcement' . . . 'The people died because they were in the line of fire in a time of crisis at the army headquarters.' . . .

'*No!*' Doodsie held on to the back of a chair.

'Ay-ay! Ay-ay! Ay! Ay!' Allan looked as he had been hit.

'Wo-o-o-y!' Jessie's eyes had an uncomprehending look. 'What dey say? Dey dead in truth, den? Carl, who dead?'

'Is like dey say, Auntie. Chief dead, an a lotta other people who support im dead. People in de crowd dead, ah suppose, although we don hear! Ministers who support im dead! Dey jus dead!'

Angel was making a strangled, sobbing sound. (*Angel* 268)

'Maurice is dead
Jackie is dead
Uni is dead
Vincent is dead
dream is dead
lesser and greater
dream is dead in these antilles' (Brand, *Chronicles* 40)

Brand's poem opposes the arsenal of U.S. imperialism to the gains of social reform (such as 'a hectare of land free from bosses' and 'women's cooperatives'), and repeatedly observes that 'you cannot fight' imperialism with any of these things. The poem concludes: 'certainly you cannot fight it with dignity/and finally you can only fight it with the silence of your dead body' (*Chronicles* 40–43).[19] The poignant conclusion of *Angel* is suffused with the same sentiments of despair and shattered hopes.

The novel identifies the conditions that led to the disintegration, suggesting that it was not inevitable. Furthermore, it reveals the extent to which the invasion forestalled a domestic solution. When Rupert leaves to join the opposition to the invaders he explains that this does not indicate his continuing support for the remaining Horizon leadership: '"I not fightin for dem . . . I fightin for us, because nobody suppose to be in we country. After ah fight wid dem, ah could fight against dem, because that fight still have to go on"' (277). The defeat of the resistance means that this does not happen; the imposition of a new regime prevents the reemergence of mass struggle. While *Angel* tries to represent the uncharted territory of revolutionary potential, the constraints of 'trans-individual' forces—the strategic location of Grenada in a world economic and political system, the weight of political trauma following the invasion—overwhelm the effort. The end of the novel gestures towards retreat in the face of a political impasse: in this sense, rather than transcending them, *Angel* epitomizes the contradictions of the moment.

The Collective Novel?

The text's extensive use of multiple narrative voices, Creole dialogue, and the epistolary form transmute the traditionally individual, private, bourgeois realist novel in to a collective, public, working-class expression, and by many measures it is successful: Patrick Taylor finds that '[I]t is in the very paradox of unity and fragmentation that the novel reaches history, neither as utopia, nor as tragic failure, but as the hope and possibility of a new future' ('Deconstruction' 16); Isabel Hoving places *Angel* in the context of 'the writing practice of writers who work from within and for a working-class community' (145); Helena Maria Lima argues that this 'historical novel recovers the discontinuities that Walter Benjamin refers to in his 'Theses,' allowing the oppressed to correct the distortions of official history' (52). The novel remains alert to the contradictions associated with such a project. If the Achilles' heel of the People's Revolutionary Government was that it came to power as the result of a minority, middle class coup *on the behalf of* the majority, the novel avoids testifying *on the behalf of* the exploited men and women who are its subject, as Collins insists, by 'drawing heavily on the reality of my existence, of the existence of those around me,' ('Writing Fiction' 25) and using established and innovative literary techniques to recreate these experiences.[20]

But particular challenges accompany any attempt to represent collective, mass, revolutionary consciousness through private, individual, middle-class literary forms. In addition to the larger question of the author 'speaking for' the people, there is the difficulty of rendering a revolutionary potential that has been historically defeated. Then also, a conscious political purpose can overwhelm artistic concerns: the realist novel depends on emotional involvement and verisimilitude; these may be preempted both by the documentary impulse to set the record straight, and by the need to organize human experience in accordance with a theoretical framework.[21] Interestingly when *Angel* is the most effectively 'collective'—in the lengthy dialogues rehearsing political arguments, written exchanges about current events, nonspecific crowd scenes—it is perhaps less compelling as a novel; conversely it is the most emotionally effective, especially at the conclusion, when it is closer to the conventional *bildungsroman*, focused on the thoughts and feelings of the central individual character and her immediate family. The shape of the novel itself reflects the promise and defeat of social transformation: While the opening scene is a broad panoramic shot of a crowd of people witnessing an emergent mass political struggle, the final one is a close-up focus on the inner emotions of the physically and emotionally traumatized central character. Even the title brings us back to the individual, and to a mysticism that is repeatedly disavowed at the level of plot. Perhaps the novel is too much within the losing paradigms of past and present to follow through on its promise to imagine something different. But what is ultimately most gripping about *Angel* is the glimpse that it gives us of *future* possibilities—of global forces and solidarities, and of new literary expressions that will answer them.

Notes

1   Grenada did, however, produce two important figures associated with earlier labor and anticolonial struggles: T. Albert Marryshow, who campaigned tirelessly for West Indian Federation, and Tubal Uriah 'Buzz' Butler, who was instrumental to the unionization of Trinidad's oil workers and in turn the mass strikes of 1937 (*Grenada* Searle 6).

2   Grenada's Creole continuum combines elements of English, French, and African languages. French Creole, sometimes referred to as 'Patois' or 'Patwa,' is still spoken by some but not by most of the younger generation: Jessie and Doodsie use it to discuss 'adult' matters (55); at one point Angel complains to her mother, "'Ah don even know Patwa. Allyou does only talk Patwa for us not to understand'" (91).

3   Angel resembles Merle Collins, who was born in Aruba in 1950 to Grenadian parents who moved back to Grenada soon after. She graduated from UWI Mona in English and Spanish in 1972 and returned to Grenada to teach. She received an MA in Latin American Studies in 1980, served as coordinator for Research on Latin America and the Caribbean in the People's Revolutionary Government, and left Grenada in 1983 after the invasion. She published *Angel* from England, where she lived and taught until 1995 when she moved to the U.S. and took up an appointment as Professor of English and comparative Literature at the University of Maryland. Her middle name is Angela.

4   Salkey talks of the book's 'gradually unfolding historical panorama' (151) and Lima calls it a 'documentary bildungsroman' (44).

5   The State of Grenada consists of the main island and also Carriacou and Petite Martinique, two of several small islands that make up the chain known as the Grenadines at the southern end of the Lesser Antilles.

6   Steele writes: 'Even though Grenada's French heritage was forced to the level of a substratum, it would survive and play a vibrant part along with the substratum of African culture in the rich mix of Grenadian culture' (151).

7   During the 1979–83 revolution Fédon was the name given to a newspaper and a publishing house in St George's (Bishop, qtd. in *Grenada* Searle 157; Hart x).

8   'vyé nèg on the ground an bakra béké on top' translates as 'old black below and white boss above.'

9   Manning Marable writes that '[t]he economic and political underdevelopment of Grenada was such that it did not experience the mass labor strikes and nationalist unrest that swept across the rest of the Caribbean in the 1930s' (200).

10 NJM combined two organizations, the Joint Endeavour for Welfare, Education and Liberation (JEWEL), and the Movement for Assemblies of the People (MAP), both developed by the returning middle class who were part of 'an active and increasingly mobilized cross-section of youth, workers and students, unwilling to put up with Gairyite arbitrariness and brutality' (*Grenada* Searle 144).

11 'Between 1946 and 1970 the number of students attending secondary school increased from 751 to 4,967, and between 1960 and 1970 the number of university-degreed persons rose from 193 to 352' (*The Jewel Despoiled* Lewis 18).

12 Lewis 88–9; McMahan 218; Meeks 129; O'Shaughnessy 112–13; McMahan 218–19; Blum 274; Searle, *Grenada*.

13 For a useful contemporaneous discussion of the legal ramifications, see 'The United States Action in Grenada:' Christopher C. Joyner, 'Reflections of the Lawfulness of Invasion;' John Norton Moore, 'Grenada and the International Double Standard;' Detlev F. Vagts, 'International Law under Time Pressure: Grading the Grenada Take-

Home Examination;' in Francis A. Boyle et al, 'Letter: International Lawlessness in Grenada.' *American Journal of International Law* 78.1 (January 1984): 131–75.

14 Collins responds to the idea that the invasion was to avenge Bishop's murder: 'U.S. forces arrived at the perfect moment for an easy psychological victory. Unless they are credited with an unfamiliar altruism, it must be agreed that theirs was cynical exploitation of a tragic situation' ('Grenada' 73). Significant evidence exists that an invasion was planned long before Bishop's assassination (Lewis 111). The students were not in danger before the U.S. invaded: they had been offered safe passage out of the country and most refused (Blum 271; McMahan 200); OECS law forbids military invasion of any member nation in the absence of a clear external threat (there was none) and the acquiescence of all members, which it didn't have (Joyner 135–8). Evidence of an imminent Cuban takeover was subsequently found to be fabricated (Lewis 105).

15 George Lamming makes the same point in his December 1983 tribute to Maurice Bishop at the Memorial Service in Trinidad: '[Walter Rodney and Maurice Bishop] were of the same generation, and had enjoyed, as you would say, similar privileges of education and social opportunity. In a region where these emblems of success were scarce and difficult to achieve, they could earn access to that minority kingdom which normally views the world of men and women from down below with habitual contempt. It had always been the function of our institutions to create these divisions in the ranks of our society; and to ensure that the social function of the professional and technocratic classes would be to reinforce and stabilise this social division of labour and status. But . . . They broke away; and they became subversive traitors to that tradition which could so easily have bestowed on them the blessings of those who proudly identify themselves as affluent consumers' (Searle, ed., *Nobody's Backyard* 3).

16 'Nyam up de ital' is a Jamaican phrase meaning 'eat up the food.'

17 Hurricane Janet hit Grenada in September of 1955, causing immense damage, killing 120 people, injuring many more, and leaving countless homeless. Seventy percent of the nutmeg trees were lost, which had a devastating impact on the economy.

18 These characteristics are also powerfully present in Collins' recent collection of poems, *Lady in a Boat*. The title refers to the nutmeg riddle: 'Lady in a boat/With a red petticoat.' The poems repeatedly return to the labor that takes place on the homeland: 'I sweat on that hill up there, in the land/I sew, cook, teach, take night and make day.' At the same time they expose the movement of goods and workers across the globe: 'leave the land, take boat, try to make me way/ go to Port-of-Spain, Oranjestaad, Brooklyn, London/see my brothers sail to Maracaibo, Cuba, Colon—/one set of poor people that travel well, my people' (44).

19 'america came to restore democracy,/what was restored was faith/in the fact that you cannot fight bombers/battleships, aircraft carriers, helicopter gunships,/surveillance planes,/five thousand american soliders/six Caribbean stooges and the american war machine,/you cannot fight this with a machete,/you cannot fight it with a handful of dirt/you cannot fight it with a hectare of land free from bosses/you cannot fight it with farmers/you cannot fight it with 30 miles of feeder roads/you cannot fight it with free education/you cannot fight it with women's cooperatives/you cannot fight it with a pound of bananas or a handful of fish/which belongs to you/certainly you cannot fight it with dignity . . ./And finally you can only fight it with the silence of your dead body.'

20 These problems are signaled by descriptions of Angel's student activism: she and her university friends (who resemble Bishop and his peers) are aware of their separation

from the poor of West Kingston whom they visit as part of the Search project: Angel and her friend Kai, 'didn't too like the idea. Is like high-up people trying to find out bout who low down, they argued' (159–60). Towards the end of the book when Angel and Rupert are fighting about the Party he accuses her: 'The *people* you siddown in you ivory tower an say you fightin for, dey know who side dey on! Fight for youself, eh, sis, because dem don have your problem. They know where they stand!' (269).

21　Julian Markels takes up these and other important questions concerning literary representations of class. Using the concepts of 'overdetermination' and 'point of entry' as Stephen Resnick and Richard Wolff use them (*Knowledge and Class.* Chicago: University of Chicago Press, 1987), Markels explores texts that employ a 'Marxian imagination' through representing both the 'overdetermined' 'push-and-pull of multiple forces as the real-life medium in which we in fact participate in structured relations like class' (19–20), while choosing the concept of class as the 'point of entry'—the analytical framework through which reality is made sense of. He speculates that '[m]imetic representation that entails the manners of a latent community may be so deeply embedded in the status quo that producing class as point of entry will be not only rare but indirect and inadvertent' (45), but convincingly shows how it does happen, in works as diverse as Shakespeare's *King Lear*, Dickens' *Little Dorrit*, and Barbara Kingsolver's *The Poisonwood Bible*.

Afterword

A Dream Deferred

Spread out before her, between the broken circle of mountains and the sea, is the capital: corrugated tin roofs, leaning shacks, high-rise hotels, flamboyants she can name from this distance by their colors, the irregular geometry of city houses and lawns, swimming pools, great bushy treetops, animal and vehicle pausing and proceeding, and the corrugated tin roofs repeating themselves all the way out to the corrugated gray water of the harbor.

Margaret Cezair-Thompson, *The True History of Paradise*

The dilemma is, I believe, the classic dilemma of the poor; a choice between death and death. Either we enter a global economic system, in which we know we cannot survive, or, we refuse, and face death by slow starvation.

Jean-Bertrand Aristide *Eyes of the Heart*

There is a major shift in the struggle for liberation. Global is the oppression of the free market: the same machine that produces more poor in Haiti is producing more poor in Detroit, in Rwanda, in the Philippines, all over the world. Global must be the force that can challenge it.

Kesta Occident 'A Stubborn Hope,' in Beverly Bell, *Walking on Fire*

Cezair-Thompson's novel opens with a young Jamaican woman standing at her veranda surveying Kingston during the 1981 state of emergency. Like other Jamaican novels of the 1980s, such as Vanessa Spence's *The Roads are Down* and Elean Thomas' *The Last Room*, this one is structured by the conflicted relationship between the middle class woman and the surrounding conditions of austerity and instability that threaten to drive her into voluntary exile (and in some cases succeed). In *True History of Paradise* Jamaica's masses are a threatening presence, the protagonist, daughter of successful petty capitalists, and her peers progressively feel trapped behind their increasingly fortified large houses and worry about the impact of the latest IMF agreement, CIA intervention, or Michael Manley's reforms, on their lives and professions. In *Roads are Down* the heroine buys a large house in the Blue Mountains that was formerly owned by British colonials, accidentally injures a poor local child while driving her car too fast, and feels guilty that the wages she pays her maid do not quite allow her to support her children. In *Last Room* even a relatively well-paid professional job is not enough to secure housing in the new elite foreign-built developments sequestered from the shantytowns. All three works are saturated with references to SAPs, U.S. businessmen, and the ouster of Michael Manley's government; all three present a bleak, jaded worldview that locates any hope for positive social change firmly in the past.

Simultaneously, all three depict a Jamaica that is simmering with discontent seeking some expression, even while doubting that any solutions will be forthcoming in the wake of a recent failed attempt. In this they resemble the fiction from Haiti, Antigua, Guyana, and Grenada considered here. While only two of the authors discussed were active participants in collective movements for social change, three of the four nations considered experienced mass struggles that find their way into the literature. Waged against imperialism and postindependence domestic regimes, the achievements and failures of these attempts have much in common with earlier collective efforts for liberation. They corroborate Fanon's analysis in 'Pitfalls of National Consciousness' that national bourgeoisies will fail to deliver on their promises and instead will adopt the mantel of colonial rule, and confirm even more sharply that national solutions will fail to address the class grievances that fuel mass protests. In addition, they suggest that when formations develop to pose an alternative, national approaches are unable to fend off the new forms of foreign domination that replace formal colonialism: Jagan is crushed by the combined might of British and U.S imperialism; the New Jewel Movement implodes from the contradictions of Grenada's location in the global system and the U.S. invasion forestalls autonomous solutions; Aristide's agreement to the terms of neoliberalism signal the demise of Lavalas; Antigua is not economically or geographically large enough alone to break free of the dependent position bargained by the Bird dynasty.

The fiction is overwhelmingly characterized by a mood of defeat, and yet offers, to differing extents, hope for renewal. For all that the literature is grappling with familiar questions of national self-determination, and in many ways looks backwards towards the past (1950s and 1960s Guyana, 1970s Grenada, 1980s Haiti), it also arguably anticipates, or looks forward towards, a future that meets global problems with global solutions. As each particular example shows, specific national contexts open up interpretive possibilities that are obscured by generic readings, making it possible to ground narrative and figurative patterns in the environments that produce them. But even as each is contextually and artistically distinct, these disparate works also share a visual and imaginative rendering of a neoliberalized terrain that looks remarkably similar everywhere: concretely in descriptions of rural poverty and urban slums, and of villages and cities rent by class polarization, and in portraits of places with particular symbolic significance, like the airport and the hospital, which are often almost interchangeable. There are reverberations too of something less explicit, a shared ambience or feeling of being besieged and invaded, and weighed down by the building pressure of cumulative wrongs. It can be seen in Nichols' description of the 'quieter waiting restlessness' of Georgetown:

> It was there in the eyes of the limers, young men who couldn't find work or who perhaps didn't want to find work, lounging around the street corners . . . in the eyes of the half-naked, under-nourished, bewildered children, standing in the dark doorways.

. . . There in the eyes of the prostitutes. . . . In the eyes of the stevedores, working through the steamy mornings. In the tired smiles of the shop and factory girls at the end of a day. (*WMS* 57)

It is in Kincaid's description of Antigua: 'It is as if . . . the beauty were a prison, and as if everything and everybody inside it were locked in and everything and everybody that is not inside it were locked out. And what might it do to ordinary people to live in this way every day?' (*ASP* 79); or again in Melville's description of Chofy's child: 'From an early age, Bla-Bla had puzzled over how he could make things better for his own people. He sensed injustice in the way they were treated and it troubled him. Sometimes, in his hammock at nights, he imagined building defences around the village to keep intruders away. He planned battles and attacks' (*VT* 318). In the works by Danticat and Collins, who are both closer to recent mass upheavals, this sense of pressure without outlet is less pervasive, but they certainly insist, sometimes literally and sometimes figuratively, that the injustices that fueled these failed revolts remain, and that the subterranean fires of rebellion will surface again in the future: because, in the words of Danticat's Guy, '[God] "gave us reasons to want to fly"' (*KK* 68); or in those of Collins's Angel, '"[w]e have to figure a way to make it"' (*Angel* 275).

Even such a small sample of recent literature in English is indicative of the tremendous creative range of this rapidly expanding field, and the texts allow for no generalization about the relationship between form and politics: the two writers who most explicitly conceptualize their writing in terms of political opposition—Jan Lo Shinebourne and Merle Collins—represent very dissimilar narrative strategies, the one turning to the realist novel and the other seeking to innovate a 'collective novel' to express the aspirations of their respective nations' peoples. Jamaica Kincaid, the writer whose work is the most pessimistic about the possibility of future mass rebellion, even while it powerfully indicts current structures of power, is generally found to use the most 'postmodern' techniques, and the author herself has acknowledged the influence of what she calls 'modernist' and 'avant garde' writing.[1] Danticat, whose fiction prefers complexity, indeterminacy, suggestion, and is laced with intertextuality and symbolism, is at the same time invested in collective projects for social justice, as can be seen in her edited anthologies and contributions to works such as *A Slave Revolution*. Taken together these works also show the ideological flexibility of literature: the middle class voice of protagonist and character may be dominant, but either directly or between the lines we often see the aspirations of the working class and dispossessed majority. There is a considerable range of perspectives, too, from the aloof privileged personae of *My Garden Book* or *True History of Paradise*, to the arduous attempt to capture a collective consciousness in *Angel*.

Regardless of the historical moment portrayed, and of the degree of explicit political engagement, the literature's voice hails from the period in which the texts were written, a period that reaped the dire consequences of neoliberal globalization. An awareness of transnational forces can be seen quite consistently, in the movement of characters (and authors) within the region or 'Away' across the globe; in the references, present in all the works, to the IMF, CIA, foreign corporations, client regimes; and in the thematic and artistic connections between these works and other postcolonial literatures. Melville's description of the Princess Street hostel in Georgetown (*VT* 336) recalls the memorable portrait by Amitav Ghosh of a residence in one of Calcutta's poor districts:

> The stairs were slippery with dirt, the bare cement walls blackened with soot and woodsmoke, the wiring strung up in bright festoons, the copper exposed at the joins where the insulating tape had worn off. It was a long matchbox-like building, not large, although it was evident from the barrack-like partitions that divided its corridors that dozens of families inhabited it. (*Shadow Lines* 132)

Kincaid's rendering of postcolonial Antigua similarly is echoed in Odun Balogun's descriptions, in *Adjusted Lives: Stories of Structural Adjustment*, of Lagos in the 1980s. And in stories like 'nineteen thirty-seven' Danticat's voice recalls that of Martinique's Chamoiseau:

> Everyone, as their hutches became more solid, began to ward off police raids with fingers crossed facing the rising sun, with drops of water splattered on the walls, three times on the right, seven times on the left, and thirty-three times in front. In the face of such turmoil, I managed to get a little chapel built out of the cliff, and I collected some coins to get us a small Virgin Mary statue which we set up with great ceremony. (*Texaco* 365)

In these and so many other ways, these authors share the spirit of the age, a combination of circumstances and moods that are distinctly global.

This period culminated with the explosion of the global justice movement, in the form of IMF rebellions; protests against the WTO, privatization, and other neoliberal mechanisms (unsuccessful in the case of Haiti; successful in Bolivia[2]); and the World Social Forums, described recently by José Corrêa Leite:

> The WSF is contributing to altering the ideological climate in today's world, helping to break the hegemony of the values of marketization, neoliberalism, and growing militarism. Giving voice to the fight against the commercialization of the world and affirming itself in opposition to multilateral organizations, the global movement as well as the WSF knows how to respond to the changes on the agenda that the Bush administration, with its unilateralism and its 'war against terrorism' imposes on the international scene. (138)

These developments are starting to find expression in literature. Sophia McClennen's comparative study of Hispanic exile literature confirms a growing consciousness of globalization and the nascent struggle against it:

> What begins at home moves to the national level and later is applied to a transnational realm. The connection between identity, exile, and geographic space is problematized after these authors recognize that their national problems are global in scale. Struggle at

the national level could not be successful because of the global reach of economic imperialism and its corresponding social ideology. (16)

The Anglophone Caribbean has not yet experienced successful coordinated organization against neoliberalism, though as we have seen, the literature reveals the conditions that make such struggle inevitable, and suggests that future solutions must be international in scale. What is certain is that the struggle for global justice will continue, in ways that we cannot even predict; what is equally certain is that Caribbean women writers will continue to add to the rich tapestry of literature that expresses these realities, that tells a 'history of horror unspeakable' (Kincaid, *Mr. Potter* 116) but also gives us 'explosions of rapture and beauty' (Danticat, *After the Dance* 152). Langston Hughes wrote his famous poem in 1951, when the mass struggles of the civil rights movement were still ahead. So too do these literary works anticipate an as yet unimaginable future.

What happens to a dream deferred?

    Does it dry up
  like a raisin in the sun?
  Or fester like a sore--
    And then run?
Does it stink like rotten meat?
  Or crust and sugar over--
    like a syrupy sweet?

    Maybe it just sags
    like a heavy load.

    Or does it explode?

Notes

1   See Selwyn Cudjoe's interview with Kincaid in his edited collection, *Caribbean Women Writers* (215–32).
2   In 2000 Bolivia's mass movement in Cochabamba, including those in labor unions as well as those fighting for indigenous rights, successfully warded off a plan to privatize water by a U.S. American transnational corporation. See Tom Lewis and Oscar Olivera. Bolivia is currently amidst a revolutionary fight against neoliberalism.

Bibliography

Adkin, Major Mark. *Urgent Fury: The Battle for Grenada*. Lexington, MA: Lexington Books, 1989.

Afzal-Khan, Fawzia, and Kalpana Seshadri-Crooks, eds. *The Pre-Occupation of Postcolonial Studies*. Durham: Duke UP, 2000.

Ahmad, Aijaz. *In Theory: Classes, Nations, Literatures*. London: Verso, 1992.

——. 'The Politics of Literary Postcoloniality.' *Race and Class* 36.3 (1995): 1–20.

Ambursley, Fitzroy, and Robin Cohen, eds. *Crisis in the Caribbean*. New York: Monthly Review Press, 1983.

Apena, Adeline. 'Guyanese Women in Action: Response and Reactions to Economic Reform,' in *Women Pay the Price: Structural Adjustment and the Caribbean*. Ed. Gloria Thomas Emeagwali. Trenton: Africa World Press, 1995. 105–20.

Appadurai, Arjun. 'Disjuncture and Difference in the Global Cultural Economy,' in *Colonial Discourse and Postcolonial Theory: A Reader*. Eds Laura Chrisman and Patrick Williams. London: Harvester, 1994. 305–23.

Aristide, Jean-Bertrand. *Eyes of the Heart: Seeking a Path for the Poor in the Age of Globalization*. Ed. Laura Flynn. Monroe, ME: Common Courage Press, 2000.

Arthur, Charles. *Haiti in Focus: A Guide to the People, Politics and Culture*. New York: Interlink, 2002.

Ashcroft, Bill, Gareth Griffiths, and Helen Tiffin, eds. *The Empire Writes Back*. New York: Routledge, 1989.

Averill, Gage. *A Day for the Hunter, A Day for the Prey: Popular Music and Power in Haiti*. Chicago: U of Chicago P, 1997.

Balch, Emily Greene, ed. *Occupied Haiti*. New York: Writers Publishing Company, 1927.

Balogun, Odun. *Adjusted Lives: Stories of Structural Adjustments*. Trenton: African World Press, 1995.

Balutansky, Kathleen. 'Naming Caribbean Women Writers: A Review Essay.' *Callaloo* 13.3 (Summer 1990): 539–50.

——, and Marie-Agnès Sourieau, eds. *Ecrire en Pays Assiégé: Haïti: Writing Under Siege*. Amsterdam: Rodopi, 2004.

Barnes, Natasha. 'Reluctant Matriarch: Sylvia Wynter and the Problematics of Caribbean Feminism.' *Small Axe* 5 (March 1999): 34–47.

Bartolovich, Crystal and Neil Lazarus, eds. *Marxism, Modernity and Postcolonial Studies*. Cambridge: Cambridge UP, 2002.

Basch, Linda, Nina Glick Schiller and Cristina Szanton Blanc, eds. *Nations Unbound: Transnational Projects, Postcolonial Predicaments and Deterritorialized Nation-States*. Langhorne, PA: Gordon and Breach, 1994.

Bell, Beverly, ed. *Walking on Fire: Haitian Women's Stories of Survival and Resistance*. Cornell: Cornell UP, 2001.

Bellegarde-Smith, Patrick. *Haiti: The Breached Citadel*. Boulder, CO: Westview Press, 1990.

Benítez-Rojo, Antonio. *The Repeating Island: The Caribbean and the Postmodern Perspective*. Trans. James Maraniss. Durham: Duke UP, 1992.

Benoît, Jean-Pierre. 'Bonne Année,' in *The Butterfly's Way: Voices from the Haitian Dyaspora in the United States*. Ed. Edwidge Danticat. New York: Soho Press, 2001. 31–35.

Bewes, Timothy. *Reification, or the Anxiety of Late Capitalism*. London: Verso, 2002.

Birbalsingh, Frank. 'Edgar Mittelhölzer: Moralist or Pornographer?' *Journal of Commonwealth Literature* 7 (1969): 88.

——. *From Pillar to Post: The Indo-Caribbean Diaspora*. Toronto: TSAR Publications, 1997.

——, ed. *Frontiers of Caribbean English in Literature*. New York: St. Martin's Press, 1996.

Bishop, Jacqueline, and Dolace Nicole McLean. 'Working out Grenada: An Interview with Merle Collins.' *Calabash: A Journal of Caribbean Arts and Letters* 3.2 (Fall/Winter 2005): 53–67.

Blackburn, Robin. *The Making of New World Slavery From the Baroque to the Modern: 1492–1800*. London: Verso, 1997.

Bloom, Harold, *Caribbean Women Writers*. Philadelphia: Chelsea House, 1997.

——, ed. *Modern Critical Views: Jamaica Kincaid*. Philadelphia, PA: Chelsea House, 1998.

Blum, William. *Killing Hope: U.S. Military and CIA Interventions Since World War II*. Monroe, ME: Common Courage Press, 1995.

Boehmer, Elleke. *Colonial and Postcolonial Literature–Migrant Metaphors*. Oxford: Oxford UP, 1995.

Booker, M. Keith, and Dubravka Juraga. *The Caribbean Novel in English: An Introduction*. Kingston: Ian Randle, 2001.

Bové, Paul. *In the Wake of Theory*. Middletown: Wesleyan UP, 1991.

——. *Mastering Discourse: the Politics of Intellectual Culture*. Durham: Duke UP, 1992.

Boyle, Francis A., et al. 'Letter: International Lawlessness in Grenada.' *American Journal of International Law* 78.1 (January 1984): 172–5.

Bragard, Véronique. 'Coolie Woman Fictionalizing Political History: Janice Shinebourne's Memories of Violence.' *Journal of Caribbean Literatures* 3.1 (2000): 13–24.

Brand, Dionne. *Chronicles of the Hostile Sun.* Toronto: Williams-Wallace, 1984.

——. 'No Language is Neutral,' interview by Birbalsingh in *Frontiers of Caribbean English in Literature.* New York: St. Martin's Press, 1996. 120–37.

Brathwaite, Edward. 'Timehri.' *Savacou* 2 (Sept 1970): 35–44.

——. Introduction in Roger Mais, *Brother Man* (1954). Oxford: Heinemann International, 1974. v–xxi.

Brecher, Jeremy and Tim Costello. *Global Village or Global Pillage: Economic Reconstruction from the Bottom Up.* Boston, MA: South End Press, 1994.

Brennan, Tim. *At Home in the World: Cosmopolitanism Now.* Boston: Harvard UP, 1997.

Brenner, Johanna. *Women and the Politics of Class.* New York: Monthly Review Press, 2000.

Brizan, George. *Grenada: Island of Conflict: From Amerindians to People's Revolution 1498–1979.* London: Zed Press, 1984.

Browdy de Hernandez, Jennifer, ed. *Women Writing Resistance: Essays on Latin America and the Caribbean.* Boston, MA: South End Press, 2003.

Brown, Suzanne Francis. 'Women No Cry: Female-headed Households in the Caribbean,' in *No Paradise Yet: The World's Women Face the New Century.* Eds Judith Mirsky and Marty Radlett. London: Panos/Zed Press, 2000. 101–18.

Burrowes, Reynold A. *Revolution and Rescue in Grenada: An Account of the U.S.-Caribbean Invasion.* Westport, CT: Greenwood Press, 1988.

Busby, M., ed. *Daughters of Africa.* London: Jonathan Cape, 1992.

Callaloo 25.3 (Summer 2002). Special Edition on Jamaica Kincaid.

Callinicos, Alex. *Against Postmodernism: A Marxist Critique.* Cambridge: Polity, 1989.

Campbell, Elaine, and Pierrette Frick, eds. *The Whistling Bird: Women Writers of the Caribbean.* London: Lynne Rienner, 1998.

Carew, Jan. *Black Midas.* London: Secker and Warburg, 1958.

——. *The Wild Coast.* Nendlen, Lichtenstein: Krause Reprint, 1972.

——. Interview with Birbalsingh, in *Frontiers of Caribbean English in Literature.* Ed. Frank Birbalsingh. New York: St. Martin's Press, 1996. 42–53.

Caribbean Quarterly 41.2 (1995). Special Edition.

Cezair-Thompson, Margaret. *The True History of Paradise.* New York: Plume, 2000.

Chamberlain, Greg. 'Up by the Roots: Haitian History Through 1987,' in *Haiti: Dangerous Crossroads.* Eds Deidre McFadyen and Pierre LaRamée with Mark Fried and Fred Rosen from the North American Congress on Latin America (NACLA). Boston, MA: South End Press, 1995. 13–26.

Chamoiseau, Patrick. *Texaco.* New York: Vintage, 1997.

Chancy, Myriam J.A. *Searching for Safe Spaces: Afro-Caribbean Women Writers in Exile*. Philadelphia, PA: Temple UP, 1997.

Changping, Li. 'The Crisis in the Countryside,' in *One China, Many Paths*. Ed. Chaohua Wang. London: Verso, 2003. 198–218.

Chin, Pat, et al. *Haiti: A Slave Revolution: 200 Years After 1804*. New York: International Action Center, 2004.

Chrisman, Laura and Patrick Williams, eds. *Colonial Discourse and Post-colonial Theory: a Reader*. New York: Columbia University Press, 1994.

Chomsky, Noam. *Deterring Democracy*. London: Verso, 1990.

——. *Year 501: The Conquest Continues*. Boston, MA: South End Press, 1993.

——. Introduction to *The Uses of Haiti*. 2nd edn. Paul Farmer. Monroe, ME: Common Courage Press, 2003. 13–44.

Cliff, Michelle. *Abeng*. New York: Dutton, 1984.

——. *Land of Look Behind*. Ithaca: Firebrand Books, 1985.

——. *No Telephone To Heaven*. New York: Vintage, 1985.

——. *Free Enterprise*. London: Penguin, 1993.

Cobham, Rhonda. '"Mwen Na Rien, Msieu:" Jamaica Kincaid and the Problem of Creole Gnosis.' *Callaloo* 24.3 (Summer 2002): 868–84.

——, and M. Collins, eds. *Watchers and Seekers: Creative Writing by Black Women in Britain*. London: Women's Press, 1987.

Collins, Merle. *Angel*. Washington, DC: Seal Press, 1987.

——. 'Grenada—Ten Years and More: Memory and Collective Responsibility.' *Caribbean Quarterly* 41.2 (1995): 71–8.

——. 'Writing Fiction, Writing Reality,' in *Caribbean Women Writers: Fiction in English*. Eds Mary Condé and Thorunn Lonsdale. New York: Palgrave Macmillan, 1998. 23–31.

——. *Lady in a Boat*. Leeds: Peepal Tree Press Press, 2003.

Condé, Mary and Thorunn Lonsdale, eds. *Caribbean Women Writers: Fiction in English*. New York: St. Martin's Press, 1999.

Cooper, Carolyn. *Noises in the Blood: Orality, Gender, and the Vulgar Body of Jamaican Popular Culture*. Durham: Duke UP, 1995.

Coram, Robert. *Caribbean Time Bomb: The United States' Complicity in the Corruption of Antigua*. New York: William Morrow, 1993.

Coulthard, G.R. *Race and Colour in Caribbean Literature*. Oxford: Oxford UP, 1962.

Covi, Giovanni. 'Jamaica Kincaid and the Resistance to Canons,' in *Modern Critical Views: Jamaica Kincaid*. Ed. Harold Bloom. Philadelphia, PA: Chelsea House, 1998. 3–12.

Craig, Christine. *Mint Tea And Other Stories*. London: Heinemann, 1993.

Cudjoe, Selwyn. *Resistance and Caribbean Literature*. Athens, Ohio: Ohio UP, 1980.

——. *Caribbean Women Writers: Essays from the First International Conference*. U of Massachusetts P dist. Amherst, MA: Calaloux Publishers, 1990.

——. 'Jamaica Kincaid and the Modernist Project: An Interview,' in *Caribbean Women Writers: Essays from the First International Conference.* U of Massachusetts P dist. Amherst, MA: Calaloux Publishers, 1990. 215–32.

Danticat, Edwidge. *Breath, Eyes, Memory.* New York: Vintage, 1994.

——. *Krik? Krak!* New York: Soho Press, 1995.

——. *The Farming of Bones.* New York: Soho Press, 1998.

——. Foreword in *Walking on Fire.* Ed. Beverly Bell, 2001. ix–xi.

——. *After the Dance: A Walk Through Carnival in Jacmel, Haiti.* New York: Crown Publishing, 2002.

——. *The Dew Breaker.* New York: Alfred Knopf, 2004.

——. 'No Greater Shame.' *Haiti: A Slave Revolution: 200 Years After 1804.* Ed. Ramsey Clark et al. New York: International Action Center, 2004. 165–72.

——, ed. *The Butterfly's Way: Voices from the Haitian Dyaspora in the United States.* New York: Soho Press, 2001.

Dash, J. Michael. *Haiti and the United States: National Stereotypes and the Literary Imagination.* 2nd edn. New York: St. Martin's Press, 1997.

Davis, Mike. 'Planet of Slums: Urban Involution and the Informal Proletariat.' *New Left Review* 26 (Mar/April 2004): 5–34.

Davies, Carole Boyce, and Elaine Savory Fido, eds. *Out of the Kumbla: Caribbean Women and Literature.* Trenton: Africa World Press, 1990.

——, ed. *Moving Beyond Boundaries Volume 2: Black Women's Diasporas.* New York: New York UP, 1995.

Dayan, Joan. *Haiti, History, and the Gods.* Berkeley: U of California P, 1995.

Denniston, Dorothy. *The Fiction of Paule Marshall: Reconstructions of History, Culture, and Gender.* Knoxville: U of Tennessee P, 1995.

Dirlik, Arif. 'The Postcolonial Aura: Third World Criticism in the Age of Global Capitalism.' *Critical Inquiry* 20.2 (1994): 328–56.

Donnell, Alison. 'Dreaming of Daffodils: Cultural Resistance in the Narrative of Theory.' *Kunapipi* 14.2 (1992): 45–52.

——. 'When Daughters Defy: Jamaica Kincaid's Fiction.' *Women: A Cultural Review* 4.1 (Spring 1993): 18–26.

——. 'She Ties Her Tongue: The Problem of Cultural Paralysis in Postcolonial Criticism,' in *Modern Critical Views: Jamaica Kincaid.* Ed. Harold Bloom. Philadelphia, PA: Chelsea House, 1998. 37–49.

Donnell, Alison and Sarah Lawson Welsh, eds. *The Routledge Reader in Caribbean Literature.* London: Routledge, 1996.

Doyle, Arthur Conan. *The Lost World.* 1912. New York: Dover, 1998.

Dreyfuss, Joel. 'A Cage of Words,' in *The Butterfly's Way: Voices from the Haitian Dyaspora in the United States.* Ed. Edwidge Danticat. New York: Soho Press, 2001. 57–9.

Dubois, Laurent. *Avengers of the New World: The Story of the Haitian Revolution.* Cambridge, MA: Belknap, 2004.

Dunn, Peter M., and Bruce W. Watson, eds. *American Intervention in Grenada: The Implications of Operation 'Urgent Fury.'* Boulder, CO: Westview Press, 1985.

Dupuy, Alex. *Haiti in the New World Order: the Limits of the Democratic Revolution.* Boulder, CO: Westview Press, 1997.

Eagleton, Terry. *The Idea of Culture.* Oxford: Blackwell Publishing, 2000.

——. *Figures of Dissent: Critical Essays on Fish, Spivak, Zizek and Others.* London: Verso, 2003.

Edmondson, Belinda. *Making Men: Gender, Literary Authority, and Women's Writing in Caribbean Narrative.* Durham: Duke UP, 1999.

Edmondson, Belinda J., ed. *Caribbean Romances: The Politics of Regional Representation.* Charlottesville: U of Virginia P, 1999.

Ellis, Pat. *Women of the Caribbean.* London: Zed Press, 1986.

Emeagwali, Gloria Thomas, ed. *Women Pay the Price: Structural Adjustment and the Caribbean.* Trenton: Africa World Press, 1995.

Engels, Frederick. *The Origin of the Family, Private Property and the State.* 1884. New York: International Publishers, 1972.

Erro-Peralta, Nora, and Caridad Silva, eds. *Beyond the Border: A New Age in Latin American Women's Fiction.* Gainesville: UP of Florida, 2000.

Esteus, Sony. 'Haiti: The Crisis Persists.' Trans. Thomas Harrison. *New Politics* 8.3 (Summer 2001): <http://www.wpunj.edu/~newpol/issue31/esteus31.htm>.

Esteves, Carmen C., and Lizabeth Paravisini-Gebert, eds. *Green Cane and Juicy Flotsam: Short Stories by Caribbean Women.* New Brunswick, NJ: Rutgers UP, 1991.

Fanon, Frantz. *The Wretched of the Earth.* 1961.Trans. Constance Farrington. New York: Grove Press, 1968.

Farmer, Paul. *Infections and Inequalities: The Modern Plagues.* Berkeley: U of California P, 1999.

——. *The Uses of Haiti.* 2nd edn. Monroe, ME: Common Courage Press, 2003.

——. 'Who Removed Aristide?' *London Review of Books.* April 15, 2004.

Fatton, Robert Jr. *Haiti's Predatory Republic.* Boulder, CO: Lynne Rienner Publishers, 2002.

Ferguson, James. *A Traveller's History of the Caribbean.* New York: Interlink Books, 1999.

Ferguson, Moira. *Jamaica Kincaid: Where the Land Meets the Body.* Charlottesville: Virginia UP, 1994.

Ferguson, Niall. 'The Empire Slinks Back.' *New York Times Magazine* (April 27, 2003): <http://www.nytimes.com/2003/04/27/magazine/27EMPIRE.html>.

Fernandez, Ronald. *Cruising the Caribbean: U.S. Influence and Intervention in the Twentieth Century.* Monroe, ME: Common Courage Press, 1994.

Fitz, Earl. *Brazilian Narrative Traditions in a Comparative Context.* New York: Modern Language Association, 2005.

Ford-Smith, Honor, and the Sistren Theatre Collective. *Lionheart Gal: Life Stories of Jamaican Women*. London: Women's Press, 1986.

Fouchard, Jean. *The Haitian Maroons: Liberty or Death*. Trans. A. Faulkner Watts. New York: E.W. Blyden Press, 1981.

French, John D., and Daniel James, eds. *The Gendered Worlds of Latin American Workers: From Household and Factory to the Union Hall and Ballot Box*. Durham: Duke UP, 1997.

Gedalof, Irene. *Against Purity: Rethinking Identity with Indian and Western Feminisms*. London: Routledge, 1999.

Ghosh, Amitav. *The Shadow Lines*. 1988. New Delhi: Ravi Dayal and Permanent Black, 1998.

Gikandi, Simon. *Writing in Limbo: Modernism and Caribbean Literature*. Ithaca, NY: Cornell UP, 1992.

Gilkes, M. *The West Indian Novel*. Boston: Twayne, 1981.

——, ed. *The Literate Imagination: Essays on the Novels of Wilson Harris*. London: Macmillan, 1989.

Gilroy, Beryl. *Frangipani House*. London: Heinemann, 1986.

——. 'Reflections,' in *Caribbean Women Writers: Fiction in English*. Eds Mary Condé and Thorunn Lonsdale. New York: Palgrave Macmillan, 1998. 11–16.

Gold, Herbert. *Best Nightmare on Earth: A Life in Haiti*. New York: Prentice Hall, 1991.

Greene, Sue. 'Report on the Second International Conference on Caribbean Women Writers.' *Callaloo* 13.3 (Summer 1992): 532–8.

Haiti Films. *Bitter Cane*. New York: 1983.

Haniff, Nesha Z. *Blaze a Fire: Significant Contributions of Caribbean Women*. Toronto: Sister Vision, 1988.

Harney, Stefano. *Nationalism and Identity: Culture and Imagination in a Caribbean Diaspora*. London: Zed Press, 1996.

Harris, Wilson. *Tradition, Writer, and Society*. London: New Beacon Books, 1967.

——. 'The Laughter of the Wapishanas.' *The Age of the Rainmakers*. London: Faber and Faber, 1971.

——. *The Guyana Quartet*. London: Faber, 1985.

Hart, Richard. Introduction to *In Nobody's Backyard: Maurice Bishop's Speeches 1979–1983: A Memorial Volume*. Ed. Chris Searle. London: Zed, 1984. xi–xli.

Heath, Roy. 'Criticism in Art: a View from the Diaspora.' *Ariel* 24.1 (January 1992): 163–72.

——. *The Murderer*. 1978. New York: Persea Books, 1992.

——. *The Shadow Bride*. 1988. New York: Persea Books, 1988.

Hodge, Merle. *Crick, Crack, Monkey*. London: Heinemann, 1970.

——. 'In the Shadow of the Whip,' in *Is Massa Day Dead? Black Moods in the Caribbean*. Garden City, NY: Anchor Books, 1974.

Hoving, Isabel. *In Praise of New Travelers: Reading Caribbean Migrant Women's Writing.* Stanford, CA: Stanford UP, 2001.

Hudson, William Henry. *Green Mansions: A Romance of the Tropical Forest.* New York: G.P. Putnam's Sons, 1904.

Hyppolite, Joanne. 'Dyaspora,' in *The Butterfly's Way: Voices from the Haitian Dyaspora in the United States.* Ed. Edwidge Danticat. New York: Soho Press, 2001. 7–11.

Ignatieff, Michael. 'Nation Building Lite.' *New York Times Magazine.* (July 28, 2002): <http://www.mtholyoke.edu/acad/intrel/bush/lite.htm>.

Ippolito, Emilia. *Caribbean Women Writers: Identity and Gender.* Rochester, NY: Camden House, 2000.

Ives, Kim. 'The Lavalas Alliance Propels Aristide to Power,' in *Haiti: Dangerous Crossroads.* Eds Deidre McFadyen and Pierre LaRamée with Mark Fried and Fred Rosen from the North American Congress on Latin America (NACLA). Boston, MA: South End Press, 1995. 41–6.

Jackson, Tommie Lee. *An Invisible Summer: Female Diasporan Authors.* Trenton, NJ: Africa World Press, 2001.

James, C.L.R. *The Black Jacobins: Toussaint L'Ouverture and the San Domingo Revolution.* New York: Random House, 1963.

——. 'Triumph,' (1929) in *Penguin Book of Caribbean Short Stories.* Ed. E.A. Markham. London: Penguin, 1996.108–25.

Jameson, Fredric. *The Political Unconscious: Narrative as a Socially Symbolic Act.* Ithaca, NY: Cornell UP, 1981.

——, and Masao Myoshi, eds. *The Culture of Globalization.* Durham: Duke UP, 1997.

Jehenson, Myriam Yvonne. *Latin American Women Writers; Class, Race, and Gender.* Albany: SUNY Press, 1995.

Journal of Haitian Studies 7.2 (Fall, 2001): Special Issue on Edwidge Danticat.

Joyce, James. *Ulysses.* 1922. New York; Random House, 1986.

Joyner, Christopher C. 'Reflections on the Lawfulness of Invasion.' *American Journal of International Law* 78.1 (January 1984): 131–44.

Kempadoo, Kamala, ed. *Sun, Sex, and Gold: Tourism and Sex Work in the Caribbean.* Lanham, MD: Rowman and Littlefield, 1999.

——, and Jo Doezema, eds. *Global Sex Workers: Rights, Resistance and Redefinition.* New York: Routledge, 1998.

Kempadoo, Oonya. *Buxton Spice.* 1998. New York: Plume, 2000.

——. Interview with Lisa Gee. <http://195.157.68.238/projects/futures/kempadoo.html>.

Kincaid, Jamaica. *At the Bottom of the River.* New York: Farrar, Straus and Giroux, 1983.

——.*Annie John.* New York: Farrar, Straus and Giroux, 1985.

——. *A Small Place.* New York: Plume, 1988.

——. *Lucy.* New York: Farrar, Straus and Giroux, 1991.

——. *Autobiography of My Mother.* New York: Farrar, Straus and Giroux, 1996.

——.*My Brother.* New York: Farrar, Straus and Giroux, 1997.

——. *My Garden Book.* New York: Farrar, Straus and Giroux, 1999.

——. *Mr. Potter.* New York: Farrar, Straus and Giroux, 2002.

Laguerre, Michel S. *The Complete Haitiana: A Bibliographic Guide to the Scholarly Literature, 1900–1980.* Millwood, NY: Kraus International Publications, 1982.

——. *The Military and Society in Haiti.* Knoxville: U of Tennessee P, 1993.

Lalla, Barbara. *Defining Jamaican Fiction: Marronage and the Discourse of Survival.* Tuscaloosa: U of Alabama P, 1996.

Lamming, George. 'Maurice Bishop Lives,' in *In Nobody's Backyard: Maurice Bishop's Speeches 1979–1983: A Memorial Volume.* Ed. Chris Searle. London: Zed Press, 1984. 1–8.

——. *In the Castle of My Skin.* 1953. Ann Arbor: U of Michigan P, 1994.

Laraque, Paul, and Jack Hirschman, eds. *Open Gate: An Anthology of Haitian Creole Poetry.* Willimantic, CT: Curbstone Press, 2001.

Larsen, Neil. 'Postmodernism and Imperialism: Theory and Politics in Latin America,' in *Reading North by South: On Latin American Literature, Culture, and Politics.* Minneapolis: U of Minnesota P, 1995.

——. 'DetermiNation: Postcolonialism, Poststructuralism, and the Problem of Ideology,' in *The Pre-Occupation of Postcolonial Studies.* Eds Fawzia Afzal-Khan and Kalpana Seshadri-Crooks. Durham: Duke UP, 2000. 140–56.

——. *Determinations: Essays on Theory, Narrative, and Nation in the Americas.* London: Verso, 2001.

Lazarus, Neil. 'Disavowing Decolonization: Fanon, Nationalism, and the Problematic of Representation in Current Theories of Colonial Discourse.' *Research in African Literatures* 24.4 (1993): 69–98.

——. *Nationalism and Cultural Practice in the Postcolonial World.* Cambridge: Cambridge UP, 1999.

Latour, Francie. 'Made Outside,' in *The Butterfly's Way: Voices from the Haitian Dyaspora in the United States.* Ed. Edwidge Danticat. New York: Soho Press, 2001. 125–31.

Leacock, Eleanor. Introduction to *The Origin of the Family, Private Property and the State.* Frederick Engels. 1884. New York: International Publishers, 1972. 7–67.

——. *Myths of Male Dominance.* New York: Monthly Review Press, 1972.

Leite, José Corrêa. *The World Social Forum: Strategies of Resistance.* Chicago: Haymarket Books, 2005.

Lens, Sidney. *The Forging of the American Empire.* New York: Thomas Crowell, 1971.

Lewis, Gordon K. *Grenada: The Jewel Despoiled.* Baltimore, MD: Johns Hopkins UP, 1987.

Lewis, Tom, and Oscar Olivera. *Cochabamba: Water War in Bolivia.* Boston, MA: South End Press, 2004.

Levenson-Estrada, Deborah. 'The Loneliness of Working-Class Feminism: Women in the "Male World" of Labor Unions, Guatemala City, 1970s,' in *The Gendered Worlds of Latin American Workers: From Household and Factory to the Union Hall and Ballot Box.* Eds John D.French and Daniel James. Durham: Duke UP, 1997. 208–31.

Levins, Richard, and Richard Lewontin. *The Dialectical Biologist.* Cambridge, MA: Harvard UP, 1985.

Lima, Maria Helena. 'Revolutionary Developments: Michelle Cliff's *No Telephone to Heaven* and Merle Collins' *Angel*,' in *Ariel: A Review of International English Literature* 24:1 (January 1993): 36–56.

Lindfors, Bernth, and Reinhard Sander. *Twentieth Century Caribbean and Black African Writers.* First and Second Series. Detroit: Gale Research Inc., 1992 and 1993.

Loewen, James. *Lies My Teacher Told Me*: *Everything Your American History Textbook Got Wrong.* New York: Touchstone, 1995.

Lorde, Audre. *Sister Outsider.* Berkeley, CA: Crossing Press, 1984.

Lukács, Georg. *History and Class Consciousness: Studies in Marxist Dialectics.* 1923. Trans. Rodney Livingstone. Cambridge, MA: MIT Press, 1988.

Macdonald-Smythe, Antonia. *Making Homes in the West/Indies: Constructions of Subjectivity in the Writings of Michelle Cliff and Jamaica Kincaid.* New York: Garland, 2001.

McAfee, Kathy. *Storm Signals: Structural Adjustment and Development Alternatives in the Caribbean.* Boston, MA: South End Press, 1991.

McClennen, Sophia A. *The Dialectics of Exile: Nation, Time, Language, and Space in Hispanic Literatures.* West Lafayette, IN: Purdue UP, 2004.

McClintock, Anne. 'The Angel of Progress: Pitfalls of the Term "Postcolonial,"' in *Colonial Discourse and Post-colonial Theory: a Reader.* Eds Patrick Williams and Laura Chrisman. New York: Columbia UP, 1994. 291–304.

——. *Imperial Leather: Race, Gender and Sexuality in the Colonial Context.* New York: Routledge, 1995.

McKay, Claude. 'Mattie and her Sweetman,' in *The Penguin Book of Caribbean Short Stories.* Ed. E.A. Markham. London: Penguin, 1996. 61–70.

McMahan, Jeff. *Reagan and the World: Imperial Policy in the New Cold War.* New York: Monthly Review Press, 1985.

McNally, David. *Bodies of Meaning: Studies on Language, Labor, and Liberation.* Albany: SUNY Press, 2001.

McTair, Roger. 'Politics Kaiso,' in *The Penguin Book of Caribbean Verse in English.* Ed. Paula Burnett. London: Penguin, 1986. 318–19.

McWatt, Mark. 'Libidinous Landscapes: Sexual Inscriptions of Place in Guyanese Literature.' *Commonwealth Essays and Studies* 25.3 (Spring 2003): 73–82.

Maes-Jelinek, H., ed. *Wilson Harris—The Uncompromising Imagination.* Coventry: Dangaroo Press, 1991.

Mandle, Jay R. 'Continuity and Change in Guyanese Underdevelopment.' *Monthly Review* 28. 4 (September, 1976): 37–51.

Manley, Robert H. *Guyana Emergent: The Post-Independence Struggle for Nondependent Development.* Boston, MA: G.K. Hall, 1979.

Marable, Manning. *African and Caribbean Politics: From Kwame Nkrumah to Maurice Bishop.* London: Verso, 1987.

Markels, Julian. *The Marxian Imagination: Representing Class in Literature.* New York: Monthly Review Press, 2003.

Markham, E.A., ed. Introduction. *The Penguin Book of Caribbean Short Stories.* London: Penguin, 1996.

Marx, Karl. *The 18th Brumaire of Louis Bonaparte.* 1852. New York: International Publishers, 1987.

Matthews, M. *Guyana, My Altar.* London: Karnak House, 1987.

Meeks, Brian. *Caribbean Revolutions and Revolutionary Theory: An Assessment of Cuba, Nicaragua, and Grenada.* Kingston: UWI Press, 1993.

Mehta, Brinda J. 'The Colonial Curriculum and the Construction of "Coolie-ness" in Lakshmi Persaud's *Sastra* and *Butterfly in the Wind* (Trinidad) and Jan Shinebourne's *The Last English Plantation* (Guyana).' *Journal of Caribbean Literatures* 3.1 (2000): 111–28.

Melville, Pauline. *Shape-Shifter.* London: Women's Press, 1990.

——. 'Beyond the Pale,' in *Daughters of Africa.* Ed. M. Busby. London: Jonathan Cape, 1992. 739–43.

——. *The Ventriloquist's Tale.* London: Bloomsbury Publishing, 1997.

——. *The Migration of Ghosts.* London: Bloomsbury Publishing, 1998.

——. 'Erzulie.' *The Migration of Ghosts.* London: Bloomsbury Publishing, 1999. 135–68.

Mintz, Sidney. *Caribbean Transformations.* Baltimore: Johns Hopkins UP, 1974.

Mirsky, Judith, and Marty Radlett, eds. *No Paradise Yet: The World's Women Face the New Century.* London: Panos/Zed, 2000.

Mittelhölzer, Edgar. *Children of Kaywana.* 1952. New York: Bantam, 1976.

Miyoshi, Masao. 'A Borderless World?: From Colonialism to Transnationalism and the Decline of the Nation-State.' *Critical Inquiry* 19.4 (Summer 1993): 726–51.

Mohammed, Patricia, and Catherine Shepherd, eds. *Gender in Caribbean Development: Papers Presented at the Inaugural Seminar of the Women and Development Studies Project of the University of the West Indies.* UWI, Trinidad, Jamaica and Barbados: Women and Development Studies, 1988.

Mohanty, Chandra Talpade, et al., eds. *Third World Women and the Politics of Feminism.* Bloomington: Indiana UP, 1991.

Momsen, Janet H., ed. *Women and Change in the Caribbean: A Pan-Caribbean Perspective.* Kingston: Ian Randle, 1993.

Monar, Rooplal. *Backdam People.* Leeds: Peepal Tree Press, 1985.
——. *Janjhat.* Leeds: Peepal Tree Press, 1989.
Mordecai, Pamela, and Betty Wilson, eds. *Her True-True Name.* Portsmouth, NH: Heinemann Educational Books, 1989.
Morrell, Carol, ed. *Grammar of Dissent: Poetry and Prose by Claire Harris, Marlene Nourbese Philip, Dionne Brand.* Fredericton, NB: Goose Lane, 1994.
Morris, Mervyn. 'Cross-Cultural Impersonations: Pauline Melville's *Shape-Shifter.*' *Ariel* 24:1 (January 1993): 79–89.
NACLA. *Haiti: Dangerous Crossroads.* Boston, MA: South End Press, 1995.
Naipaul, V.S. *The Middle Passage.* London: Andre Deutsch, 1962.
Nash, June, and Maria Patricia Fernandez-Kelly, eds. *Women, Men, and the International Division of Labour.* Albany: SUNY Press, 1983.
Nasta, Susheila, ed. *Motherlands: Black Women's Writing from Africa, the Caribbean, and South Asia.* London: The Women's Press, 1991.
Neptune, Miriam. 'In Search of a Name,' in *The Butterfly's Way: Voices from the Haitian Dyaspora in the United States.* Ed. Edwidge Danticat. New York: Soho Press, 2001. 147–51.
Nichols, Grace. *I Is a Long Memoried Woman.* London: Karnak House Publishers, 1983.
——. *Whole of a Morning Sky.* London: Virago, 1986.
Niebylski, Dianna C. *Humoring Resistance: Laughter and the Excessive Body in Contemporary Latin American Women's Fiction.* Albany: SUNY Press, 2004.
Niesen de Abruna, Laura. 'Jamaica Kincaid's Writing and the Maternal-Colonial Matrix,' in *Caribbean Women Writers: Fiction in English.* Eds Mary Condé and Thorunn Lonsdale. New York: St. Martin's Press, 1999. 172–83.
Norris, Christopher. *What's Wrong with Postmodernism?: Critical Theory and the Ends of Philosophy.* Baltimore, MD: Johns Hopkins UP, 1990.
——. *Uncritical Theory: Postmodernism, Intellectuals, and the Gulf War.* Amherst: U of Massachusetts P, 1992.
——. *The Truth About Postmodernism.* London: Blackwell, 1993.
O'Callaghan, Evelyn. *Woman Version—Theoretical Approaches to West Indian Fiction by Women.* London: Macmillan, 1993.
——. *Women Writing the West Indies, 1804–1939: 'A Hot place, Belonging to Us.'* London: Routledge, 2004.
Occident, Kesta. 'A Stubborn Hope,' in *Walking on Fire: Haitian Women's Stories of Survival and Resistance.* Ed. Beverly Bell. Ithaca, NY: Cornell UP, 2001. 228–30.
Olmos, Margarite Fernández, and Lizabeth Paravisini-Gebert. *Remaking a Lost Harmony: Stories from the Hispanic Caribbean.* Fredonia, NY: White Pine Press, 1995.
O'Shaughnessy, Hugh. *Grenada: An Eyewitness Account of the U.S. Invasion and the Caribbean History that Provoked It.* New York: Dodd, Mead, 1984.

Osirim, Mary Johnson. 'We Toil All the Livelong Day,' in *Daughters of Caliban: Caribbean Women in the Twentieth Century.* Ed. Consuelo Lopez Springfield. Bloomington: Indiana UP, 1997. 41–67.

Paravisini, Lizabeth. *Jamaica Kincaid: A Critical Companion.* Westport, CT: Greenwood Press, 1999.

Paravisini, Lizabeth, and Barbara Webb, eds. 'On the Threshold of Becoming Caribbean Women Writers.' *Cimarron* 1.3 (1988): 106–31.

Parry, Benita. *Postcolonial Studies: A Materialist Critique.* London: Routledge, 2004

Payen, Nikol. 'Something in the Water…Reflections of a People's Journey,' in *The Butterfly's Way: Voices from the Haitian Dyaspora in the United States.* Ed. Edwidge Danticat. New York: Soho Press, 2001. 66–82.

Peake, Linda. 'The Development and Role of Women's Political Organizations in Guyana,' in *Women and Change in the Caribbean: A Pan-Caribbean Perspective.* Ed. Janet H. Momsen. Kingston: Ian Randle, 1993. 109–31.

Pearce, Jenny. *Under the Eagle: U.S. Intervention in Central America and the Caribbean.* Boston, MA: South End Press, 1981.

Perry, Donna. 'Initiation in Jamaica Kincaid's *Annie John,*' in *Caribbean Women Writers: Essays from the First International Conference.* Ed. Selwyn Cudjoe. U of Massachusetts P dist. Amherst, MA: Calaloux Publishers, 1990. 245–54.

Petras, James, and Morris Morley. *Latin America in the Time of Cholera: Electoral Politics, Market Economics, and Permanent Crisis.* New York: Routledge, 1992.

Plant, Roger. *Sugar and Modern Slavery: A Tale of Two Countries.* London: Zed Press, 1987.

Plummer, Brenda Gayle. 'The Afro-American Response to the Occupation of Haiti, 1915–1934.' *Phylon* 43 (June 1982): 125–43.

——. *Haiti and the Great Powers, 1902–1915.* Baton Rouge: Louisiana State UP, 1988.

Pollard, Velma. 'Dread Talk.' *Caribbean Quarterly* 26.4 (1980): 32–41.

Poynting, Jeremy. '"You Want to Be a Coolie Woman?" Gender and Ethnic Identity in Indo-Caribbean Women's Writing,' in *Caribbean Women Writers: Essays from the First International Conference.* Ed. Selwyn Cudjoe. U of Massachusetts P dist. Amherst, MA: Calaloux Publishers, 1990. 98–108.

Premdas, Ralph R. *Ethnic Conflict and Development: The Case of Guyana.* Avebury: United Nations Research Institute for Social Development, 1995.

Quayson, Ato. *Postcolonialism: Theory, Practice or Process?* Cambridge: Polity, 2000.

Reddock, Rhoda. 'Feminism, Nationalism, and the Early Women's Movement in the English-Speaking Caribbean (with Special Reference to Jamaica and Trinidad and Tobago),' in *Caribbean Women Writers: Essays from the First International Conference.* Ed. Selwyn Cudjoe. U of Massachusetts P dist. Amherst, MA: Calaloux Publishers, 1990. 61–81.

Rees, John. *The Algebra of Revolution: The Dialectic and the Classical Marxist Tradition.* London: Routledge, 1998.

Reiter, Rayna R., ed. *Toward an Anthropology of Women.* New York: Monthly Review Press, 1975.

Renda, Mary A. *Taking Haiti: Military Occupation and the Culture of U.S. Imperialism 1915–1940.* Chapel Hill: U of North Carolina P, 2001.

Renk, Kathleen. *Caribbean Shadows and Victorian Ghosts: Women's Writing and Decolonization.* Charlottesville: U of Virginia P, 1999.

Resnick, Stephen and Richard Woolf. *Knowledge and Class.* Chicago: U of Chicago P, 1987.

Rodríguez, María Cristina. *What Women Lose: Exile and the Construction of Imaginary Homelands in Novels by Caribbean Writers.* New York: Peter Lang, 2005.

Rody, Caroline. *The Daughter's Return: African-American and Caribbean Women's Fictions of History.* Oxford: Oxford UP, 2001.

Rodney, Walter. *How Europe Underdeveloped Africa.* London: Bogle-L'Ouverture, 1972.

——. *A History of the Guyanese Working People.* Baltimore: Johns Hopkins UP, 1981.

Rosaldo, Renato. *Culture and Truth: The Remaking of Social Analysis.* Boston: Beacon Press, 1989.

Roy, Arundhati. *Power Politics.* 2nd edn. Boston, MA: South End Press, 2001.

——. *War Talk.* Boston, MA: South End Press, 2003.

Rutherford, A., L. Jensen, and S. Chow. *Into the Nineties.* Coventry: Dangaroo Press, 1994.

Said, Edward. *Orientalism.* New York: Pantheon, 1978.

——. *The World, the Text, and the Critic.* Cambridge, MA: Harvard UP, 1983.

——. 'Criticism/Self Criticism.' *Linguafranca* 2.3 (1992): 37–43.

——. *Culture and Imperialism.* New York: Knopf, 1993.

——. *Reflections on Exile and Other Essays.* Cambridge, MA: Harvard UP, 2000.

——. 'Between Chance and Determinism: Lukács's Aesthetik,' in *Reflections on Exile.* Cambridge, MA: Harvard UP, 2000. 61–9.

——. 'History, Literature and Geography,' in *Reflections on Exile.* Cambridge, MA: Harvard UP, 2000. 453–73.

——. 'Introduction,' in *Reflections on Exile.* Cambridge, MA: Harvard UP, 2000. xi–xxxv.

——. 'Opponents, Audiences, Constituencies, and Community,' in *Reflections on Exile.* Cambridge, MA: Harvard UP, 2000. 118–47.

——. 'Traveling Theory Reconsidered,' in *Reflections on Exile.* Cambridge, MA: Harvard UP, 2000. 436–52.

Salkey, Andrew. Interview with Birbalsingh in *Frontiers of Caribbean English in Literature.* New York: St. Martin's Press, 1996. 29–41.

Sassen, Saskia. *The Mobility of Labor and Capital: A Study of Investment and Labor Flows.* Cambridge: Cambridge UP, 1988.

Savory, Elaine. 'The Truth is in the Clothes.' Review of *Shape Shifter. CRNLE Reviews Journal* 1 (1994): 123–31.

Sayers, Janet, Mary Evans and Nanneke Redclift, eds. *Engels Revisited: New Feminist Essays.* London: Tavistock Publications, 1987.

Schmidt, Hans. *The United States Occupation of Haiti, 1915–1934.* New Brunswick, NJ: Rutgers UP, 1971.

——. *Maverick Marine: General Smedley D. Butler and the Contradictions of American Military History.* Lexington: UP Kentucky, 1987.

Schoenhals, Kai P., and Richard A. Melanson. *Revolution and Intervention in Grenada: The New Jewel Movement, the United States, and the Caribbean.* Boulder, CO: Westview, 1985.

Scott, Helen. 'Replacing the "Wall of Disinformation:" *The Butterfly's Way, Krik? Krak!,* and Representation of Haiti in the USA.' *Journal of Haitian Studies* 7.2 (Fall 2001): 78–94.

——. 'Capitalist Modernity and the Origins of Racism,' in *Marxism, Modernity and Postcolonial Studies.* Eds Crystal Bartolovich and Neil Lazarus. Cambridge: Cambridge UP, 2002.167–82.

——. '"Dem tief, dem a dam tief:" Jamaica Kincaid's Literature of Protest.' *Callaloo* 25.3 (2002): 977–800.

——. 'Haiti Under Siege.' *International Socialist Review* 35 (May-June, 2004): 19–28.

——. '*Ou libéré?* History, Transformation, and the Struggle for Freedom in Edwidge Danticat's *Breath, Eyes, Memory*,' in *Ecrire en Pays Assiégé: Haïti: Writing Under Siege.* Eds Kathleen Balutansky and Marie-Agnès Sourieau. Amsterdam: Rodopi, 2004. 459–78.

Searle, Chris, *Grenada: The Struggle Against Destabilization.* London: Writers and Readers Publishing, 1983.

——, ed. *In Nobody's Backyard: Maurice Bishop's Speeches 1979–1983: A Memorial Volume.* London: Zed Press, 1984.

Sen, Gita. *Development, Crises, and Alternative Visions: Third World Women's Perspectives.* New York: New York UP, 1987.

Senior, Olive. *Working Miracles: Women's Lives in the English Speaking Caribbean.* Cave Hill, Barbados: Institute of Social and Economic Research, UWI, 1991.

Shacochis, Bob. *The Immaculate Invasion.* New York: Viking, 1999.

Shaw, Donald L. *The Post-Boom in Spanish American Fiction.* Albany: SUNY Press, 1998.

Shea, Renee H. 'Bearing Witness and Beyond: Edwidge Danticat Talks about Her Latest Work.' *Journal of Haitian Studies* 7.2 (Fall 2001): 6–20.

Shepherd, Verene, et al. *Engendering History: Caribbean Women in Historical Perspective.* New York: St. Martin's Press, 1995.

Shinebourne, Janice. *Timepiece*. Leeds: Peepal Tree Press, 1986.

———. *The Last English Plantation*. Leeds: Peepal Tree Press, 1988.

———. 'Twin Influences: Guyana in the 1960s and Anglophone Caribbean Literature,' in *Caribbean Women Writers: Essays from the First International Conference*. Ed. Selwyn Cudjoe. U of Massachusetts P dist. Amherst, MA: Calaloux Publishers, 1990.

Shohat, Ella. 'Notes on the "Post-Colonial,"' in *The Pre-Occupation of Postcolonial Studies*. Eds Fawzia Afzal-Khan and Kalpana Seshadri-Crooks. Durham: Duke UP, 2000. 126–39.

Siegel, Paul N. *The Meek and the Militant: Religion and Power Across the World*. London: Zed Press, 1986.

Simmons, Dianne. *Jamaica Kincaid*. New York: Twayne, 1994.

Sims, Peter. *Trouble in Guyana: An Account of People, Personalities and Politics as They Were in British Guiana*. London: George Allen and Unwin, 1966.

Sinclair, Norma. *Grenada: Isle of Spice: An Introduction and Guide*. 1987. 3rd edn. Oxford: Macmillan, 2002.

Singh, R. *Garland of Stories*. Ilfracombe: Stockwell, 1960.

———. *Days of the Sahib are Over*. Georgetown: 1960.

———. *Collection of Poems*. Georgetown: privately published, 1976.

Slemon, Stephen, and Helen Tiffin, eds. *After Europe: Critical Theory and Post-Colonial Writing*. Mundelstrup, Denmark: Dangaroo Press, 1989.

Smith, Ashley. 'Aristide's Rise and Fall.' *International Socialist Review* 35 (May–June, 2004): 29–35.

Sniader Lanser, Susan. 'Compared to What? Global Feminism, Comparatism, and the Master's Tools,' in *Borderwork: Feminist Engagements with Comparative Literature*. Ed. Margaret Higonnet. Ithaca: Cornell UP, 1994. 280–300.

Sokal, Alan. *Fashionable Nonsense: Postmodern Intellectuals' Abuse of Science*. New York: Picador, 1998.

Spence, Vanessa. *The Roads are Down*. Oxford: Heinemann, 1993.

Spinner, Thomas J. *A Political and Social History of Guyana, 1945–1983*. Boulder, CO: Westview, 1984.

Spivak, Gayatri Chakravorty. 'Three Women's Texts and a Critique of Imperialism.' *Critical Inquiry* 12 (Autumn 1985): 243–61.

Springfield, Consuelo Lopez, ed. *Daughters of Caliban: Caribbean Women in the Twentieth Century*. Bloomington: Indiana UP, 1997.

Steele, Beverley. *Grenada: A History of Its People*. Oxford: Macmillan Caribbean, 2003.

Stotzky, Irwin P. *Silencing the Guns in Haiti: The Promise of Deliberative Democracy*. Chicago: U of Chicago P, 1997.

Suleri, Sara. 'Woman Skin Deep: Feminism and the Postcolonial Condition.' *Critical Inquiry* 18 (Summer 1992): 756–69.

Taylor, Patrick. *The Narrative of Liberation: Perspectives on Afro-Caribbean Literature, Popular Culture, and Politics*. Ithaca: Cornell UP, 1989.

——. 'Deconstruction and Revolution: Merle Collins's *Angel.' The CLR James Journal* (January 1991): 12–17.

Thomas, Clive Y. 'Bread and Justice: the Struggle for Socialism in Guyana.' *Monthly Review* 28.4 (September 1976): 23–36.

——. *The Poor and the Powerless: Economic Policy and Change in the Caribbean.* New York: Monthly Review Press, 1988.

Thomas, Elean. *The Last Room.* London: Virago, 1994.

Tiffin, Helen. 'Postcolonial Literatures and Counter-Discourse.' *Kunapipi* 9.3 (1987): 17–34.

——, and Stephen Slemon, eds. *After Europe: Critical Theory and Post-Colonial Writing.* Coventry: Dangaroo Press, 1989.

——. 'Cold Hearts and (Foreign) Tongues: Recitation and the Reclamation of the Female Body in the Works of Erna Brodber and Jamaica Kincaid.' *Callaloo* 16.4 (Fall 1993): 909–21.

Toussaint, Eric. *Your Money or Your Life! The Tyranny of Global Finance.* Trans. Raghu Krishnan with Vicki Briault Manus. London: Pluto, and Dar Es Salaam: Mkuki na Nyota Publishers, 1998.

Trotsky, Leon. *Permanent Revolution.* 1930. New York: Pathfinder, 1976.

——. *Literature and Revolution.* 1925. Trans. Rose Trunsky. Ed. William Keach. Chicago: Haymarket, 2005.

Trouillot, Michel-Rolph. *Haiti, State against Nation: The Origins and Legacy of Duvalierism.* New York: Monthly Review Press, 1990.

——. 'The Odd and the Ordinary: Haiti, the Caribbean, and the World.' *Cimarron* 2 (Winter 1990): 3–12.

Volek, Emil, ed. *Latin America Writes Back: Postmodernity in the Periphery.* New York: Routledge, 2002.

Wagner, Geoffrey. *Red Calypso.* Washington, DC: Regnery Gateway, 1988.

Walrond, Eric. 'The Wharf Rats,' in *The Penguin Book of Caribbean Short Stories.* Ed. E.A. Markham. London: Penguin, 1996. 95–107.

Waugh, Alec. *Love and the Caribbean: Tales, Characters and Scenes of the West Indies.* 1958. New York: Farrar, 1959.

Webb, Barbara. *Myth and History in Caribbean Fiction: Alejo Carpentier, Wilson Harris, and Edouard Glissant.* Amherst, MA: U of Massachusetts P, 1992.

Welsh, Sarah Lawson. 'Pauline Melville's Shape-Shifting Fictions,' in *Caribbean Women Writers: Fiction in English.* Eds Mary Condé and Thorunn Lonsdale. New York: St. Martin's Press, 1999. 144–71.

Wilentz, Amy. *The Rainy Season: Haiti Since Duvalier.* New York: Simon and Schuster, 1989.

Williams, Brackette F. *Stains on My Name, War in My Veins: Guyana and the Politics of Cultural Struggle.* Durham: Duke UP, 1991.

Williams, Eric. *Capitalism and Slavery.* Chapel Hill: U of North Carolina P, 1944.

——. *From Columbus to Castro: The History of the Caribbean 1492–1969.* 1970. New York: Vintage, 1984.

Williams, Raymond. *Marxism and Literature*. Oxford: Oxford UP, 1977.

Williams, Wyck. 'Talent Rising: Review of Oonya Kempadoo's *Tide Running*.' (August 8, 2003): <www.guyana.caribbeanpolitics.com>.

Wisker, Gina. *Post-Colonial and African American Women's Writing*. New York: St. Martin's Press, 2000.

Wood, Ellen Meiksins. *The Retreat from Class: A New True Socialism*. London: Verso, 1986.

Wucker, Michele. *Why the Cocks Fight: Dominicans, Haitians and the Struggle for Hispaniola*. New York: Hill and Wang, 1999.

Wynter, Sylvia. 'Beyond Miranda's Meanings: Un/silencing the "Demonic Ground" of Caliban's Woman,' in *Out of the Kumbla: Caribbean Women and Literature*. Eds Carole Boyce Davies and Elaine Savory Fido. Trenton: Africa World Press, 1990. 355–67.

Yardan, Shana. *The Listening of Eyes*. Georgetown, 1976.

Zwerneman, Andrew J. *In Bloody Terms: The Betrayal of the Church in Marxist Grenada*. South Bend, IN: Greenlawn Press, 1986.

Index